Applications of Task-Based Learning in TESOL

Edited by Ali Shehadeh and Christine Coombe

Maria Dantas-Whitney, Sarah Rilling, and Lilia Savova, Series Editors

TESOL Classroom Practice Series

Teachers of English to Speakers of Other Languages, Inc.

Typeset in ITC Galliard and Vag Rounded
by Capitol Communication Systems, Inc., Crofton, Maryland USA
Printed by Gasch Printing, Odenton, Maryland USA
Indexed by Pueblo Indexing and Publishing Services, Pueblo West, Colorado USA

Teachers of English to Speakers of Other Languages, Inc.
1925 Ballenger Avenue, Suite 550
Alexandria, Virginia 22314 USA
Tel 703-836-0774 • Fax 703-836-6447 • E-mail tesol@tesol.org •
http://www.tesol.org/

Publishing Manager: Carol Edwards
Copy Editor: Sarah J. Duffy
Additional Reader: Terrey Hatcher
Cover Design: Capitol Communication Systems, Inc.,

ISBN 9781931185684
Library of Congress Control No. 2010921274

Table of Contents

Series Editors' Preface   v

Chapter 1
Introduction: From Theory to Practice in Task-Based Learning   1
   Ali Shehadeh and Christine Coombe

Innovative Applications

Chapter 2
Talking It Up: A Small-Group Discussion Task for the Classroom   11
   Gregory Strong

Chapter 3
An EFL Dictogloss Task: Three Teachers, Three Contexts,
Three Perspectives   21
   Steven Herder, Mark A. de Boer, and Kirsten A. Anderson

Chapter 4
Cooperation, Communication, and Critical Thinking Through
Content-Based Investigative Tasks   35
   R. T. Olivia Limbu and Tara A. Waller

Chapter 5
Task-Based Cultural Awareness Raising Through Learner Ethnographies . . .   49
   Andrew Reimann

Chapter 6
Poetry in Second Language Task-Based Learning.   67
   Patrick Rosenkjar

Chapter 7
Task-Based Templates for Multilevel Classes.   79
   Jennifer M. Herrin

Technology

Chapter 8
Multitasked Student Video Recording 97
Tim Murphey and Jodie Sakaguchi

Chapter 9
Learning Through CALLaborative Projects Using Web 2.0 Tools 111
Carla Arena and Erika Cruvinel

Chapter 10
The Harmonica Project: Task-Based Learning Beyond Words 123
Betty Litsinger

Evaluation, Testing, and Assessment

Chapter 11
I Can! Bringing Self-Evaluation to a Task-Based Syllabus
for Language Learning Success 137
Jan Edwards Dormer

Chapter 12
Knowing Who's in Your Audience: Task-Based Testing
of Audience Awareness 149
Betty Lanteigne

Chapter 13
Assessing Task-Based Activity in a Speech Training Class 161
Aiden Yeh

Chapter 14
Using Online Tasks for Formative Language Assessment 173
Paula M. Winke

References 187

Index 201

Series Editors' Preface

The TESOL Classroom Practice Series showcases state-of-the-art curricula, materials, tasks, and activities reflecting emerging trends in language education and in the roles of teachers, learners, and the English language itself. The series seeks to build localized theories of language learning and teaching based on students' and teachers' unique experiences in and out of the classroom.

This series captures the dynamics of 21st-century ESOL classrooms. It reflects major shifts in authority from teacher-centered practices to collaborative learner- and learning-centered environments. The series acknowledges the growing numbers of English speakers globally, celebrates locally relevant curricula and materials, and emphasizes the importance of multilingual and multicultural competencies—a primary goal in teaching English as an international language. Furthermore, the series takes into account contemporary technological developments that provide new opportunities for information exchange and social and transactional communications.

Each volume in the series focuses on a particular communicative skill, learning environment, or instructional goal. Chapters within each volume represent practices in English for general, academic, vocational, and specific purposes. Readers will find examples of carefully researched and tested practices designed for different student populations (from young learners to adults, from beginning to advanced) in diverse settings (from pre-K–12 to college and postgraduate, from local to global, from formal to informal). A variety of methodological choices are also represented, including individual and collaborative tasks and curricular as well as extracurricular projects. Most important, these volumes invite readers into the conversation that considers and so constructs ESOL classroom practices as complex entities. We are indebted to the authors, their colleagues, and their students for being a part of this conversation.

Based on insights gained from using tasks as research tools, this volume shows how teachers can use tasks as teaching tools. Task-based pair and group activities ensure that students take responsibility for much of the work and have greater involvement in the learning process. At the same time, such activities free the teacher to focus on monitoring students and providing relevant feedback. Authors in this volume found that using task-based applications in their classrooms builds a sense of community, develops critical-thinking skills and intercultural communicative competence, increases cultural awareness, and encourages cooperation, all of which prepare learners to engage in real-world language and culture. In addition, this volume inspires with ideas from teachers who skillfully integrated technology with task-based learning using video and audio recordings, music, and the Internet, including Web 2.0 tools.

Maria Dantas-Whitney, Western Oregon University
Sarah Rilling, Kent State University
Lilia Savova, Indiana University of Pennsylvania

CHAPTER 1

Introduction:
From Theory to Practice in
Task-Based Learning

Ali Shehadeh and Christine Coombe

Task-based learning (TBL) is an approach to second/foreign language (L2) learning and teaching and a teaching methodology in which classroom tasks constitute the main focus of instruction (R. Richards, Schmidt, Platt, & Schmidt, 2003). A *classroom task* is defined as an activity that (a) is goal-oriented, (b) is content focused, (c) has a real outcome, and (d) reflects real-life language use and language need (for a review, see Shehadeh, 2005). The syllabus in TBL is organized around activities and tasks rather than in terms of grammar or vocabulary (R. Richards et al., 2003).

Why are many teachers around the world moving toward TBL? Why are they making the change to TBL? This shift is based on the strong belief that TBL facilitates second language acquisition (SLA) and makes L2 learning and teaching more principled and more effective. This belief is supported by theoretical as well as pedagogical considerations. In the first half of this introduction, we briefly summarize the various perspectives that have tried to account for how TBL can facilitate L2 learning. In all cases, we present the perspective proposed, the theoretical conclusions based on that perspective, and the way in which tasks are seen to facilitate learning from that perspective.

THE INPUT PERSPECTIVE

According to the input perspective, interaction provides learners with an opportunity to receive feedback on the level of their comprehension in the L2, which results in negotiated modification of conversation with their speech partners that leads to comprehensible input, which, in turn, is necessary for SLA (e.g., Krashen, 1998; Long, 1996). Likewise, negotiation serves to draw learners' attention to the formal properties of the target language (i.e., to focus their attention on form) as they attempt to produce it. Learners' noticing of and paying attention to linguistic form is also a necessary requirement for L2 learning (Long, 1998; Schmidt, 1998). Therefore, it can be concluded that negotiation of meaning and modification of input are necessary for L2 learning. How do tasks facilitate L2 learning according to this perspective? Research has shown that they provide learners with excellent opportunities for negotiating meaning, modifying input, and focusing on the formal properties of the L2 (e.g., Ellis, Tanaka, & Yamazaki, 1994; see also Ellis, 2003).

THE OUTPUT PERSPECTIVE

According to Swain (1995, 1998, 2000), learner output plays an important role in the acquisition process because it (a) forces learners to move from semantic to more syntactic analysis of the target language (TL), (b) enables them to test hypotheses about the TL, and (c) helps them consciously reflect on the language they are producing. All of which makes it possible for learners to notice a gap between what they want to say in the L2 and what they can say, which prompts them to stretch their current interlanguage capacity in order to fill the gap. This represents "the internalization of new linguistic knowledge, or the consolidation of existing knowledge" (Swain & Lapkin, 1995, p. 374). In other words, output presents learners with unique opportunities for active deployment of their cognitive resources (Izumi, 2000). Learner output is not just a sign of acquired knowledge, but also a sign of learning at work (Swain, 1998, 2000). Research has shown that tasks provide learners with an excellent opportunity to modify their output in order to make it more comprehensible (e.g., Iwashita, 1999; Shehadeh, 2001, 2003, 2004).

THE COGNITIVE PERSPECTIVE

The cognitive perspective on L2 learning stipulates that learner performance has three basic aspects: fluency, accuracy, and complexity. *Fluency* refers to the learner's capacity to communicate in real time, *accuracy* to the learner's ability to use the TL according to its norms, and *complexity* to the learner's ability to use more elaborate and complex TL structures and forms (Skehan, 1998, 2003). These three aspects can be influenced by engaging learners in different types of production and communication. To do so, it is necessary to identify what task types, variables, and dimensions promote fluency, accuracy, and complexity in L2 learners and use them accordingly. These three aspects of learner performance are important for both effective communication (fluency and accuracy) and progress and development (complexity) of the L2 (Skehan, 1998).

Research has shown that task-based instruction can promote fluency, accuracy, and complexity in learners (Ellis, 2005b). For instance, if a teacher wants to promote fluency, he or she engages learners in meaning-oriented tasks; and if the goal is to promote accuracy or complexity, the teacher engages learners in more form-focused tasks.

THE SOCIOCULTURAL PERSPECTIVE

According to Vygotsky (Rieber & Carton, 1987), external activities that learners participate in are the main source of mental and cognitive activities. When individuals interact, their cognitive processes awaken. These processes, which occur on the interpsychological (or social) plane, include both cognitive and language development. The language development moves from the intermental plane to the intramental plane on the assumption that what originates in the interpsychological sphere will eventually be represented intrapsychologically, that is, within the individual. In other words, external activities are transformed into mental ones through the processes of approximation and internalization. With respect to L2 learning, this means that learners collaboratively construct knowledge as a joint activity. This co-construction of knowledge engages learners in cognitive processes that are implicated in L2 learning. Thus, social interaction mediates learning, as explained by Ellis (2000): "Learners first succeed in performing a new function with the assistance of another person and then internalise this function so that they can perform it unassisted" (p. 209), a process often referred to as *scaffolding*. Collaborative construction of knowledge in a joint activity is an important source of L2 learning.

Research has shown that tasks are successfully accomplished by learners as a joint activity and that this process of joint accomplishment indeed contributes to L2 learning (e.g., Lantolf, 1996; LaPierre, 1994). Also, studies have shown that jointly performed tasks enable students to solve linguistic problems that lie beyond their individual abilities (Swain & Lapkin, 1998).

THE RESEARCH–PRACTICE INTERFACE PERSPECTIVE

Tasks have attracted both researchers and teachers: Researchers use them as a research tool to collect and analyze learner data and learner language (so that they can make principled conclusions on how languages are learned), and teachers use them as a teaching tool. These two groups have worked pretty much independently in the past, with little or almost no cooperation. However, with TBL there are now more serious attempts to make pedagogical decisions to use tasks as a teaching tool based on insights gained from tasks used as a research tool (see, e.g., Ellis, 2003; Van den Branden, 2006b). With task-based learning and instruction, there is now more collaboration between researchers and teachers. In fact, tasks and TBL have brought researchers and teachers, and by implication, learning and teaching, closer together than ever before, which makes L2 learning and teaching more principled and more effective (see also Samuda & Bygate, 2008).

THE STUDENT AUTONOMY AND
STUDENT-CENTERED INSTRUCTION PERSPECTIVE

Recent approaches to L2 teaching methodology emphasize student autonomy and student-centered instruction as effective ways of learning. This is because (a) students take much of the responsibility for their own learning; (b) they are actively involved in shaping how they learn; (c) there is ample teacher–student and student–student interaction; (d) there is an abundance of brainstorming activities, pair work, and small-group work; and (e) the teacher's role is more like a partner in the learning process, an advisor, and a facilitator of learning than an instructor or lecturer who spoon-feeds knowledge to learners (see, e.g., Edwards & Willis, 2005; Mayo, 2007). Therefore, internally driven devices (e.g., self-noticing), as opposed to external techniques and external feedback (e.g., clarification requests), must be encouraged in the L2 classroom because strong empirical evidence suggests that internal attention-drawing devices are more facilitative of L2 learning than external attention-drawing techniques (Izumi, 2002; Shehadeh, 2004).

Task-based instruction is an ideal tool for implementing these principles in the L2 classroom. For instance, research has shown that task-based pair and group activities that are generated by students or are sensitive to students' preferences ensure not only that students take responsibility for much of the work but also that students have greater involvement in the learning process. At the same time, such activities free the teacher to focus on monitoring students and providing relevant feedback (e.g., Shehadeh, 2004).

There is no wonder, therefore, that many teachers around the world are moving toward TBL; that task-based pair work and group work are now considered standard teaching and learning strategies in many language classrooms around the world; and that many publications, symposiums, seminars, colloquiums, academic sessions, and even whole conferences are specifically devoted to TBL. The most notable of these is the formation in 2005 of an International Consortium on Task-Based Language Teaching (ICTBLT), which holds a biennial international conference on the topic.

A BRIEF OVERVIEW OF THE VOLUME

As stated earlier, TBL has brought researchers and practitioners closer together than ever before, and perhaps more so than any other L2 learning and teaching approach. This volume provides a new forum for these professionals to come even closer together and further explore the usefulness of TBL. Can tasks be used with learners at all levels? Is deeper restructuring of knowledge really taking place with TBL? How should task-based language courses be designed? How is the syllabus in TBL organized? What is the methodology of task-based teaching? How are learners tested in a task-based language learning and teaching context? How should task-based language learning and teaching be assessed? The contributors to this volume provide answers to these and other questions based on their application and use of TBL in various classroom contexts.

Given the practical emphasis of the volume and the growing interface between practice and research, we believe that this volume will be of real interest not just to practitioners but also to research students and SLA researchers worldwide, who will get firsthand knowledge from practitioners and be able to evaluate their theories and research in light of what happens in the classroom.

Innovative Applications

In this section, the contributors describe how TBL can be implemented in different learning and teaching contexts and from different perspectives; how it can be used for specific classroom activities, for a semester or a full academic curriculum; and how it can be used with multilevel, mixed-ability students. In chapter 2, Strong describes the development of a small-group discussion task with Japanese English for academic purposes students and illustrates how to implement a single task with a number of teachers and across several courses. In chapter 3, Herder, de Boer, and Anderson demonstrate how an English as a foreign language dictogloss task can be implemented from three different perspectives and in three different contexts in Japan: a girls' private junior-senior high school, a private language school, and a public junior high school.

In chapter 4, Limbu and Waller describe an innovative academic year curriculum that encourages cooperating, building a sense of community, and developing critical-thinking skills through content-based investigative tasks. Applying an ethnographic methodology, in chapter 5 Reimann describes a task-based approach to developing intercultural communicative competence and an increased sense of cultural awareness, which prepares learners to engage in real-world language and culture, pursue relevant and meaningful goals, and develop communication skills and strategies.

Rosenkjar, in chapter 6, describes a literature-based lesson that demonstrates how tasks can integrate focus on form with focus on meaning. In chapter 7, Herrin proposes task-based templates for multilevel students. She describes three such templates that can successfully engage students in speaking, reading, writing, and listening by focusing on exchanging information, communicating, and understanding meaning rather than on practice of form.

Technology

This section examines how technology such as the Internet, video recording, and music can be used to enhance learning and progress in the L2 in a TBL classroom context. In chapter 8, Murphey and Sakaguchi describe a longitudinal project in which students record video of their conversations and perform a variety of related tasks. They demonstrate how this multitasked, longitudinal, and self-evaluated recording allows students to become more successful and autonomous learners. Arena and Cruvinel, in chapter 9, explain how learners can easily be creators of content and how teachers can promote interaction in the TL through carefully designed tasks that lead to meaningful connections through collaborative projects using Web 2.0 tools. In chapter 10, Litsinger describes the Harmonica Project, which involved students in a nonlinguistic pursuit and resulted in language growth as well as improved classroom climate for her multilevel, mixed-grade, middle school English as a second language students, who had been accustomed to teacher-centered instruction and rote learning.

Evaluation, Testing, and Assessment

The chapters in this section address the most challenging issue for TBL: how learners are evaluated, tested, and assessed. In chapter 11, Dormer discusses how students in Brazil and Indonesia took responsibility for their own learning via a syllabus that incorporated self-evaluation. They learned how to monitor their own language acquisition as they pursued effective communication. Lanteigne, in chapter 12, describes a semester-long task-based teaching and assessment project in an undergraduate public speaking course at an English-medium university in the Middle East. She points out how well students can implement what they have been taught about audience awareness and audience analysis in their informative speeches.

In chapter 13, Yeh describes a blended task-based activity designed for intermediate- and advanced-level students in speech or oral training classes. She also presents the pedagogical framework and assessment tools used to evaluate student performance. In chapter 14, Winke explains how to use online tasks for formative language assessment, which is defined as assessment that is used in "evaluating students in the process of 'forming' their competencies and skills" (Brown, 2004, p. 6). She demonstrates how these tasks provide continuous feedback to the teacher and learners, and how this feedback can be used for making decisions about ongoing instructional procedures and classroom tasks.

All contributions are classroom based or classroom motivated, and all fall within the framework of TBL, broadly defined, and the perspectives to TBL outlined earlier. Similarly, all contributions are highly accessible to TESOL practitioners worldwide who come from a broad range of formal and informal educational settings that serve a wide range of language learners.

Ali Shehadeh has a PhD from Durham University and is an associate professor in, and past chair of, the Department of Linguistics at United Arab Emirates University. He is the current chair of TESOL's Applied Linguistics Interest Section, and he has written for top-tier international journals, including Language Learning, TESOL Quarterly, System, Journal of Applied Linguistics, *and* ELT Journal.

Christine Coombe has a PhD from The Ohio State University and is currently a faculty member at Dubai Men's College, in the United Arab Emirates. She is a past member of the TESOL Board of Directors and chaired the 40th Annual TESOL Convention and Exhibit. Her publications focus on assessing English language learners, leadership in English language teaching, teacher research, and evaluating teacher effectiveness.

Innovative Applications

CHAPTER 2

Talking It Up:
A Small-Group Discussion
Task for the Classroom

Gregory Strong

This chapter describes the ongoing development of a small-group discussion
task with Japanese students in a large-scale university language program. In that
respect, it offers a perspective on implementing a single task with a number
of teachers and across several different courses. The chapter also provides an
overview of the literature on discussion skills for English for academic purposes
(EAP), a description of the task itself, and the current iteration of a rating scale
for students leading discussions.

CONTEXT

Numerous writers on the needs of language students have emphasized the importance of providing classroom opportunities for the improvement of speaking and
listening skills (Brown, 2000; Hadley, 1993; J. C. Richards, 2003). Yet there are
important differences between the needs of English language students in English
as a second language (ESL) contexts and those in English as a foreign language
(EFL) ones.

   In the former context, discussion skills have important applications in postsecondary education. Surveys of ESL students and their instructors at the college
level in the United States suggest that the students are reluctant to participate in
large- or small-group discussions. Ferris and Tagg (1996) report that among 234
content area instructors in a variety of disciplines at four tertiary institutions in
California, there was a high level of concern about ESL students' abilities. Ferris
and Tagg found that in addition to note taking during lectures, classes required
a number of other tasks, including the ability to lead a discussion, participate in a
debate, and communicate with native speakers in order to complete course work.
Numerous statements from respondents led Ferris and Tagg to conclude that

language students needed better preparation for the type of interactions typical of U.S. university classrooms. In another study, Ferris (1998) noted the apprehension among 476 ESL students at three postsecondary institutions about answering oral questions in classes and interacting in small groups. Overall, the instructors and students in the two studies agreed on the need for further development of ESL students' speaking abilities.

However, in EFL contexts, the need for discussion skills is rarely vital for academic success, due in part to the range of contexts in which English language instruction occurs. In many places, although speaking ability is seen as desirable because English serves as a technical language, the language of global business, or the lingua franca of intercultural communication, there are actually few opportunities for its daily use. This is certainly true in my context, a large English department in a prominent Tokyo university in which most of the content courses in English literature, linguistics, and communications are taught in Japanese.

This situation notwithstanding, many students in the department seek to develop their speaking ability while in the Integrated English Program (IEP), a 2-year combined language skills program for 650 freshmen and sophomores, which I coordinate. The program consists of 6 hours of weekly instruction in speaking, listening, writing, and reading. Upon entering the program, students take a placement test and, based on the results, are put into classes at one of three levels of ability. They are then taught by Japanese teachers using English in the classroom or, more frequently, by native English speakers. Each of the levels is organized into themes, and students engage in a number of activities and tasks, both in class and as homework assignments, including writing journals or blogging; reading books and reporting on them; and writing paragraphs in such standard rhetorical modes as persuasion, comparison-contrast, and classification before advancing to essay writing and a use of quotations and references.

When the IEP began, the teachers in it were dissatisfied with the offerings in course books designed to develop speaking skills. Many of the activities contained in them seemed to be variations on the drill-and-practice exercises in earlier generations of textbooks. When textbooks did contain conversations, they did not provide much motivation for students to speak.

CURRICULUM, TASKS, MATERIALS

Developing and Implementing the Task

As a result of these factors, the other IEP teachers and I began developing a small-group discussion task. We started with an informal "topic of the week" activity in which students in small groups took turns telling each other about something that they had heard on the radio or watched on television (see Figure 1). Ellis (2005a) highlights the strong support among language researchers for this type of small-group work in which students have extensive opportunities for social interaction that will produce linguistic output and provide opportunities for them to negotiate meaning. Ellis also notes the importance of giving topic choice to language learners in order to motivate them to strive toward better communication. Our initial small-group discussions were also authentic in that they had all the appropriate features of a task that might take place in a U.S. classroom, including the open-endedness of a discussion and the manner in which the discussion could be shaped by participants' contributions and the discussion management skills of the group leader.

For these reasons, our small-group discussion task fits the definition of a "real-world task" that J. C. Richards and Rogers (2001) summarize as one of those classroom tasks "that are found to be important in a needs analysis and turn out to be important and useful in the real world" (p. 231). Our task offered the potential to incorporate content that was meaningful to students into a task that was appropriate pedagogically and yet had applications in the world outside of the classroom.

Today, students at all levels of the IEP engage in this task, several times during each semester as discussion leaders and in all other classes as discussion participants. To accommodate the differences in student ability at the three levels of proficiency in the program, task difficulty can be adjusted by requiring students to read and summarize longer articles, attempt readings with more difficult

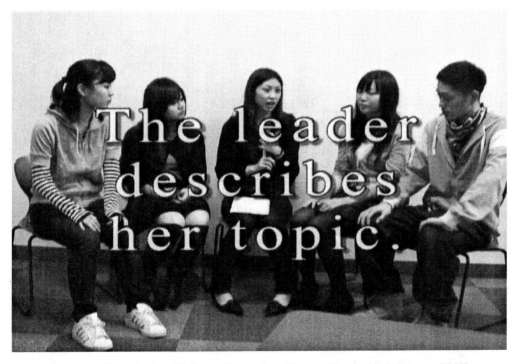

Figure 1. Screen Shot of a Small-Group Discussion (Source: Rucynski & Strong, 2007)

vocabulary and structure, and reach a higher level of performance as a discussion leader. The task takes about 45 minutes of class time in a weekly double period of 180 minutes.

Before class, each discussion leader selects a newspaper article; records the author, title, and publication information according to MLA reference style; and then takes notes on it by reading to find key information (e.g., who it is about, where it takes place, what happened, when it happened, why it happened, how many people were involved). Next, the discussion leader writes down the key vocabulary in the article and decides which words will have to be explained to other students. Afterward, based on his or her notes, the discussion leader writes a paragraph summarizing the article, expresses a written opinion about it, and lists several questions for use in discussion. In class, the oral performance aspect of the task consists of each discussion leader managing a small group of four or five students and employing eye contact, gaze direction, and gestures as well as appropriate language for turn-taking, questioning, expressing agreement and disagreement, and paraphrasing the comments of group members. Finally, with the whole class as an audience, each group leader makes an oral summary of the different comments made by each of his or her partners (see Figure 2 for steps in the process).

As part of the syllabus, throughout the semester the teacher instructed students in the fundamental parts of the task, describing and summarizing their articles and questioning and using follow-up questions when a group member's answers needed further clarification or were in some other way inadequate. In addition, during discussions the teacher moved from group to group, modeling appropriate language, recasting phrases and words correctly when students made errors or could not express themselves, and encouraging students to make thoughtful comments and contributions to the discussion. Videotaping discussion leaders regularly and showing them the tapes for self-evaluation and peer assessment were other aspects of teaching the small-group discussion.

Assessing the Task

We started assessing this discussion task soon after introducing it into the IEP. Robinson, Strong, Whittle, and Nobe (2001) tested it by comparing three classes in which it was taught. The pre- and posttest discussions were videotaped, and a 5-point rating scale was constructed for assessing the four categories of turn-taking, eye contact and gesture, language, and discussion content. Scoring of the videotaped pre- and posttests of the students in different groups, which was done by three raters, showed statistically significant improvement on the posttests by all three groups in all four categories.

In 2007, we reassessed the task, initiating an action research cycle of data collection, analysis, and refinement of the problem for further research (Burns, 1999). The process included videotaping small-group discussions in a number of

Introducing the Task

1. Initially, the teacher describes the components of a discussion: turn-taking, eye contact and gesture, phrasal or turn-taking language, and discussion content. Students view and rate a DVD of others engaging in a discussion.

2. In class, students are given a short, high-interest newspaper article with a captioned photograph (features that make it easier to comprehend). They read it individually, find the key information, and compare this information with a partner.

3. Individually, students prepare written summaries and compare these in a small group, choosing the best one. These are shared with the class and commented on by the teacher. In groups, students discuss their opinions and generate questions. To prepare students to start doing weekly discussions, the teacher reviews the steps of reading an article, taking notes, and then sharing the article with classmates. Each student in the class then signs up to serve as a discussion leader for three dates later in the term.

Follow-Up Classes

4. In another class, the teacher sensitizes students to eye contact by having them draw slips of paper identifying them as high- or low-eye-contact participants in a subsequent discussion. Afterward, they guess who drew which slip. Similar activities follow for the use of gestures.

5. In subsequent classes, the teacher presents examples of functional language, such as expressing agreement and disagreement (see the Appendix). Students practice using the expressions and then employ them in a discussion.

6. In later classes, students compare each other's performance in a discussion. On alternate weeks, the discussion leaders are videotaped and the leaders prepare transcripts, read them, and comment on them.

Figure 2. Steps Involved in the Small-Group Discussion Task

teachers' classes. After viewing these and discussing the results with the teachers, a number of differences became apparent. The challenge that emerged, especially among students with lower levels of language ability, was that student discussion leaders were reading too much from the notes that they had made about their news articles. In one case, a well-intentioned teacher actually directed the leaders to provide photocopies of their news articles and their summaries to each of their group members. That approach, the least successful of all those observed, led to a student discussion that appeared to be almost scripted—hardly a discussion at all. And because each leader would read from his or her notes, eye contact, gestures, and turn-taking were even further curtailed.

However, in the best case, an instructor had set up the task in such a way as to circulate the leaders from one group to another so that they repeated their discussions several times. The repetitions did not tire the leaders because each time they spoke, they had new audiences that were hearing their topics for the first time. At the same time, with each repetition the group leaders exhibited greater confidence and spoke without reading as much from their papers. The results were visible in these students' increased fluency and confidence. After several repetitions of their subjects, the leaders read very little from their texts. The discussions that they led seemed more authentic, with the students responding more frequently to each other's ideas.

Changing the Task

Our observations led us to introduce three important changes to the small-group discussion task. The first was recognition of the importance of repetition for the discussion leader. The second was the focus of our instruction. The third involved creating a new scale for assessing task performance.

Recognizing the Importance of Repetition

The importance of repetition is validated in the literature on task-based language use, which states that performance will likely be improved by repeating a task because there will be less planning and fewer errors, and therefore fewer self-corrections, and greater fluency. Bygate (1996) investigated how a nonnative English speaker narrating a story twice showed significant improvements on the second performance of the task. The transcript of the second performance showed a smaller number of errors, a wider range of vocabulary items, and fewer inappropriate word choices, which suggests that "learners may learn through repeated experience of the same or of similar or parallel tasks, and teachers may be able to use task familiarity to help learners' language to develop" (Bygate, 1996, p. 145). Bygate (2001) also conducted a study of 48 foreign students who were studying English and had them complete a narrative task and an interview task about a video that they had seen 10 weeks earlier, and he found greater levels of fluency, accuracy, and complexity. He concludes that "previous experience of a task is available for speakers to build upon subsequent performance to assist them in formulating more complex and/or more fluent performance" (Bygate, 2001, pp. 43–44).

In addition, T. Lynch and Maclean (2001) examined the effect of repetition on three students making an oral presentation to their classmates about a poster they had prepared that summarized a medical journal article of 800–1,000 words. The presentation took the form of an interaction, answering questions from six other students, one at a time, about each of the posters. Lynch and Maclean found that the subjects, who represented a range of linguistic abilities, corrected and improved their task performances, making corrections or adding linguistic complexity if they had greater language ability.

As a result of what we had seen in our classrooms and our review of the literature, we directed the instructors in the IEP to change the way they set up the task. Now, each discussion leader would rotate from one group to another, taking up the same topic a number of times within the same class.

Shifting the Focus of Instruction

We realized that the focus of instruction in class should be the discussion leader instead of the discussion behavior of an entire small group, which was difficult for a classroom teacher to assess without recourse to videotaping. Furthermore, during the discussion part of a class, the teacher had to interact with only six or seven discussion leaders, assessing their small-group discussion management skills as well as their eye contact, gesture, turn-taking, and use of language, and providing them with feedback. The teacher also could more easily comment on things said in discussions, amplifying the more thoughtful remarks and demonstrating to students that they were making their points clearly.

Creating a New Assessment Scale

As a result of these changes, we created a new assessment scale for teachers to use in evaluating the classroom performance of the student discussion leaders (see Table 1). After testing several versions with teachers using the scale to rate videotaped discussions, our newest iteration distinguished between the categories of Explaining and Questioning. We found that we could use the former for the retelling aspect of the task, in which students describe their article and paraphrase other students' remarks. Questioning, on the other hand, was the aspect of the task that involved eliciting responses from other group members. Finally, we combined eye contact and gestures into a single category of Nonverbally Communicating because we found it easier to teach them in that way and we noticed that

Table 1. Assessment Scale for Discussion Leaders

	Explaining	Questioning	Nonverbally Communicating
3	(a) Described the main points of the article without reading (b) Explained vocabulary when needed, using only English (c) Paraphrased partners' comments accurately	(a) Asked partners questions, used their names, and encouraged their participation (b) Used follow-up questions and rephrased them as necessary (c) Employed questioning to direct the discussion and clarify points	(a) Made frequent, natural eye contact (b) Used appropriate, helpful gestures (c) Had good posture and sensitivity to the body language of other group members
2	Any combination of two descriptors from (a), (b), and (c)	Any combination of two descriptors from (a), (b), and (c)	Any combination of two descriptors from (a), (b), and (c)
1	One descriptor from (a), (b), or (c)	One descriptor from (a), (b), or (c)	One descriptor from (a), (b), or (c)
0	Read the article aloud	Read the questions aloud	No eye contact or gestures

many students seemed to use both more frequently as their confidence increased. Once this version of the scale was complete, we made a simplified checklist from it in order to evaluate students' performances.

As a result of these changes to the task, we have found that the discussion group leaders tend to improve after each repetition of their topic discussion. Their confidence appears to grow, and because they lead a discussion with a different group each time, they are not bored by the repetitions. Even though teachers concentrate on only a few students in each class, the other students in the class see the corrections and benefit from interacting with better student models.

REFLECTIONS

One challenge in implementing a small-group discussion task in a large language program concerns the number of teachers involved. In our case, there are 28 instructors in the program, almost all of whom are adjunct faculty at other institutions in Tokyo, with heavy teaching loads of up to 23 classes of 90 minutes each. Furthermore, as much as 25% of the foreign teaching staff turn over every year, many departing from Japan altogether to return to their countries of origin. Under these conditions, our experience suggests a few measures for the successful implementation of this task and of other curricular innovations: (a) offering a preservice orientation for new teachers to the program; (b) conducting annual orientations for existing instructors; and (c) providing support to teachers in the form of materials for classroom use, including print materials produced in house and recorded samples of student discussion leaders demonstrating different levels of task performance.

Students and teachers in our language program have reacted very positively to these small-group discussions. Previously, in class evaluations at the end of term, students frequently commented that they wished they had had more opportunities to speak in class. We seldom get these comments now because students have so many opportunities to discuss topics of interest to them. In addition to more general topics such as bullying in elementary and high schools, teenage suicide, and the impact of divorce on a family, students have brought up issues such as government support for homeless young people who are working part-time or temporary jobs and are forced to stay overnight at Internet cafes, and whether the "baby drop" at a private Catholic hospital where unwanted children can be left saves lives or simply encourages young people to become more irresponsible.

For teachers, the small-group discussion task provides a welcome change from other classroom activities. Their role becomes that of a facilitator. While monitoring the different groups in class, they also interact with students, responding to their ideas and participating in some of the discussions. In short, these classroom discussions elicit something approaching authentic communication, one of the premier goals of language programs.

In terms of versatility, the task can be implemented with students who have different levels of language proficiency. Although a complex task, it can be introduced in increments over a series of classes. Initially, the teacher should emphasize that discussion leaders should use their partners' names and employ turn-taking phrases. In later classes, as students become more skilled at leading discussions, the teacher should ask them to summarize their partners' remarks to the whole class.

For students at lower levels of proficiency, a number of web sites offer news stories in modified language and sometimes other teaching aids, too. The California Distance Learning Project's (2005) *Adult Learning Activities* seeks to improve access to the news by providing a database of several hundred easy-to-read news articles of about 250 words each that have been rewritten to control for grammar and vocabulary. By clicking a button on the web site, students can also listen to the story being read aloud, which offers the possibility for student self-access and the use of news items with students at elementary levels of language ability. Some of the stories have video content as well. Another web site, *Learning Resources* (Literacyworks, 2006), provides news stories from CNN and CBS. To aid student comprehension, it provides original news stories, abridged versions, outlines, and multiple-choice reading comprehension and vocabulary questions. An additional resource for student small-group discussions is an online video of a discussion among advanced English language students that can be found on the web site of the Hong Kong Polytechnic University's English Language Centre (2000–2009). In it, students discuss the transition from high school to university life.

In summary, research suggests that tasks incorporating productive language, such as the speaking task described in this chapter, will aid in language acquisition. The task is highly motivating because it enables students to choose topics that interest them and to interact with one another. By simplifying the written part of the task or assigning shorter and more easily comprehensible newspaper articles, teachers can easily adjust the task for different levels of student ability. Because the students in a class using the task are organized into small groups, they also have more opportunities to engage in productive linguistic output than in a more teacher-centered classroom. If thoughtfully implemented in a language program through a careful and comprehensive description of the task, accompanied by the means of implementing and assessing it and supported by appropriate classroom materials in print and on DVD, the small-group discussion task will prove popular with teachers and students alike.

Gregory Strong is a professor and program coordinator at Aoyama Gakuin University, in Tokyo, Japan, and has also worked in China and Canada as a teacher educator and curriculum designer. He coedited Adult Language Learners: Context and Innovation *(TESOL, 2009), in the TESOL Classroom Practice Series, and has published fiction as well as the biography* Flying Colours: The Toni Onley Story *(Harbour Press, 2002).*

APPENDIX: QUESTIONING AND TURN-TAKING PHRASES

Asking Opinions	Agreeing	Disagreeing
What do you think? What's your opinion? What's your idea? What do you have to say? How do you feel about it? Could you tell me . . . ? I'd like to ask . . . I'd like to know . . . I'm interested in . . .	I agree. I have the same opinion. I feel the same way. Yes, this is what I think. Likewise for me. Certainly, that's true. Me too. Likewise.	I disagree. I can't believe that. I have a different opinion. I have another idea. I feel differently. I don't think so. I can't agree.
Interrupting	**Clarifying**	**Giving Reasons**
Excuse me for interrupting, but . . . May I say something? Pardon me. Sorry, but . . . Wait a minute! I might add here . . . I'd like to say something.	Would you mind repeating that? I didn't catch the last part. Sorry, I don't follow you. What was that? I didn't get that.	The main reason is . . . Because . . . Seeing as how . . . This is the reason why . . . That's why . . . Furthermore . . . And another thing . . .

CHAPTER 3

An EFL Dictogloss Task: Three Teachers, Three Contexts, Three Perspectives

Steven Herder, Mark A. de Boer, and Kirsten A. Anderson

Dictogloss is a versatile activity that balances listening, writing, speaking, and grammar all in one task. The dictogloss task as outlined by Wajnryb (1990) comes in four stages:

- *Preparation:* The teacher prepares learners for the text topic through warm-up activities, introducing new vocabulary, explaining the task, and organizing learners into groups.

- *Dictation:* Learners listen to the text twice—first listening and letting it "wash" over them and then listening and taking notes for the reconstruction.

- *Reconstruction:* Learners work in groups to reconstruct their version of the text by using their notes.

- *Correction:* The teacher directs students to analyze, compare, and correct their work.

When we first came across this task-based learning (TBL) activity, we were somewhat surprised. If the dictogloss was such a versatile task, why wasn't it already part of our English as a foreign language (EFL) teaching repertoire? Intrigued by this introduction to dictogloss, and impressed by its potential, we agreed to collaboratively undertake a classroom research project designed to investigate it further. Our initial discussions led to an agreement that if we were to research dictogloss, we wanted to know how adapting it can confirm or disconfirm "new" task types for use in the classroom and whether dictogloss would fit into our understanding of current second language acquisition (SLA) theory. Therefore, we developed these specific research questions:

1. How adaptable is dictogloss within three different EFL contexts: a private junior high school, a language school, and a public junior high school?

2. How effective is dictogloss in supporting learner autonomy as an experiential learning tool within a balanced approach to learning?

CONTEXT

Researcher Triangulation

One point that Wajnryb (1990) makes is that dictogloss is not appropriate for learners younger than 15 years old. Even so, we wanted to determine whether it could be used with young lower level learners because these learners need English activities beyond the one-dimensional, grammar-translation lessons they currently endure within the Japanese context.

For this classroom experiment, we all used junior high school (JHS) students, who provided an excellent research opportunity because they are full of energy yet often are a challenging group of beginning learners. Conveniently, the three of us were employed in markedly different teaching environments: a private junior-senior high school for girls (Herder), a private language school (de Boer), and a public school (Anderson). Interestingly, even though we were colleagues from the University of Birmingham's MA TEFL/TESL course, with 3–18 years of EFL teaching experience at the time, we approached the dictogloss from different perspectives. Our three separate approaches focused on process, teacher and learner autonomy, and student engagement (see Figure 1). Although we each focused on one main perspective, we found ourselves constantly overlapping in an intensely satisfying series of online collaborative discussions. The rich and varied contexts in which we researched applications of dictogloss offer insights that we believe can be useful to many other EFL educators.

CURRICULUM, TASKS, MATERIALS

We modified Wajnryb's (1990) original model for the benefit of teachers who are looking to expand their teaching and learning methods. Only two rules were standardized at the outset of the process: The dictogloss passages had to focus on the study of the past tense, and all of the subjects of the study had to be Grade 8 students. Beyond that, many adaptations were made to complement each teaching situation. The following three qualitative descriptions detail how the dictogloss was used and how the students responded to it. The discussion that follows highlights implications for classroom adaptation and reflections on the process of collaborative research.

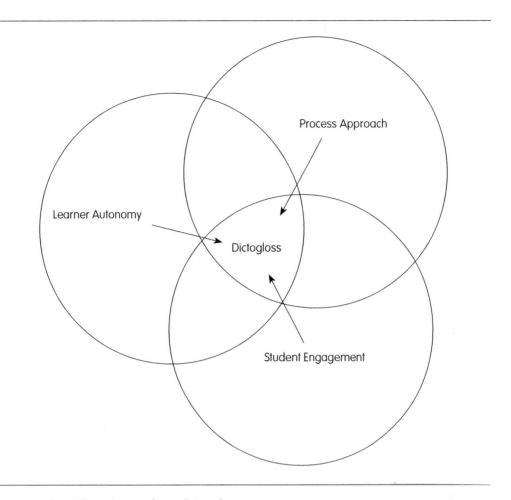

Figure 1. Our Three Approaches to Dictogloss

Private Junior–Senior High School for Girls (Herder)

This research took place at a Catholic private girls' school in Osaka, Japan, where since 1992 I have had full teaching and testing responsibility for more than 500 students in Grades 7–12. One-half of two Grade 8 classes (n = 14 and n = 12) took part in the study.

A quasipsychological understanding of current Japanese students is useful, especially when implementing a new idea as cognitively demanding as dictogloss. Two recent attitudinal changes have had a great effect on the classroom in Japan: Many students have lost the famous Japanese sense of *gaman* (perseverance, patience), and many have abandoned the unquestioned willingness to make an effort. These days, without even a blink, students say, "I can't do this" when faced with a difficult task. This doesn't mean that students are bad; it is simply a testament to the fact that it is no great embarrassment to join the vast number of

Japanese who have failed at English. Within this reality, I was challenged to get the girls to make an effort and not give up so easily.

What if I introduced a series of graded, feasible tasks that would add success upon success and ultimately enable the students to do the dictogloss? This simple question clarified my perspective for this research. The process of introducing and preparing students for a task-based lesson like dictogloss would determine its ultimate usefulness.

Having abandoned textbooks in April 2007, my lessons are now based on the tenets of my own theory of learning and practice. I always ask the following three questions to prepare my lessons, and I did so in approaching dictogloss:

1. Does dictogloss balance the need to "use English" with "studying English?" Yes. In fact, dictogloss offers an excellent opportunity to both study and use English overtly, by focusing on communicating meaning in a grammatically correct form (Wajnryb, 1990).

2. Will students be motivated to do the activity? Students are always inter- ested in my young children's lives, so telling a true story about one of them would be a good way to introduce dictogloss. As part of my theory of practice, I want to actively share my life with my students. In return, I am interested to learn about them using English to interact whenever the window of opportunity opens.

3. Does the task build confidence? Unfortunately, dictogloss initially seemed too challenging for my JHS students' fragile confidence. Therefore, I determined that they would have to develop the following skills in order to succeed with this activity:
    *   listening globally for meaning
    *   taking notes in the first (L1) or second language (L2)
    *   working together
    *   self-correcting
    *   working within time limits

To develop these skills, I introduced the tasks outlined in Table 1. Figure 2 presents the dictogloss that I developed for this research.

On the day of the final treatment, the lesson began as usual except for the video camera set up at the back of the room. Two large pictures of Sarah and Kenji and the prospect of a love story easily captured students' attention. Students were put into teams of three or four, and the rules of the game were explained:

1. First listening—no writing, only listening for overall meaning.

2. Check with your neighbor to confirm what you understood.

3. Second listening—take notes in any form.

Table 1. Activities Leading Up to Dictogloss

Activity	Description
Sleeping Sentences	Individual students receive one or two words; then teams race to construct sentences.
Five Things I Did Yesterday (But One Is a Lie)	The teacher's model focuses on listening and note taking; students' creation focuses on using grammar to convey meaning.
Translation Teams	Teams work together to translate a simple yet enthralling story about my kids or me.
Running Dictation	The "runner" must memorize, dictate, and monitor a text that the "writer" documents. They switch at the halfway point.
Scrambled Sentences	Teams race to unscramble questions about the teacher, run to ask the teacher, and then record the questions and answers in their notebook.

4. Work alone to try to reconstruct the dictogloss.

5. Work in a group to negotiate a set of five answers about the story.

6. Hand in the group's final five answers.

The students were eager to understand the story. More important, they were now better armed with the skills needed to succeed at this TBL activity. Substantially more students were engaged in the dictogloss than in usual lessons. The information they were working with was real, and they were emotionally connected to finding the answers. There was a palpable sense of "English in use" during the lesson. Whereas working alone was frustrating for many, the group reconstruction stage was quite satisfying for everyone: Lower level students could catch up, and higher level students could feel satisfaction as helpers. Students who knew some grammar were perceived as "cool" and "useful" (based on several students' comments). Learning was visibly happening in the room (as one student commented, smiling, "I understand what you said, but I can't write it down . . . yet"). The slight sense of competition between groups increased the time that

---

1. (Sarah **met** a boy **named** Kenji, and she loves him very much.)

2. He **lived** in America for 2 years.

3. They **started to study** English together 6 months ago.

4. (Last week Kenji **went back to** America, so Sarah <u>is</u> very sad.)

5. Kenji **didn't want to** leave his friends in Japan.

Bold = past tense; <u>Underline</u> = grammar beyond students' level; ( ) = mixed tenses in one sentence.

Figure 2. The Dictogloss on Which the Research Was Based

they spent finalizing their answers. Overall, the dictogloss succeeded on many levels and students left the classroom happy. I realized that I had another keeper to add to my cache of effective lesson ideas.

Private Language School (de Boer)

I work in a private English language school in a country setting in northern Japan. I have the flexibility to implement and test programs without any influences from the Ministry of Education or a school principal. I can focus my lessons on student autonomy and student-centered learning. The students come to the school of their own volition, especially at the junior high level, so there are very few motivational problems. Students also are open to new teaching methodologies that differ from their regular school classroom setting. One key difference between my school and their traditional classroom English lesson is that I teach the students at their level of understanding rather than adhering to a curriculum timetable. In addition, class size is small, with a maximum of six students.

During the course of my graduate study, I developed a new TBL methodology that is supported by the concept of Vygotsky's (1978) zone of proximal development (ZPD). The key to this methodology is social interaction in the classroom whereby students who are more capable assist those who are unable to understand the language on their own. The teacher's role is to provide scaffolding for students (Wood, Bruner, & Ross, 1976) and to focus on doing the following:

- Use a *beyond methods* approach (Kumaravadivelu, 2003). Continually challenge students by looking for learning opportunities in the classroom.

- Eliminate the use of display questions. Questions are used by students to get information that they need rather than by the teacher to verify knowledge.

- Exploit social interaction in the classroom. Students are encouraged to look to other students as well as the teacher for support in order to become more autonomous learners. They become aware of the chances they have for learning and for acquiring language.

- Challenge students. For students to work through their ZPDs, exposure to known language is important, yet exposure to small amounts of unknown language or grammatical structures is equally important. Through interaction, the unknown language becomes known and students begin to understand its use.

- Give students more freedom. It is difficult to avoid "teaching" at the front of the classroom, but by stepping out of that role, the teacher helps students become more engaged and make the language their own when given the freedom to do so.

The dictogloss passage I used was a conversation called "What Did You Do on the Weekend?" taken from a popular textbook series. The grammar focus was simple past tense. Students were allowed to listen to the conversation a total of three times, and between listening sessions they were given time to make notes and discuss what they had heard. The use of Japanese was not discouraged because students used it as a tool to negotiate English meaning within the reconstruction stage. Students were permitted to discuss their notes, but without showing their notebooks to each other. One final draft of the conversation was handed in at the end of the lesson.

The objective of the lesson was not to complete the conversation verbatim. The concept of this task shows that, through social interaction, students are able to learn how to acquire language for the purpose of understanding a conversation. They are exposed to past tense forms of English but are not explicitly taught them at this school.

To facilitate learning within the classroom, I redirected many of the students' questions back to the class. In the following conversation excerpt, students are discussing the language until one student directs a question to me. I redirect the question back to the class. Another student attempts the answer, which is incorrect, so I use a clarification check to provide scaffolding. The student picks up on his mistake and corrects it himself. As the lesson progresses, I play a lesser role and students elicit information from each other. Students tended to rely on each other because they knew I would redirect the questions back to the class anyway. The classroom moved from a teacher-centered or teacher-involved one to a classroom in which students relied on each other solely for information, which increased the opportunity for students to assist each other in language acquisition:

S1:   *So, the first part was something, something*—good weekend?*

S2:   Did you had a good weekend.

S3:   *Isn't it*—Did you have?

S1:   *Ah right!* Did you have a good weekend?

S4:   How do you spell weekend? (directed to the teacher)

T: Does anyone know? (redirect)

S2:   w-e-k-e-n-d.

T: w-e-k-e-n-d? (scaffolding check)

S2:   *Ah right! It's* e-e! w-e-e-k-e-n-d.

S4:   Thanks.

The dictogloss exercise using a standard conversation from a textbook worked well in this context. Through interaction with each other and with the teacher, students learned to decipher language despite maybe never having previously

_____

*Italics indicate use of Japanese.

heard or understood it. Students may not usually be encouraged to ask each other questions in a traditional Japanese classroom, but in this context they were fully engaged. Despite my lack of formal teaching, the classroom was an effective learning environment for the students. They needed to rely on the resources they had available, and through this social interaction in the classroom, they were given the opportunity to rely on each other's knowledge and understanding in order to complete the reconstruction of the conversation. The objectives of the lesson—social interaction and discussing the language to reconstruct the conversation—were met. The objective in this task was not for students to reconstruct the conversation, but instead to interact and work together in order to assist each other through their ZPDs. The reconstruction of the conversation occurred as a result. Students left the lesson much more satisfied with what they had learned than in traditional lessons.

Public Junior High School (Anderson)

With a concrete gray façade, a dirt baseball field, a dilapidated pool, and an unused sumo *dohyo* (ring), the junior high school where I teach resembles many rural public schools in Japan. Each class has between 30 and 40 students, making it a challenging EFL setting. As an assistant language teacher (ALT), my major goal and concern was to keep students engaged and motivated in order to actively participate in communicative-focused language learning activities. However, these motivational concerns are completely dictated by the structural limitations of the team-teaching context, depending on what I can negotiate with my partner, the Japanese teacher of English. The reality of the team-teaching classroom ranges wildly, from strict adherence to the government-mandated syllabus to a more meaning-focused approach incorporating TBL. For this research, I was fortunate to have a cooperative Japanese teaching partner.

Before the dictogloss research model, we tried several preparatory lessons to test students' skill levels and assess their ability to successfully complete a dictogloss task. The first attempt at a dictogloss-like lesson indicated that students did not have L2 note-taking skills and stumbled with issues such as word order, spelling, and missing information. Consequently, I modified the dictogloss activity into smaller feasible tasks (Thornbury, 1999) to build up the learners' self-confidence (Table 2).

Subsequent modifications to the listening section of the lesson helped encourage student participation as follows:

- After the first listening session, students were asked to confirm with their partner the information that they had heard.

- Following that confirmation, suggestions of teachers who might fit a certain profile were elicited from students to increase their interest.

Table 2. Dictogloss Stages Adapted From Wajnryb (1990)

Wajnryb's Dictogloss	Additions
Preparation	Note-taking review Warm-up quiz
Dictation (listen only, then listen and take notes)	Postlistening comprehension pair checks Note taking on worksheet
Reconstruction	Reconstruction in pairs
Analysis and correction	Self-evaluation activity Class correction and analysis on the board

- Before the second listening session, students were given a note-taking and reconstruction worksheet that showed them exactly what to write and where to write it.

- Two teachers read the text as an interview. To minimize the cognitive listening load, students were instructed to take notes only about the answers to five questions asked.

An interview-style text (Table 3) had been created from the results of a brief questionnaire previously distributed to all teachers in the school. The purpose of the questionnaire was to gather potentially interesting information about teachers' junior high school experiences that would intrigue and motivate students to participate (Thornbury, 1999).

After the reconstruction, students were asked to self-evaluate the grammatical correctness of their reconstructed sentences. This step was designed to help them reflect on the reconstruction stage as a consciousness-raising activity. During the last stage, volunteers wrote their reconstructions on the board. All students were

Table 3. Interviewing a Mystery Teacher

Questions	Sample Answers
Where did you go to junior high school?	I <u>lived</u> in Nyuzen and <u>went</u> to Nyuzen West Junior High School.
What subjects were you good at?	I <u>was</u> good at social studies and physical education.
What sports did you play?	I <u>did</u> *kendo* and <u>played</u> basketball and baseball.
What food did you often eat?	I often <u>ate</u> *takoyaki* and *okonomiyaki*, but I <u>didn't eat</u> raisins.
Where did you go for your junior high school trip?	I <u>went</u> to Hiroshima, Kyoto, and Nara on my school trip.

encouraged to make corrections to their own work as the teachers evaluated each sentence. Finally, students voted on who they thought the mystery teacher was, then the answer was revealed and several students applauded.

Impressively, more than 90% of the class reconstructed four or more sentences. These completed reconstructions had a range of errors, but this task was successful in that most of the students participated and were engaged. Nonetheless, the following task-oriented problems arose, which are partly inherent to a large junior high classroom setting. Some problems may be addressed by integrating more task-based lessons into the curriculum, thus training learners in learner autonomy.

Unwillingness to Share Information

Some pairs of students were obviously mismatched in terms of ability. In this situation, students with greater ability sometimes tried to hide their work and needed to be encouraged to share and help their partners, and students with less ability were often too shy or embarrassed to ask for help. However, some students demonstrated a great deal of patience and willingness to help students with less ability by working with them each step of the way.

Inability to Take Adequate Notes

This activity was not new to the students, and we discussed successful note-taking strategies before reading the text. However, this was still a difficult and challenging element of the task. Several students had to be reminded or coaxed to take notes. A few were immediately overwhelmed, could not take notes in English or Japanese, and relied on their partner during the reconstruction stage.

Student Inertia

During the reconstruction, some students were stumped by one word or sentence and unable to move on. Asking them how they might begin to reconstruct their notes helped them refocus and continue the task. Additionally, other students were so focused on one point that they were unable to move on to the other sentences without prompting or encouragement.

REFLECTIONS

This section highlights the similarities and differences observed in the three case studies. It also discusses how dictogloss can be modified for young EFL learners and supports current SLA theory, thereby validating TBL activities in the classroom. Based on our individual dictogloss research and the collaborative analysis of those studies, we concur that these experiences validate collaboration in classroom research.

Similarities

Dictogloss was a new TBL activity for all three of us. After 4 months of trialing and testing dictogloss, we finished the research with a much greater respect for its pedagogical merits.

Ellis (2003) and D. Willis and Willis (2007) note that an essential component of a TBL activity is that an outcome be realized. In our contexts, dictogloss resulted in students' satisfaction in having a better understanding of the meaning of the text. This outcome, coupled with the focus on grammatical form, leads us to recommend dictogloss as an effective teaching tool.

The need to adapt the dictogloss from its original methodology was another similarity. Herder realized that to use dictogloss effectively with his students, a series of scaffolding pretasks would be necessary; de Boer's adaptations involved exploiting the dictogloss for its inherent social interaction opportunities; and Anderson saw the opportunity to increase student engagement with the dicto-gloss by embedding it in a quiz about a popular teacher at school.

Tweaking dictogloss for our respective contexts led to more student engagement. More than 90% of paired students in Anderson's class finished the reconstruction section, and 100% of Herder's teams did so. Based on observing considerable focused interaction and the positive way students left the classroom, all three of us unequivocally plan to continue using dictogloss in our classrooms for the following reasons:

- It is an effective TBL teaching tool.

- It can be adapted to individual EFL contexts.

- We observed that students were highly engaged in dictogloss activities.

- Dictogloss can be approached from many perspectives.

Differences

Initially, we tried a few of Wajnryb's (1990) lessons with other groups of students, attempting to get a feel for what dictogloss had to offer as a pedagogical tool. We met once or twice a week online (via Skype) to discuss our methodologies and fresh observations. Almost immediately, we realized that dictogloss was a highly adaptable activity because we noticed we were focusing on completely different areas: Herder's process, de Boer's social interaction, and Anderson's student engagement. In other words, Herder was concerned primarily with what to do before attempting the dictogloss, de Boer observed learning opportunities during the dictogloss, and Anderson focused on what to do with the information after the dictogloss. Obviously, this led to many stimulating pedagogical discussions and opportunities to hear different perspectives. Through our debates and observations, the lesson reinforced once again that for any activity or lesson that we choose to undertake, context is key, and all lessons should be planned based on one's students and one's context. Therefore, we conclude that motivations for using dictogloss can be different, different teachers can have a different focus throughout the lesson, and the degree of adaptations should be related to individual contexts.

Validating Task-Based Learning

Originally, we asked whether dictogloss could stand the test of time and whether it could be used in an EFL context with low-level learners. Our observations overwhelmingly support its use as both a TBL approach in the classroom and a pedagogical activity steeped in the following key elements of current SLA theory.

Learner Autonomy

Students learn to decipher the language as a group, which creates social interaction in the classroom. In the traditional Japanese teacher-centered classroom, the teacher asks the majority of questions (most of which are display type). In dictogloss, students can ask questions that they feel are relevant to their own learning needs, which results in the classroom language becoming more authentic. As learners assist each other, they help each other progress through their ZPDs, which promotes learner autonomy. The teacher's role changes to that of an autonomous learner providing scaffolding during the reconstruction stage. Additionally, this provides significant learning opportunities both cognitively and motivationally for all those involved. Students are focused on collaborating and negotiating both the meaning and the form of the text.

Experiential Learning

Dictogloss addresses EFL learners' overwhelming need for greater opportunities to learn English by actually using it, especially in the reconstruction stage, as they collaborate in pairs or groups (Thornbury, 1999). In the context of the three case studies presented here, students were not only encouraged but expected to become part of the learning process. They had to work with their peers to create a new text, having taken notes in the L1 or L2 (sometimes even using pictures and symbols). This allowed students to play with English. Working in a relatively teacher-free zone and at their own pace allows students to contribute to the discourse in ways that they are comfortable with.

Balanced Approach to Teaching

Dictogloss encourages learners to pay attention to and balance both a focus on form and a focus on meaning through social interaction during the reconstruction and error-analysis stages (Long, 2007). Highly learner-centered tasks such as dictogloss are not usually the norm in EFL contexts like Japan. However, dictogloss is accessible to teachers because, at first glance, it resembles traditional grammar-focused lessons. It can be used to balance a traditional curriculum by encouraging students to actually use English with each other.

Adaptability

Wajnryb (1990) suggests that dictogloss is not appropriate for learners younger than 15 years old. However, seeing immense potential in dictogloss, we decided to challenge her age restriction by testing it with Japanese JHS students, who are just beginning their SLA process. We saw an opportunity to adapt a task meant to encourage learner autonomy while focusing on both the form and the meaning of the text. This adaptability was central to our success in using dictogloss by incorporating it into a broader task and using short texts that were perceived as feasible, even by beginners (Thornbury, 1999; Wajnryb, 1990). For our case studies, dictogloss was malleable in various contexts.

In this chapter, we set out to better understand Wajnryb's (1990) dictogloss. Coincidently, the two major findings from this exploration of dictogloss are pedagogically linked. First, it is an effective TBL tool. Second, our collaborative research process was an invaluably effective professional development opportunity. Whereas we asked students to discuss, negotiate, and ask questions among themselves, we as teachers also ended up in a similar ongoing collaborative discussion. This proved to be an incredibly valuable lesson; the knowledge we gained and the process we explored can be used to pave the way for future collaborative research projects. If we are going to expect students to learn through the negotiation of ideas and language, we as teachers should also be committed to those same expectations.

Steven Herder has an MA in TEFL/TESL from the University of Birmingham and teaches at Seibo Jogakuin and Kyoto Sangyo University, in Kyoto, Japan. He has a never-ending commitment to learning and is interested in extensive writing and defining the EFL context.

Mark A. de Boer has an MA in TEFL/TESL from the University of Birmingham and owns a chain of English language schools in Japan. He is active in MASH collaboration (Meet, Ask, Share and Help, an international teachers network) and is always seeking new ways to develop professionally. His research centers on the discourse that ensues from using Vygotskian principles in the EFL classroom.

Kirsten A. Anderson has an MA in TEFL/TESL from the University of Birmingham and is currently an American India Foundation William J. Clinton Service Fellow at AID India, in Tamil Nadu, India, where she is developing a reading curriculum and materials for government schoolchildren. Formerly, she taught English in Japan in the JET Programme and at Tibet Charity, in Dharamsala, India.

CHAPTER 4

Cooperation, Communication, and Critical Thinking Through Content-Based Investigative Tasks

R. T. Olivia Limbu and Tara A. Waller

Although content- and task-based learning are not new concepts in English language teaching, they have yet to be fully integrated into many language program curricula, particularly in Japan. At Kanda University of International Studies (KUIS), in Chiba, Japan, learners in the International Languages and Culture Department (ILC) have been introduced to a new content- and task-based learning approach in their second year of the English language program. This new curriculum was created to promote cooperative learning, communication, and critical thinking through content-appropriate tasks that are related to learners' needs within the ILC.

In this chapter, we explain the context and rationale for developing the new curriculum. We also describe the full academic-year curriculum that focuses on building a sense of community, encouraging cooperation, and developing critical thinking skills through investigative tasks. For the purposes of this chapter, *investigative tasks* are defined as classroom tasks and activities that involve an element of investigation—the presentation of a situation that progresses to the evolution of a theory behind how this situation came to be.

CONTEXT

The English Language Institute of KUIS has 60 instructors who hail from a variety of backgrounds. All of the institute's instructors teach English language courses within one of the following departments: English, Chinese, Spanish, Korean, International Communication, and International Languages and Culture.

The curriculum described in this chapter was developed for the ILC between 2004 and 2006. Learners in this department are double-language majors in English and one of the following: Indonesian, Portuguese, Thai, or Vietnamese. Learners in the ILC divide their language learning hours between their two languages, which results in only four 90-minute periods a week in English. This is in contrast with learners in other departments, who focus on English in six to eight periods a week. Due to this difference in English exposure, learners in the ILC have language learning needs that are quite different from those in the general English or International Communication departments, whose learners focus solely on one language. This lesser exposure to English also explains why many learners in the ILC lack motivation to study English and why their skills tend to be lower than those of other learners at KUIS.

With these factors in mind, we decided to reevaluate the content and activities of the ILC curricula starting with Sophomore English. The existing curriculum displayed solid ideas and a general direction but seemed to lack creativity, consistency, and cohesion. In addition, the full Sophomore English curriculum did not appear to have an overall goal. The primary concern of teachers regarding this curriculum was that it contained materials that were too abstract and intangible for Japanese learners to understand, reproduce, and expand upon. During formal primary and secondary education, Japanese students are rarely trained in completing abstract tasks, in contrast with their counterparts in English-speaking countries. In addition to the lack of preparation for these abstract tasks, learners lacked the language to accurately express their ideas.

It became apparent that a curriculum needed to be developed that addressed the department's and university's mission to produce learners who think critically. We felt that it was important to first give learners the necessary skills (tools) before allowing them to move onto more abstract tasks (Nunan, 2004). Thus, we decided that the sophomore year would be broken down into two pedagogically different semesters, the first focusing on skill building and the second focusing on the application of these first-semester skills.

The second-semester curriculum was inspired by the popular 1980s children's computer game and television show *Where in the World Is Carmen Sandiego* and the popular television show *CSI*. Although our initial impetus was to provide learners with more motivation to learn English language skills, we eventually developed a multifaceted task-based curriculum that not only engaged students but also challenged them in terms of language and content. We sought to make classes more enjoyable, yet academic, based on our own views of teaching and learning and as recommended by K. Graves (2000). Thus, we chose to create a task-based curriculum using Van den Branden's (2006a) definition of a task as "an activity in which a person engages in order to attain an objective, and which necessitates the use of language" (p. 4). By using this definition, we upheld our desire to improve learners' language acquisition. Furthermore, it was our desire to keep learners interested in the course materials because "tasks, as long as they provide a 'reasonable challenge,' will be cognitively involving and motivating" (Ellis, 2003, p. 209).

CURRICULUM, TASKS, MATERIALS

A new first-semester course was designed around the merits of the original curriculum. The unit themes of identity and culture were retained, and the theme of community was added. We wanted the first semester to focus on building skills that learners would need in order to successfully complete the second semester's investigative tasks. In essence, the entire first semester could be considered a large-scale pretask phase during which students gain background knowledge related to the unit theme and consider the skills they will need to apply during the task cycle (Shehadeh, 2005) throughout the entire semester. Subsequently, the second semester would be the task cycle in which learners would apply their understanding of the topics in order to accomplish the tasks. Of course, in reality, there are multiple task cycles within each semester's curriculum.

Rationale

The ILC instructors shared the belief that it was crucial to develop not only learners' language skills, but also other related skills, including those having to do with presentations, project writing, team work, and critical thinking. Through the units in the first semester, learners would be made aware of these skills and given the opportunity to practice them in controlled conditions before fully applying them, as they interpreted them, in the second semester.

In the ILC, it is important that learners discover their own and others' cultures. In order to examine culture, we felt that it was important to first look at the self and then connect one's self to one's culture. This approach to studying culture was inspired by Bronfenbrenner's (1979) ecological systems theory, which suggests that bidirectional influences occur between a person's immediate environment (the self included) and the macrosystem (culture). After determining that using this theory as a model was the best way to achieve the goal of learning about culture, we decided that learners would first learn to define identity before defining culture.

However, one pedagogical factor gave the instructors and materials developers pause: the multilevel classroom. This was an area of concern mainly due to the varying language abilities of learners. Would they be able to accurately convey their ideas and discuss their opinions with their peers? Would learners with lower language abilities feel inferior to learners with higher language abilities? More important, would the different ability levels cause a rift in the language classroom? To address these concerns, a third thematic unit—community—was added to the first semester's curriculum.

First Semester Overview

Community

Of the three units in the first semester, the Community unit is seen as the most important. The goal of this unit is not focused on learners being able to define and identify communities, but on learners studying the ideas behind communities and building their own classroom community in order to become involved in one another's learning. This idea stems from Lave and Wenger's (1991) concept of communities of practice. By creating their own communities of practice, we hope that learners may become more autonomous with their learning and foster deeper cooperative and participatory skills in class.

The early weeks of the first semester are the most crucial. During this time, learners are involved in various team-building and motivational activities. Each lesson revolves around one team-building activity, and learners are subsequently asked to complete a reflective journal entry regarding the activity. The objective of the reflective journal is for learners to discover for themselves what they learned from a particular activity and how they may extend that learning to future tasks or situations. By the end of this unit, learners bond with one another and become more comfortable in their classroom environment. Due to their increased understanding of themselves and how they relate to the larger classroom community, learners begin to define themselves as members of this community, which leads into the second unit: Identity.

During the Community unit, the first focus that is introduced and taught to learners is presentation skills. Learners are given the opportunity to practice these skills within the context of community, and they conclude the unit by presenting their learning to their peers.

Identity

It was important for the first third of the semester to be devoted to building comfort in the classroom because it is generally uncommon for Japanese people to openly talk about themselves before others, as is common in the West. Comfort is key when encouraging Japanese learners to begin to look at their own identity. However, the topic of identity is broad and inexhaustible. To create a more manageable unit, the topics of personality and nature versus nurture were selected as the focus of the lessons (see Appendix A). For the Identity unit, writing skills became the main skill to focus on. The aim by the end of the unit was for learners to be able to accurately state an opinion about the formation of personalities in the form of an essay with supporting arguments and examples.

Culture

The final unit of the first semester's curriculum brings us to one of the overall aims of the curriculum: to think deeper. Unlike the former two units, this unit is not about the self. When examining the idea of community, it is easy to visualize the relationship between the self and the broader community. When discussing identity, it is virtually impossible not to discuss one's self in relation to one's identity. However, it is often not so easy to place the self in culture.

To many people, the idea of culture refers to the arts—history, language, music, theater, and crafts. For this particular curriculum, the sociological aspect of culture is the main focus. Through looking at stereotypes and the material possessions of different ethnic groups, learners are able to draw inferences about the differences and similarities between groups. The final goal of this unit is for learners to understand the reasons for cultural misunderstandings and conflicts. The focus skill is to be able to put together a presentation that combines presentation skills, writing skills, and Microsoft PowerPoint skills. Learners compare and contrast two cultures and present their findings to their peers as a culmination of the semester's work.

First Semester Wrap-Up

Overall, the three units were designed to complement one another and enable a logical and clear transition from one to the next. The units are also structured to ease learners into the content and tasks of the second semester. All skills have already been introduced by the end of the first semester, and learners are poised to begin working on more abstract tasks and understanding the outcomes of their learning at a deeper level.

Second Semester Overview

During this semester, learners participate in an ongoing investigation that is carried over the course of 14 weeks. The semester is divided into three storylines through which learners work to catch a suspect, Mr. X. Each storyline presents a different scenario with more cognitively challenging content that is related to what was foundationally covered in the first semester.

Identity

The first storyline is related to the topic of identity. Our suspect has stolen a credit card and used it to travel to different countries, purchased tickets to a variety of events, and pretended to be someone he is not. The content related to identity theft is directly connected to one of the topics covered in the first semester: considering one's identity. From the clues, learners investigate how one's identity can be stolen through credit cards and why it is important to consider this current issue as it becomes easier to access personal information in the ever-changing modern world.

History and Culture

In the second storyline, learners receive clues about a plot to vandalize a number of historic places (World Heritage Sites) in order to reduce costs for the expansion of a Japanese resort to other countries. The story touches on issues related to modernization at the expense of cultural artifacts and heritage, which was also considered in the first semester's curriculum. Furthermore, learners gain knowledge about current events and are exposed to different cultural values as they investigate in detail different World Heritage Sites in Japan as well as the rest of the world.

Community

Finally, in the third storyline learners are asked to consider the community of English speakers around the world as they compare and contrast the similarities and differences in English used in a variety of native-English-speaking countries and as they narrow in on catching the suspect who is hiding within these countries. Learners address the first-semester topic of community in a broader sense as it relates to the world and not just their school or neighborhoods. Learners expand their understanding of other English-speaking countries outside of the obvious choices of the United States, the United Kingdom, and Australia, investigating how English is spoken in India, Singapore, Jamaica, and other countries.

Through these three storylines, learners are challenged to deepen their understanding of the topics addressed during the first semester as well as expand their knowledge of content as it relates to these topics in their daily lives, the news, and the world around them.

Second Semester Materials

Step 1

The materials are designed to first introduce the storyline topic by providing learners with some background information, address any vocabulary that they may need, and prepare them to be able to critically discuss the importance of the content to their own lives. This background information is provided in introduction packets that allow learners to conduct pretask planning (Ellis, 2005b; Nunan, 2004).

The introduction packets generally begin with a reading from a newspaper article or other text that asks learners to consider the concept of identity, culture, or community as it applies to the world around them. A list of new words is also included to help learners begin building familiarity with appropriate vocabulary. Finally, learners are asked to begin expressing their thoughts about the reading and incorporating the new words into their vocabulary through controlled discussions. Once they have enough background knowledge, they become amateur sleuths and move on to the second step, when they are given clues to investigate and decipher (see Appendix B).

Step 2

For a class of approximately 25–30 learners, there will be five groups. Each group is given one set of clues. Learners may be given authentic materials for their clues, such as real ticket stubs from events, maps of areas they are to investigate, URLs to access web pages, movie clips, or music samples. Alternatively, learners may receive created materials such as postcards, letters, recordings of messages or conversations, and so on. Instructions for each clue set are given in written format, and learners receive only clarification but no guidance from the instructor. In this manner, they are forced to negotiate meaning, agree on a method to solve the clues, and discuss and come to agreement on the group's conclusion regarding the significance of the clues.

This method of dividing up the storyline into five sets of clues creates a gap activity that uses the three types of gap tasks described by Prabhu (1987, as cited in Leaver & Willis, 2004). The first type is a simple information gap task in which learners have only a small piece of the storyline: the clues. The second type is a reasoning gap task that requires learners to work out the best method to solve the clue they receive; this is combined with an opinion exchange task in which learners need to give their opinions and conclusions on what they think is the significance of their clues. The exchange of information then comes in Step 3.

Step 3

This step further develops learners' presentation skills, which they first started working on with PowerPoint in the first semester. Also, because each clue set does not provide enough information for one group to understand the whole storyline, it is important for learners to present to the class what they have uncovered from their clues. Therefore, as a large-scale jigsaw activity, the penultimate part of this activity is group presentations of the clues and conclusions to the whole class so that learners can collectively piece together the entire storyline.

Step 4

The final step of this activity is for each learner to continue developing his or her writing skills by writing an essay about the activity. Learners are asked to describe their clues and how their group went about solving the mystery, share their group's conclusions, speculate on what they think happened, and express their own opinions about the significance of the concept in terms of their own lives and country.

In all of the scenarios, learners are exposed to a variety of clues that require them to use a particular language skill. Listening, speaking, reading, and writing skills reviewed in the first semester are further developed and honed during the second semester. In this way, learners receive both theoretical and practical knowledge of how to build a sense of community through multiple textual practices, cooperate with one another, and develop critical-thinking skills.

REFLECTIONS

Learners' Responses

After each of the investigative scenarios, learners were asked to complete a survey about their learning experience as well as the materials. This provided us with feedback to make improvements the following years. In response to the question, "Did you enjoy the process of investigating?" the majority of the learners answered yes. The following are a few of their comments:

- "I could knew the way of investigation. And I think that my listening ability become more better."

- "I enjoyed guessing and investigating about this problem. This was exciting."

- "It was exciting, I enjoyed decoding."

In response to the question, "Did you feel that you learned any English through this process?" many learners said yes, specifically mentioning that they increased their vocabulary, improved their writing skills, enjoyed collaborating within a community of learners, and so on.

Some learners mentioned that they did not feel as if they were learning any English because they are used to a more traditional method of teaching in Japan whereby language is taught explicitly rather than using an inductive teaching method. However, during free conversations with learners in the course, other teachers reported that the learners were speaking animatedly and intelligently in English about the storylines and clues from class. If production is a mark of success, then it seems that the curriculum is a success.

Teachers' Responses

Until now, this method of classroom task development has been quite rare, or perhaps not present at all, in the English language learning context in Japan. Investigative tasks have been designed for native English speakers in the sciences for years, but to the best of our knowledge a full curriculum based on investigative tasks for English language learners has not yet been developed outside the United States. These tasks can, of course, be easily adapted for other classrooms by changing the scenarios while maintaining the idea of an investigation. However, the most exciting feature of the curriculum described in this chapter is that learners from all levels are able to complete the tasks using information from pre-task planning as well as their prior knowledge—in effect, grading their own tasks and showing production results in accuracy and fluency (Ellis, 2005b) according to their ability and learning styles.

Furthermore, the content- and task-based curriculum allows for a cooperative learning environment as described by Johnson and Johnson (1994), in which learners are motivated by a common goal and are held accountable by one another to engage in the tasks in order to piece together a complete story. By engaging in tasks that promote critical thinking, ILC English language learners develop their language skills while investigating content that is appropriate for them.

First Semester

Compared to the teaching of the original, more traditional curriculum 2 years prior, the change is astounding from instructors' perspectives. It is easy to see the cohesion in the units because they were designed with an end goal in mind. This helps maintain continuity for learners and instructors (Nunan, 2004), which was lacking in the previous curriculum.

The curriculum continues to help learners develop important language and cognitive skills, but further development in subsequent language courses is necessary to solidify these skills. For example, more time should be allocated in the future for the teaching of additional skills (essay writing, presentation, and research) so that learners can more comprehensively understand the concepts behind these skills. The timing and pacing of each unit could also be modified for future cycles. More time could be spent on the Culture unit for learners to gain a better understanding of cultural differences in the world around them.

Second Semester

From the perspective of materials developers, the time spent developing these materials was well worth it. By participating in a curriculum infused with the element of investigation, learners appear to have been able to gain motivation to study both the English language and the content. This manifests in their drive to be able to communicate and articulate their thoughts and ideas about the investigation and their desire to uncover the outcome of the investigation.

The process of developing this new curriculum was long and often time-consuming, especially at the planning and design stage, when the ILC instructors initially had varied ideas on how to develop the curriculum. However, the merits of this curriculum lie in the fact that the materials challenge learners and encourage them to use all the skills they have learned and apply them to the various stages of investigation. The clues that learners are given challenge them to think outside the box. They must think of creative ways to interpret the messages they receive and work as a team to agree on an interpretation. The materials allow learners to produce as much output as they possibly can—with the only limitation being their imagination. As long as learners continue to engage their imaginations, the scope of the investigations could be virtually limitless. Instructors could encourage learners to keep including alternative solutions and ideas in their investigation reports.

The Full Curriculum

In looking at two full-year runs of the entire curriculum, it seems that it has greatly changed learners' motivation and production of language. It was rewarding to hear them speak to one another about the topics and storylines covered in class. Many learners wanted to know just who Mr. X really was or would speculate about whether they were going to meet a real person. Also, learners were found discussing whether the storylines were true because they were imbued with as many realistic qualities as possible. This kind of informal feedback confirmed that the work we had put forth was worth it.

The curriculum has a forward momentum for learners to develop their language skills and content knowledge. In contrast, the previous curriculum did not have a clear goal at the end, thus making it difficult to know what the learners were supposed to achieve and what the instructor as well as the learners were meant to do in order to bring about the desired result. Therefore, although the new curriculum needs more work related to assessment and fine-tuning of the materials, we feel that it is innovative and has achieved the goal of engaging and challenging learners to improve their English language ability, develop critical thinking skills, and work cooperatively in the classroom.

R. T. Olivia Limbu is an editor in New York City, in the United States. Formerly a lecturer at Kanda University of International Studies, in Japan, her research focused on classroom methodologies and materials development relating to confidence and motivation. She has graduate degrees from the University of Hong Kong and Teachers College, Columbia University.

Tara A. Waller teaches at Zayed University, in Abu Dhabi, in the United Arab Emirates, and is pursuing a doctorate through Macquarie University, focusing on leadership training for EFL professionals. She has worked with a variety of age groups and levels in primary, secondary, and tertiary education in Japan and the United States. Her research interests are in curriculum development, content- and task-based learning and teaching, and professional development.

APPENDIX A: NATURE VS. NURTURE
READING AND DISCUSSION TASK

(In-house materials from the Kanda University of International Studies English Language Institute)

What Is Nature and Nurture?

<u>Nature</u> refers to your genes (DNA), which you inherit from your parents.

<u>Nurture</u> means your life experiences, including your family, the way you were brought up, your early experiences, your childhood friends, even the kind of TV shows you watched when you were small.

The debate over nature versus nurture concerns which one is more important for determining your personality, intelligence, sexual orientation, and so on.

Discussion: Which do you feel is more important, nature or nurture, for:

   (a) **personality**
   (b) **intelligence**
   (c) **some diseases**
   (d) **sexual orientation**
   (e) **the language people speak**

Clear-Cut Cases

In a few clear-cut cases, it makes sense to say that a trait is due almost entirely to nature or almost entirely to nurture. In the case of some diseases (e.g., Huntington's disease), nature seems to be the right answer; basically, you will get the disease only if you have a certain gene. In the case of which particular language you speak, nurture seems to be the right answer. Any human being can learn a language. Which language you learn depends completely on which language you were exposed to as a child.

What Scientists Think About Nature and Nurture

The issue is a very complex one, and scientists do not have the answers yet. Most scientists nowadays believe that nature does not determine (i.e., decide) personality traits, but it probably influences them.

Identical twins (with exactly the same genes) who have been raised separately (i.e., with different family and experiences) have often been found to live similar lives and have similar personalities and levels of intelligence. For example, they might have similar unusual habits (e.g., always separating their white clothes from their colored clothes when they put them in the closet) and have similar favorite things (e.g., they both love green tea ice cream). However, not all cases show this, and often some aspects of their personality might be similar, but other aspects quite different. There has been a lot of discussion in the media about the so-called gay gene, but actually the research suggests it is much more complicated than this. In fact, scientists have not discovered a gene that "makes people gay." It is possible, however, that the presence of a gene might make it more likely that a person is homosexual compared to people who do not have the gene. Again, the evidence is still unclear.

Discussion: Which aspects of your personality do you feel you inherited from your parents (e.g., your short temper, your sense of humor), and which parts do you feel come from your experiences? Do you feel it is possible to separate them?

APPENDIX B: POSTCARD CLUE SAMPLE

(In-house materials from the Kanda University of International Studies English Language Institute)

Dear Jesse,

I've met a girl! What a lady! She's so classy and elegant. She's French! Oh-la-la!
She gave me 2 presents yesterday for my birthday – a cactus plant with 7 spikes and a cellular phone!
My new number is: 07041776

Wish you were here,
Mr. X.

Jesse Hsu
Kanda University of International Studies
1-4-1 Wakaba, Mihama-ku
Chiba City, Chiba 261-0014
JAPAN

Mr. X. has written a postcard to Jesse. He has hidden four important pieces of information in the postcard. Your mission is to find the information in the postcard and put them together to find out ONE place where Mr. X. went. Answer each question, and by the end of this section you should be able to reach the goals of the mission.

1. **What are the FOUR clues in the postcard?** (Please put them in the order found on the postcard)

   a. _____

   b. _____

   c. _____

   d. _____

2. **What's important about answer (b)? Why did this happen?**

   _____

   _____

   _____

   _____

3. **What does answer (c) mean?**

   _____

   _____

   _____

   _____

4. **Answer (d) is very important. Why?**

   _____

   _____

   _____

   _____

5. **Where did Mr. X. go?**

   _____

   _____

CHAPTER 5

Task-Based Cultural Awareness Raising Through Learner Ethnographies

Andrew Reimann

In the pursuit of creating practical language learning methodologies tailored more toward learners' goals, needs, and potential experiences in the real world, task-based learning has been at the forefront in developing and promoting essential skills. Considering that the environment in which most language learners will be communicating in the future is becoming increasingly more intercultural and diverse, language tasks should reflect this by focusing on developing the skills required for navigating and understanding these new and unfamiliar contexts.

Although intercultural communicative competence has been considered an important goal of English as a foreign language (EFL) for some time (Byram, 1997; Kramsch, 1993), many of the methods and materials used to train learners or raise cultural awareness are limited in scope to learning about culture rather than learning from culture (Widdowson, 1998). Materials tend to provide irrelevant and largely trivial snapshots of cultural knowledge, and tasks and methods often fail to actively engage learners or promote skills required for negotiating meaning.

According to J. Willis (1996), an appropriate classroom task is "a goal-oriented activity in which learners use language to achieve a real outcome" (p. 53). Willis also suggests that language use in tasks should reflect language use in the outside world. However, language use in the outside world is quite ambiguous, and activities and tasks based on predetermined or structured scenarios tend to miss the nuances and subtleties of meaning negotiation, which is essential to accurate and successful communication. Nunan (1989) similarly states that a task "is a piece of classroom work which involves learners in comprehending, manipulating, producing, or interacting in the target language while their attention is principally focused on meaning rather than form" (p. 10). As such, according to Nunan, a language learning task is an activity that has a nonlinguistic purpose or goal with a clear outcome and that uses any or all of the four language skills in its accomplishment by conveying meaning in a way that reflects real-world language use.

This approach to language learning and teaching is practical on a local or class-room level. However, the problems that persist center more on what exactly con-stitutes real-world language use and how meaning can be created or negotiated through a common target language between people of different backgrounds and communication styles in unfamiliar contexts, where even basic common sense, values, and perspectives are in a perpetual state of flux. Acquisition of these skills requires a refocusing of goals and ideas for communicative competence. Shehadeh (2005) concludes that "what is needed, therefore, is an approach to L2 [second language] learning and teaching that provides a context that activates language acquisition processes" (p. 14). However, if such contexts are indeed constantly changing and unpredictable, how can they be reproduced in a classroom or structured language learning environment for the purpose of practicing tasks in order to acquire real-world skills?

Widdowson (1998) asserts that learners cannot be rehearsed in patterns of cultural behaviour because these are too unpredictable and cannot be repro-duced in the classroom. However, he also suggests that the classroom context is a community with its own cultural reality and conventions, and that this offers a unique environment in which language and culture are not just learned but learned from. Tasks more representative of the real world can then be integrated into the classroom as a methodology that will provide for communicative com-petence by functional investment, engaging the learners in problem-solving tasks as purposeful activities but without the rehearsal requirement that they should be realistic or "authentic" as natural social behavior. These tasks should then con-nect systematically to the things learners need to do in the real world, incorporate what is known about the nature of successful communication, and embody what is known about second language acquisition (Widdowson, 1987).

Similarly, Bygate (1987) suggests that through oral interaction routines or tasks in which participants are constantly negotiating meaning, such as an interview or a dinner party, learners are able to practice skills such as evaluation, explanation, justification, and predication, and generally learn how to manage interaction in terms of who is to say what, to whom, when and about what.

Addressing the lack of a clear intercultural pedagogy, Byram (1997) proposes that "learners need to see their role not as imitators of native speakers but as social actors engaging with other social actors in a particular kind of communica-tion and interaction which is different from that between native speakers" (p. 21). Byram's model provides that the ultimate goal of language teaching should not be to become a native speaker but an intercultural speaker. In addressing the requirements for an intercultural speaker, Byram establishes a comprehensive model of intercultural communicative competence geared toward developing culture-specific as well as general knowledge and skills for learning about, becoming involved in, and successfully negotiating intercultural communicative interactions. This model consists of a combination of the knowledge and skills needed to be an intercultural speaker and participate in communication in any context.

To put this into practice and prompt learners to acquire the range of real-world skills needed for negotiating meaning and communicating in ambiguous, unfamiliar, and evolving environments, a critical and autonomous task-based approach is required. Applying an ethnographic methodology using a form of participant observation and critical inquiry (outlined in Spradley, 1979, and described in more detail later in the chapter), learners are able to engage real-world language and culture, pursue relevant and meaningful goals, and develop communication skills and strategies such as critical thinking, evaluation, flexibility, and tolerance for differences that will prepare them to communicate at an intercultural level. This chapter describes a task-based approach to developing intercultural communicative competence and an increased sense of cultural awareness, incorporating Byram's (1997) model as part of a basic EFL training curriculum.

CONTEXT

The ethnography project depicted here was inspired by Roberts, Byram, Barro, Jordan, and Street (2000) but was designed to be carried out entirely in the target language and more easily adapted to accommodate various levels, contexts, class sizes, environments, or purposes. The flexible nature of these intercultural communication activities stems from the fact that they incorporate tasks in which differences are not obstacles to be overcome; rather, they are used as valuable resources to explore and understand communication styles and culture. Most of any language learning context, whether homogenous or diverse, is rich with individual differences and subsequent curiosities that form the basis for ethnographic research as well as an impetus for communication. Moreover, these differences serve as strong motivators and incentives to engage learners' interests in relevant communication tasks and activities. If learners can harness the target language to meet the basic needs they have for communication with their peers, then substantial progress toward competence will likely follow.

The initial context in which this project was tested consisted of five classes of Japanese university students. The class sizes ranged from 15 to 80 students. Each class met once per week for 90 minutes and varied in terms of goals, structure, and methodology. The classes included (a) a basic English conversation component in which the focus was on developing fundamental speaking and listening skills, (b) an intermediate-level content-based component on comparative culture in which exploring and learning about cultural differences in English was the primary goal, and (c) a more advanced research English component geared toward more structural aspects of language as well as the skills required for inquiry, such as critical thinking, organization, analysis, and interpretation.

CURRICULUM, TASKS, MATERIALS

As an introduction to ethnographic methodology, students are given some basic explanation, readings, and practice exercises based on materials and ideas from Spradley's *The Ethnographic Interview* (1979) and *Participant Observation* (1980). These include a brief synopsis of what ethnographic research entails, how it is conducted, how conclusions are reached, and how results are interpreted. The process of triangulation—which involves viewing some social phenomena on three separate occasions, from three different perspectives, and using varied techniques or measurements to obtain a more objective and unbiased interpretation—is particularly relevant at this stage. It is important here to explain to students that their conclusions are flexible and open to interpretation, reevaluation, and modification, and are not so much conclusions as detailed descriptions of a particular event, in a particular context, at a particular time and can be used only to try to better understand certain aspects of the community in question and not as an overall generalization for the population. A clear understanding of this process, its limitations, and purpose is essential to developing related intercultural communication skills.

Part of this introduction also involves having students review examples of ethnographic studies and complete a hypothesis development exercise with which to brainstorm ideas, speculate on causes and effects of social behaviour, consider the best means by which to observe or otherwise collect relevant data, and generally develop ideas and a plan of action for conducting their own ethnographic studies (see Tables 1 and 2).

Essentially, an ethnography, in the sense of an anthropologist living among natives, is a portrait or picture of an example of human behavior or activity at a specific time and in a specific context. To be considered valid, this type of research requires detailed "thick description" of events, observations, and circumstances of data collection. The following is an outline provided for the classes involved in this project:

Table 1. Examples of Ethnographic Activities That Can Be Done Locally

Phenomenon	Hypothesis	Method
Some lunch specials are more popular than others.	Teachers prefer rice dishes; students prefer noodle dishes.	Observation, interview
Male/female behavior between classes is different.	Men usually smoke alone; women talk in groups.	Observation, survey
Different age groups use mobile phones differently.	Young people use games, music, mail; older people check news, weather, mail.	Interview, survey

Table 2. Questions to Answer When Exploring Cultural Behavior

Who	Who is involved? How many? What are their roles/relationships? What is their background information?
What	What exchanges, actions, and events occur? What type of communication or interaction?
Where	Where does the behavior take place? What are the context and situation?
When	When does the behavior occur? What time, day, season? What events affect or are affected by it?
Why	What is the purpose of this behavior? Is it conscious, unconscious, planned, or spontaneous?
How	How are the actions involved related? What kind of verbal/nonverbal communication is used?

Ethnography is the process of describing a culture. It means creating a portrait of a people. Ethnography is a written description of a particular culture, including communities, perspectives, people, products, and practices. This type of research is based on information collected through fieldwork that usually involves a process known as triangulation. Triangulation is a way of getting accurate and unbiased data by using at least three different sources or methods; typically these are interviews, observation, or surveys.

The goal of ethnographic research is to get an insider perspective and understanding of another way of life. Rather than studying people, ethnography focuses on learning from them in order to better understand how we perceive others and social differences (Spradley, 1979).

There are many situations and ways in which ethnographic research can be done. In fact, each one of us unconsciously does ethnographic research every day. Whenever we enter a new environment, try something new, or meet new people, we automatically try to get as much information as we can by observing the situation and others' behavior, asking questions, participating, listening, or reading.

Ethnographic research is a cycle with no real beginning or end. Because social behavior is unique and unpredictable, it is impossible to make any final conclusions that can be generalized to all people of a particular group. There are, however, some important steps that make getting started easier, as Spradley (1980) states:

1. Identify a problem; observe some interesting behavior, something you don't understand or would like to know more about.

2. Create some research questions; brainstorm ideas; try to develop a hypothesis by identifying possible causes, reasons, or explanations for what you have observed.

3. Think about the best way or method to answer your questions or prove/test whether your hypothesis is true or false.

After the introduction to the basic principles of ethnographic research, learners can engage in small interview and brainstorming activities in which they explore the diversity of the classroom or practice the basic skills required for conducting ethnographic research, such as interviewing, critical analysis, and interpretation. Several of these preliminary activities are described in the remainder of this section of the chapter.

Task 1: Perception and Perspective Analysis

Activity: Visual illusions and abstract picture interpretation

Goal: To illustrate how preconceptions influence people's interpretation of reality

Procedure: Students are shown pictures of visual illusions as well as ambiguous and abstract images and asked to write a description of what they see (see Figure 1). Each picture is viewed only briefly and is followed by a comparison with others and a detailed explanation.

Rationale: People tend to see only what they expect or want to see. Individual differences of perception and perspective affect how they experience reality. Stereotypes, generalizations, and prejudices lead people to interact with the world in a limited way. By understanding this process, learners are able to broaden their outlook by reevaluating their first impressions and initial expectations, which enables them to become more tolerant and flexible.

Materials: The materials for this task consist of a set of images large enough to be presented as a slideshow.

Perceptual Set (We See What We Want to See)

Often our expectations, beliefs, and values influence how and what we perceive, and as a result our reactions and interpretations may not be accurate. This usually results in illusion, ethnocentrism, prejudice, stereotypes, racism, and discrimination. When this happens between people and cultures, communication becomes very difficult or impossible.

Questions

Where do you think a person's worldview originates?

Do you think all people of a culture share exactly the same worldview? Why?

What do you think shapes a person's worldview?

Without lifting your pencil off the paper, connect all nine dots using only four straight lines.

Look at the following pictures. Write down your impressions.

What did you see? Do others agree with your interpretations?

How is it possible for individuals to look at the same picture and have different interpretations?

What do you see?

Figure 1. Ambiguous Images and Illusions

Task 2: Self and Group Awareness

Activity: Discovering, exploring, and comparing public and private identities

Goal: Determining subcultures, communities, and social influences

Procedure: Students are given a series of questionnaires and communication tasks in which to explore their backgrounds and understand the influences in their lives as well as the factors that make them unique members of their communities.

Rationale: By looking inward and understanding the influences that shape their identity, students are able to understand the extent to which individual differences can vary and how diverse their communities really are.

Materials: The materials for this task consist of an Experience and Perspective Survey, a Life Experience Timeline (Figure 2), group membership analysis, and an Identity and Critical Incident Activity (Figure 3).

Experience and Perspective Survey

Answer the following questions and compare your responses with others. Think about how your different experiences shape the person you are and how you view the world and others. How similar are your responses to those of other students in the class?

Background

Describe your family.

What sort of things does your family do together?

What are some important memories of your childhood? Do they affect your view?

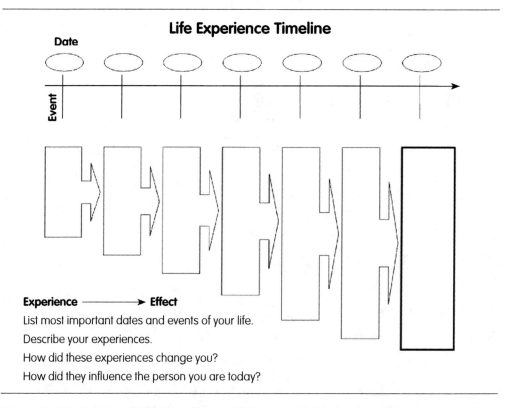

Figure 2. Life Experience Timeline (Source: Reimann, 2005)

Make two lists about your identity. Think about how you see yourself compared with how others see you. Include information about family, friends, community membership, roles, and relationships.	
Private Identity	**Public Identity**
I see myself as…	Others see me as…

How are the lists different? How are you influenced by others and by your culture? Is your identity/personality consistent? How do you change in different situations? Write down your feelings about or reaction to the following situations.

Situation	Your Character/ Actions
You have to give a presentation in class. It's a nice, sunny day.	
You have to give a presentation in class. Your dog just died.	
You promised to invite a friend for dinner, and you just got paid.	
You promised to invite a friend for dinner, and your wallet just got stolen.	
Your father asks you about school, and you just got an A on a report.	
Your father asks you about school, and you just failed an important test.	
How do your actions/feelings change depending on the situation?	

Figure 3. Identity and Critical Incident Activity (Source: Reimann, 2005)

Age

How old are you?

In what ways does your age affect your outlook?

How has your worldview changed as you have grown older?

Home

Where do you live?

Have you experienced any big moves or changes?

How does your location affect your view?

Relationships

Who are your closest friends?

Which family members are you closest to?

Why are these people important to you? How do their opinions influence yours?

Travel

Where have you traveled?

What experiences did you have during your travels?

How have they influenced you?

Values

Describe your religious beliefs (if you have any).

What are the most important things in life?

How do these beliefs affect your outlook?

Education

What schools did you attend when you were younger?

Describe your teachers, classmates, and education?

How do these influence your view?

Interests

What books, television shows, movies, and other media have influenced your worldview?

How do you spend your free time?

What are your hobbies?

How do these affect your view?

Task 3: Exploring Core Values

Activity: Short story interpretation and character analysis

Goal: To gain insight into the common value and belief systems of a community and to understand that, although basic values and the notion of common sense are largely culturally determined, they cannot always be universally extended to each member of that community

Procedure: Students read "The Parable" and rank the characters in order of preference. They also provide reasons for their choices and make a list of each character's strengths and weaknesses. The teacher then writes the preferences of the entire class on the board to make a group comparison and gain some perspective on individual differences in values. As an extra activity, students can discuss the role of gender and whether it would make a difference to the outcome or ranking if the gender of the characters was reversed.

Rationale: Students are generally surprised by the range of differences in the evaluation and ranking of basic qualities and values. Believing firmly that they are a member of the group, it is quite an eye-opener to discover that not all of their peers interpret actions or regard basic values in the same way.

Materials: The materials for this task consist of the following parable.

The Parable (Alligator River)

Mary is a woman of about 21 years of age. For several months she has been engaged to a young man named Greg. The problem she faces is that between her and her fiancé there lies a river. No ordinary river, but a deep, wide river filled with hungry alligators.

Mary wonders how she can cross the river. She remembers Kevin, who has the only boat in the area. She then approaches Kevin, asking him to take her across. He replies, "Yes, I'll take you across if you'll stay with me for one week." Shocked at this offer, she turns to another acquaintance, Rob, and tells him her story. Rob responds by saying, "Yes, Mary, I understand your problem. But it's your problem, not mine." Mary decides to return to Kevin and stays with him for one week. Kevin then takes her across the river.

Her meeting with Greg is warm. But on the evening before they are to be married, Mary feels she must tell Greg how she succeeded in getting across the river. Greg responds by saying, "I wouldn't marry you if you were the last woman on earth."

Finally, Mary turns to her friend Mark. Mark listens to her story and says, "Well, Mary, I don't love you . . . but I will marry you." And that's all we know of the story.

Source: Holmes & Guild, 1973, p. 1

Analysis

1. Read the story and rank each of the five characters in order of your approval of them. (1 = best, 5 = worst)

2. Write a short comment for each character explaining your reasons for ranking.

3. In the space next to the characters' names, assign qualities or faults that you think these people have (e.g., kind, mean, cheerful).

4. Compare your answers with your fellow students. How are they different? Why are they different?

5. What can these answers tell you about your values and those of others?

6. If you had to be one of the characters in the story, which would you be? Why?

7. Do you think your answers would be different if the roles of male and female characters were reversed? Why or why not?

Task 4: Participant Observation and Fieldwork in the Classroom

Activity: Anthropology exercise

Goal: To practice observation, interpretation, analysis, and taking field notes

Procedure: Divide the class into three groups: Culture A, Culture B, and a team of anthropologists. But do not explain why or how you are separating them. Give groups A and B a simple communication or question-and-answer task or activity to complete, and explain to the anthropologist group that they are to observe and try to interpret any differences or interesting behavior. Finally, provide groups A and B with different, opposite, or conflicting communication rules or guidelines to which they must strictly adhere. These can be improvised as appropriate to the class but should include some obvious differences in communication styles such as eye contact, touch, personal space, gestures, and other aspects of nonverbal communication. The group of anthropologists is to observe and describe the communication of groups A and B, taking careful field notes that can be recorded on the chart in Table 3.

Rationale: All students are under the impression that they are simply completing a basic communication exercise. Once their partners begin to act in a manner outside of what they consider normal, communication difficulties and even total failure might occur. Students will need to adapt quickly in order to complete the activity and observers will be able to witness, record, and interpret firsthand some typical difficulties characteristic of intercultural communication.

Materials: The materials for this task consist of instruction cards for the basic question-and-answer task and a chart on which to record field notes, comments, and reflections (see Table 3).

Upon completing these introductory activities, students will have gained some perspective concerning individual differences and the existence of subcultures in their classroom community. Now that their curiosity and awareness have been

Table 3. Chart for Field Notes and Reflections

Write down any questions, ideas, insights, or new information from your experiences exploring culture.	
Language What new words, phrases, expressions, and communication styles or strategies did you learn, use, or experience?	
Culture What interesting information did you learn about identities, communities, people, actions, perspectives, or values?	
Observations Watch your classmates and friends closely. How do they act, react, and interact differently in different situations?	
Discoveries What did you find out about yourself and others? How have your perspectives changed?	
Reflection How do you feel about what you've seen, experienced, and learned? Do you think any of this has changed you?	

raised and stimulated, they are in an ideal position to begin questioning the basic elements of their culture, common values, and beliefs, and are therefore also ready to conduct a self-directed ethnographic study of behavior or phenomena in their local community.

Task 5: Local Ethnographic Project

Activity: Engaging in fieldwork

Goal: The primary purpose of this activity is to gain a better understanding of individual differences and a broader perspective of social interaction and communication on different levels by considering a basic aspect of culture or society and critically analyzing, evaluating, and questioning all factors involved in the phenomena, including the origins, reasons, participants, contexts, artifacts, meanings, consequences, relationships, and perspectives. In short, students dissect an element of social behavior (x), isolating the variables and placing them under a microscope to better understand: Why does x happen? Does everyone do x? When? Where? With whom?

Procedure: After reflecting on some sample studies and reviewing the basic principles of Spradley's (1979, 1980) observation and interview procedures, the ethnographic project begins with students brainstorming topics and developing research questions. To help them visualize some of the more abstract aspects of cultural phenomena, some guidance in determining significant and observable features is provided. Moran (2001) developed a model for categorizing cultural dimensions in a way that can be easily understood and applied to the investigation and understanding of learners' specific contexts. Moran's cultural dimension diagram (see Figure 4) clearly shows how simple elements of culture are interconnected to create a larger social entity. This type of deconstruction is useful in formulating ideas and parameters for creating the ethnographic study.

Materials: The materials for this task consist of charts and tables designed to help learners develop and organize their ideas in order to create practical goals for fieldwork research and group membership analysis.

Learners can use Moran's (2001) model to analyze their own cultures and to visualize more concretely how the dimensions are interconnected as well as how the combination of influences and variables in their lives is unique.

Depending on the dynamic of the class, these initial activities can be carried out in pairs, in groups, or independently. Most of the planning, however, should be completed as homework, with class time being used mainly for receiving advice and feedback from peers and the teacher. Once students have contemplated an area of interest and determined a viable hypothesis and research questions, they can begin to formulate the logistics of their research, including method of data collection; type of subjects; and timeframe for collecting, analyzing, and organizing data in order to make a formal report and presentation of their experience and

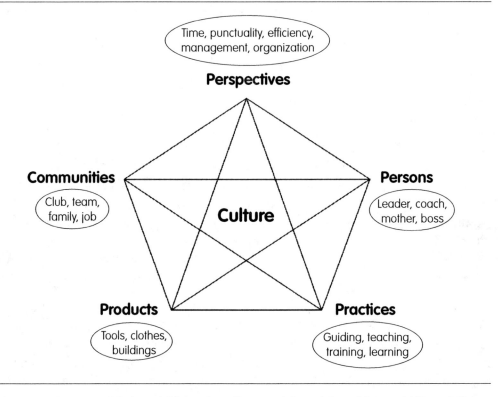

Figure 4. Diagram of Cultural Dimensions (Source: Adapted from Moran, 2001, p. 24)

results. At this point, it is important that the teacher review students' plans and provide guidelines regarding subject matter and feasibility. It is also necessary to make it clear to students that they should not be intrusive in their fieldwork and must respect their subject's privacy, state their intentions, and ask permission to use the data obtained.

The flow charts in Figures 5 and 6 can be used to help students brainstorm, develop, and visualize their ideas, formulate a research plan, and work out a feasible method of data collection. As indicated by the arrows, all ideas contribute to the development of a thesis or testable hypothesis. Similarly, the arrows in Figure 6 indicate that the ethnographic cycle is a continuous reevaluation of data and has no beginning or end.

The following are examples of topics that students' hypotheses and research questions have focused on:

- types of exchanges and rapport between customers and employees at convenience stores

- individual differences in shyness and the use of personal space

- male/female differences in eye contact and power distance

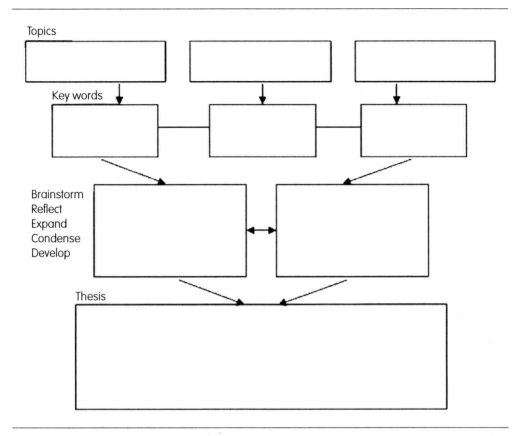

Figure 5. Topic and Hypothesis Development Chart

- investigation of the "unnatural" right-handedness phenomenon in Japan
- differences in cell phone dependence and usage among university students
- cross-cultural differences in expressing and displaying affection publicly
- variations in interaction between male and female university students
- English usage among young people; exploring "Japanglish"
- acceptability of silence in conversation (Is silence golden or uncomfortable?)
- intercultural variations in dating rituals
- individual differences and preferences in brand selection (toothpaste)
- variations in fashion trends and clothing preferences by students of different faculties

After completing their fieldwork and analyzing data, students begin to process their results in a clear and concise way that is suitable for making a presentation to

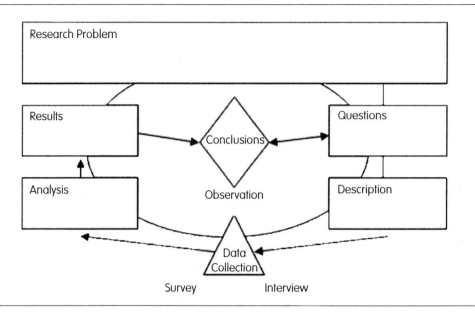

Figure 6. Diagram and Flowchart of the Ethnographic Cycle

the entire class. The extent to which students are able to empirically support their findings can vary according to experience and other curriculum requirements. For the purpose of this project, however, statistical significance of results is considered secondary to more holistic qualities such as overall experience, personal interpretation, and reflection. It is more important that students are able to view their culture from different perspectives rather than establish whether their hypotheses are true or false.

The final task in this project is to create a Microsoft PowerPoint presentation introducing the topic, describing results, and highlighting experiences and insights for the purpose of stimulating discussion and reflection, thereby promoting critical thinking skills and raising the awareness of the entire group.

Each presentation is planned for 10–15 minutes, including time for questions and discussion. Depending on class size, time restrictions, and student abilities this can be shortened considerably to less than 5 minutes or changed entirely to a simultaneous group poster presentation in which all members present their work interactively. The format in this case is kept flexible and informal to encourage audience participation and to reduce the anxieties of the presenters. Students are primarily evaluated on their ability to interpret and reflect on the significance of their research and on their participation in discussions. To accommodate the different levels and goals of particular classes, assessment criteria can be expanded to include more structural aspects of presentation delivery, quality of data collection and analysis, or overall originality of research. However, if the curriculum goals are indeed raising cultural awareness and developing intercultural communicative competence, then a more holistic consideration of students' experiences is best.

REFLECTIONS

Overall, the results indicate that the project was successful in that students responded well to the tasks and classroom activities, comments were positive, research topics were creative and insightful, and methods were innovative. The quality of discussion stimulated during the presentations was also high, indicating that students were indeed able to develop a critical and more flexible approach to viewing their communities and thereby broadening their perspectives and perhaps also their worldviews.

Although the ethnographic project does not duplicate the travel-abroad experience, it is able to re-create the experience of difference and diversity that is in essence the crux of living in a foreign community comfortably and being able to communicate successfully. The analysis of student work and subsequent feedback indicates that an ethnographic approach to developing intercultural communicative competence, exposing students to local differences and opening their eyes to the diversities at home, is the first step to developing global understanding.

Whether the learning environment is homogenous or diverse, there is a wealth of ethnographic information and opportunity for the average language learner. Every classroom is full of subcultures, microcultures and co-cultures that have nothing to do with nationality. All students differ in their backgrounds, memberships, interests, perspectives, and other sociopsychological or affective traits. After exploring their own identities and perspectives, learners can turn this reflexive information outward and explore differences among their peers, communities, and social circles. Through self-directed ethnographic research such as observation, interview, or survey, students can delve deeper into everyday life, bringing to the surface new information and understanding of differences and diversity at home that they previously ignored or were oblivious to.

EFL educators should strive to foster metacultural or ethnographic competence with which learners are able to rise above their preconceptions, stereotypes, and generalizations—in a sense, transcending the part of their identity rooted in culture and nationality (Reimann, 2005). Achieving such an objective and unbiased worldview is fundamental to communication with people of different backgrounds in unfamiliar contexts, using a common language, and it is both a desirable and essential part of intercultural communicative competence. If EFL learners can develop skills that allow them to become sensitive and aware of differences within their own communities, then they will be better equipped to handle ambiguities and differences that exist elsewhere. As a result, they will become much more competent communicators and well-rounded global citizens.

Andrew Reimann (PhD, Applied Linguistics, Macquarie University) is associate professor of international studies at Utsunomiya University, in Tochigi, Japan. He is editor of Canadian Content Journal *and member of the JALT editorial advisory board. His publications focus on raising cultural awareness and developing effective methods for building intercultural communication skills.*

CHAPTER 6

Poetry in Second Language Task-Based Learning

Patrick Rosenkjar

This chapter describes how tasks can integrate focus on form with focus on meaning in a literature-based lesson. The term *task* has had numerous definitions in education, but it has recently come to have a specific meaning in the fields of second language acquisition (SLA) and English language teaching. J. Willis (2005) explains the characteristics of language learning tasks thus:

> So what characteristics do the tasks in this book have in common?
>
> - In carrying out a task the learners' principal focus is on exchanging and under-standing meanings, rather than on practice of form or pre-specified forms or patterns.
>
> - There is some kind of purpose or goal set for the task, so that learners know what they are expected to achieve by the end of the task, for example, to write a list of differences, to complete a route map or a picture, to report a solution to a problem, to vote on the best decorated student room or the most interesting/memorable personal anecdote.
>
> - The outcome of the completed task can be shared in some way with others.
>
> - Tasks can involve any or all four skills: listening, speaking, reading, and writing.
>
> - The use of tasks does not preclude language-focused study at some points in a TBL [task-based learning] lesson, though a focus on specific grammar rules or patterns will not generally come before the task itself, as this could well detract from the real communicative purpose of the subsequent interaction. (p. 3)

This chapter seeks to show how all of the characteristics can come into play in a lesson based on a poem and further seeks to support the claim that the very nature of the language used in poetry lends itself directly to the integra-tion of focus on form and meaning through tasks. This is possible because of what Widdowson (1992) calls the *representational* nature of literary language, which means that literary texts are intended to give readers the feeling of (re)experiencing some emotion or event, rather than merely to convey information. Widdowson contrasts the nature of literary texts, which are representational, with that of nonliterary texts, which he terms *referential* to indicate that conveying information is exactly the focus of the latter.

The method by which a poem represents experience is through foregrounding of certain elements of the text. This means making specific sections of a poem "perceptually prominent" (Short, 1996, p. 11) through skillful use of a variety of linguistic devices: parallelism; repetition of sounds, words, phrases, or sentences; other patterning at the levels of graphology, phonology, lexis, grammar, or discourse; or deviation from the norms of the language or from some pattern previously established in the poem. For students in the poetry-based English to speakers of other languages (ESOL) classroom, perceiving such foregrounded effects can be accomplished through stylistic analysis utilizing tasks that ask the learners to find and interpret specific features of a poem's language. Indeed, these foregrounded features become the task outcomes.

If Widdowson's (1992) insight into the nature of literary language is valid, then the connection between form and meaning in poetry is central, because the linguistic form is precisely the means by which the poet creates the illusion that mere words represent actual experience. Therefore, focusing on the formal features of a poem can lead to the ability to perceive its represented meaning. This is the fundamental principle underlying the use of stylistic analysis in lessons relying on tasks to elucidate poems (see, e.g., Rosenkjar, 2006). In lessons based on a stylistic approach, form-focused tasks lead students to discover the salient linguistic features for themselves. They then possess objective evidence that allows them to move on to more meaning-focused tasks for interpreting what the poem represents, to use Widdowson's term. Indeed, the more kinds of evidence encompassing a variety of linguistic features of a poem that students can find and coherently relate to their developing interpretation, the more solid and supportable that interpretation becomes. Tasks, in J. Willis's (2005) sense, are both the means by which this evidence is found and the context in which students discuss and negotiate their interpretations.

When students learn that they can use their existing knowledge of English to achieve a clear and solid understanding of a poem based on discoverable, objective linguistic evidence, they often become interested in and even excited about poetry. Moreover, current SLA theory maintains that a balance between focus on form and focus on meaning is necessary for learners to acquire a second language (see, e.g., Skehan, 1998). Thus, there are strong theoretical reasons to include poems in the ESOL course syllabus and to teach them through lessons based on stylistic tasks.

CONTEXT

Stylistic tasks are tasks that require students to identify various formal features found in a specific text at the levels of phonology, grammar, lexis, or discourse structure and to use those features to fashion an interpretation of the communicative effect of the text. That is, stylistics leads learners to interpret poems on the basis of the objective linguistic evidence they find in them.

The stylistic tasks demonstrated in this chapter are used in an Introduction to Poetry undergraduate course in the College of Liberal Arts and a Literature in Language Teaching graduate course in the TESOL master's program at Temple University, Japan Campus, in Tokyo. In addition to teaching these courses, I use the same tasks in occasional public seminars for Japanese high school teachers to demonstrate how the stylistic approach to teaching literary texts works and to raise their awareness of student-centered, task-based methods and the important role of focus on meaning in language lessons oriented to the acquisition of actual communicative competence. For Japanese teachers of English, these ideas tend to be eye-opening because of the heavy emphasis in Japanese foreign language classes on the traditional *yakudoku* (translation/reading) method.

The weakness of the *yakudoku* method to teach literary texts is precisely that it treats them as referential rather than representational. The method tends to put great weight on the informational content of poems, to consider translation of an English poem into Japanese to be equivalent to understanding its communicative intent and effect, and to emphasize teacher-fronted lecture in Japanese about the authorized meaning of the poem. The most usual net result of these lesson features is to stifle interest in English poetry because students come to believe that English poems are difficult, boring, and of little communicative value or purpose. This chapter seeks to counter such negative evaluations by offering a lesson to demonstrate that poems can be interesting, motivating, and oriented to communication between writer and reader and among readers. This is achieved through tasks.

CURRICULUM, TASKS, MATERIALS

The poem chosen for this lesson is "Coat," by Vicki Feaver. A copy of the full text is available in Maley and Duff's (1989) *The Inward Ear,* but I recommend that readers of this chapter first work through Activities 1–3 before viewing the text of the poem so that they might experience the lesson as students and public seminar participants would. J. Willis (1996) provides a useful classification of six task types that may be incorporated into lessons: listing, ordering and sorting, comparing, problem solving, sharing personal experiences, and creative tasks. Each activity presented here is followed by a discussion of its objective and of its place in Willis's classification scheme.

Activity 1

Work with a partner or small group to do the following two tasks:

1. List as many words or phrases as you can that describe the positive side of human relationships (e.g., *close friendship*).

2. Similarly, list as many words or phrases as you can that describe the negative side of human relationships (e.g., *jealousy*).

Activity 2

Imagine that you had a close relationship that you decided to bring to an end. List as many reasons as you can for ending that relationship.

Activities 1 and 2 are prereading schema-setting tasks that ask students to create lists in pairs or groups. The outcome is the students' lists in response to the questions, and the pair or group work is normally followed by a whole-class discussion of items from the lists.

Activity 3

(Adapted from Maley & Duff, 1989, p. 72)

Write the words that you think go in the spaces (only one word per space). Afterward, the whole class will discuss the choices each group made and the reasons for them.

Coat
by Vicki Feaver

Sometimes I have wanted
to throw you off
like a _____ coat.

Sometimes I have said
you would not let me
breathe or move.

But now that I am free
to choose _____ clothes
or none at all

I feel the _____
and all the time I think
how _____ it used to be.

Activity 3 is a kind of problem-solving cloze task, the purpose of which is to induce students to read the text carefully and consider the range of lexical choices available to the poet as she wrote the poem.

Activity 4

Answer the following grammar questions:

- How many grammatical sentences are in the poem? What are they? Write them out, or highlight them in alternating colors.

- Find the main verb(s) in each sentence, and circle them. Circle the main verb in independent clauses.

- In what grammatical tense is each main verb? Alternatively, if you do not know the words for the English verb tenses, group the verbs into two groups based on similarity of grammatical form.

In the terminology of Pica, Kanagy, and Falodun (1993), Activity 4 is a convergent task (i.e., a closed task that has definite right answers) that requires students to analyze various grammatical features of the poem. The purpose is partly to establish understanding of the propositional meaning and partly to begin listing features of grammar that can serve as the basis for the task in Activity 5. Students should see that stanzas 1 and 2 are each full sentences with main verbs in the present perfect tense ("have wanted," "have said") and that stanzas 3 and 4 comprise a single full sentence with main verbs in the simple present tense ("feel," "think").

Activity 5

With your partner(s), decide how to divide the poem into two parts, and draw a horizontal line separating the two parts.

- What are the two parts?

- Why did you choose to divide the poem in that way?

- What do you think each part represents?

- What do you think happened between the first part and the second part?

Activity 5 implicitly asks students to use the grammatical information gathered in the previous activity to determine where to divide the poem into two parts based on their understanding of the meaning. It is thus a problem-solving or decision-making task with an outcome of a line drawn somewhere in the poem. Students usually place the division between stanzas 2 and 3, partly on the basis of differences in the verb tenses, partly on the use of "but" at the beginning of stanza 3, and partly on general understanding of the change in the speaker's situation.

Activity 6

Find all the personal pronouns in the poem.

- Which pronouns are used?

- In which parts of the poem (based on your division in Activity 5) are they found?

- Does the distribution of pronouns support how you divided the poem into two parts? Why or why not?

Activity 6 again asks students to find and list instances of a specific grammar feature and provides further evidence for a division of the poem after stanza 2. Students should see that the first two stanzas contain both first and second person pronouns, whereas the third and fourth stanzas have only first person pronouns.

Activity 7

Divide the following list of words from the poem into two groups, name each group, and explain the reasons for your decisions:

Group 1 = _____   Group 2 = _____

breathe

choose

free

heavy coat

light clothes

move

none at all

(not) breathe

(not) let

(not) move

throw off

Activity 7 is a sorting task based on the notion of lexical sets, that is, groups of words that are related because they all pertain in some way to the same domain of experience. The expected answer to this task is a grouping of words into the two categories of Control and Freedom; however, because this is potentially a divergent task (Pica et al., 1993), students sometimes offer unexpected answers that contain insights into the poem. Also, the item "throw off" is ambiguous and may be placed in either list, with the reasons for the decision offering a rich source of communication among students.

Activity 8

In the last sentence of the poem, there are two words that are opposite in meaning. What are they?

Activity 8 is a simple convergent task in which students are expected to answer with a two-item list of "cold" and "warm" and to consider the meaning of these terms for their developing interpretations of the poem.

Activity 9

Work with your partner or group to mark the following sentences T (true) or F (false). Be prepared to give reasons for your choices.

- _____ In this poem, a woman is speaking to her former husband.

- _____ The speaker is satisfied with the present situation.

- _____ The speaker wishes to return to the former relationship.

Activity 9 presents a series of decisions that students must make about the poem based on their understanding of the human situation that it represents. This activity also allows students to express their original understanding of what the poem represents. It is ideal if students disagree with one another on the answers because that provides the need to communicate about their individual interpretations of the poem. One of the items in Activity 9 has a fairly definite right answer ("The speaker is satisfied with the present situation"). However, the other two items are ambiguous or have more than one possible answer. Thus, this activity would be classified as a problem-solving task.

Activity 10

Work with your partner or group to decide the answers to the following questions:

- What does the word "coat" mean in this poem?

- To the speaker, what is the role of the coat?

- What kind of situation is represented by a heavy coat?

- What do the words "breathe" and "move" represent in the poem?

- What do "light clothes" or "none at all" represent in the poem?

- In the last sentence, how has the speaker's feeling about a heavy coat changed?

- What does the speaker mean when he or she says, "All the time I think how warm it used to be"?

- How would you feel if you were in a relationship with someone who controlled you too much? What would you do to try to improve the situation?

- What does this short, simple poem have to say about human relationships?

Activity 10 is similar in purpose to Activity 9 and can be viewed as a set of traditional comprehension questions or as a springboard to discussion of individual students' interpretations of the poem. Again, some of the items have more or less definite answers (e.g., "What does the word 'coat' mean in this poem?"), whereas others are more ambiguous or dependent on individual interpretation (e.g., "What does this short, simple poem have to say about human relationships?").

Activity 11

As a follow-up task, pretend that you are the person who is "you" in the poem. Write a letter to the speaker explaining your view about why the relationship with the speaker ended and how you feel about it.

Activity 11 is an exploitation activity, in which students must use their imaginations and understanding of the poem to create something new, in this case a letter from the opposite viewpoint to that of the speaker. Thus, per J. Willis (1996), it is a creative task.

One reasonable interpretation of what this poem represents is the ambivalence of feeling experienced by someone who has ended an intimate relationship because the other person was too controlling. Yet the speaker who is now free of the control formerly exercised by the other also feels the lack of closeness and notices the negative side to being alone. It is an open question whether this means that the speaker wants to go back to the old relationship. Perhaps so, but equally possible is that the speaker recognizes the emotional warmth of the previous intimacy without minimizing its cost in lack of independence and does not wish to go back. The final sentence of the poem clearly implies regret, but it does not clearly express a wish to repair the breach in the relationship. Perhaps the competing human needs for closeness to others and for personal autonomy are irreconcilable, and the poem represents and expresses this profound and universal human dilemma.

The lesson follows a standard format for reading lessons, with activities before, during, and after reading. Further, all of the activities in the sequence fulfill J. Willis's (2005) definition of task characteristics because the focus is on meaning exchange in each one, each has a clear goal or outcome (e.g., finding a specific set of linguistic features, explaining a personal interpretation based on them), the outcome is shared with others, all four language skills are potentially involved, and various points of grammar arise naturally in the activities and can be the springboard for more language-focused study if desired.

REFLECTIONS

It should be noted that, although the lesson presented in this chapter focuses primarily on determining and expressing meaning with regard to interpreting the poem, there is also a large role for a focus on form. Indeed, a major claim is that the inherent closeness of form and meaning in poems lends itself to a balanced focus on both in poetry-based lessons. Certainly, the lesson plan aims to put students' attention on various formal features as a means to working out an interpretation. In addition, several language points salient in the poem could be addressed in form-focused instruction. These include basic sentence structure; dependent and independent clauses; verb morphology, tense, and aspect; pronoun use; and the nature of metaphorical extension of word meaning. Decisions about which points to take up and when and how to do so are up to individual teachers, but the poem definitely provides a meaning-focused environment within which to situate form-focused lesson objectives. Current notions of effective pedagogy hold that this is a key to acquisition of those language features. For example, Nation (2001) recommends that language courses consist of roughly equal attention to four factors: meaning-focused input, form-focused instruction, meaning-focused output, and fluency development. In a similar vein, Brown (2007) suggests that focus on grammatical form should be integrated with communicative activities.

How have teachers reacted to a presentation of this lesson? In a recent seminar on using literature in language teaching, graduate students and practicing teachers were asked to work on the task sequence reported here. Afterward, they responded in writing to three questions on the poem and the lesson:

1. How do you feel about "Coat" after the lesson?

2. What is your reaction/evaluation of the tasks of the lesson?

3. More generally, what do you think about this stylistic approach to teaching poems?

To the first question, one seminar participant offered this response:

> When I first read the poem, I was reading it as if it were a referential material. I wasn't interested in the message that the poet was trying to convey either. As I did the activities, however, the poem became more personal and it truly came to life. I started [to] sympathize and empathize with the speaker. I wanted to know more about her and her life. In order to do so, I tried to relate the poem to my personal experience. Then I found it exciting to be able to share [a] similar experience with someone on this earth. I might have felt a sense of security in it, too, knowing that I wasn't the only person in the world who was feeling what I was feeling. In the end, the poem was speaking for me and became mine.

Another seminar participant wrote:

> The poem "Coat" looked very simple and clear at first, but as I read it I came to
> realize that it has deep meanings underneath which the author elaborately conveys to
> us by using simple words and grammar. This poem can be a good reading material for
> beginners as well as for more advanced English learners.

A third participant contributed the following comment:

> It is not a difficult poem to read before the activities, but I read it again after doing
> the exercises and participating in the discussion in class, and I began to appreciate it
> more. I became more conscious of the absence of "you" in the second [part] and it
> made me realize even more how effective[ly] the poet was able to make the readers
> feel that the speaker is now alone.

Seminar participants also had a great deal to say about the second question,
which asks them to evaluate the lesson and its tasks. One person offered the following comment:

> Each task is designed to be simple but focused. It is not difficult at all to complete
> each task. Some tasks may not look helpful for us to understand the meaning of the
> poetry at first, such as grammar activities, but as you do the task, you will come to see
> how closely forms and meanings are related to each other. They're thoughtfully and
> carefully designed to guide students to see the poem from many different perspec-
> tives. They scaffold students so that the poem becomes accessible. The students will
> be equipped with skills to find clues to appreciate poems.

Another person wrote:

> The activities to 4 are appropriate for beginners and the rest of them can be used
> for more advanced learners. I myself enjoyed doing these activities because they are
> carefully arranged from the easier tasks to more difficult ones.

With regard to the third question on the value of the stylistic approach generally, the comments were also positive. Here is one typical comment:

> In general, the stylistic approach is extremely useful. For me, it has changed the way
> I can look at a poem. Before . . . a poem would be read through once or twice, and I
> would either get it or not, like it or not (quite often it would be the latter). By break-
> ing it down and seeing the parts of it, I can now appreciate the whole, and actually
> feel it.

Another teacher had this to say:

> It made me look at poems in a different way. I am beginning to look for more "ele-
> ments" when reading a poem and because there are more things that I think I can do
> with it, I enjoy spending more time analyzing it and discussing it with classmates who
> seem to share the same interest. I will no longer hesitate to help a language learner
> whose task in the mainstream class is to analyze a poem because I know the questions
> to ask to help the student think for himself. I think that because I am beginning to

enjoy reading and looking at poems, I can make analyzing poems an interesting task for language learners, too.

Another of the teachers participating in the seminar offered the following insightful comment:

> This analytic approach to teaching poems is very useful in teaching English, although teachers need very careful and thoughtful preparation, especially an appropriate selection of poems is crucial.

What can language teachers interested in using a task-based approach to poems learn from this simple lesson on a simple poem? The first point is the one made in the last teacher comment—that it is vital to choose poems that are suitable for the students and to prepare lessons on them carefully and thoughtfully. Criteria for selecting appropriate poems are discussed by Rosenkjar (2006) and summarized here:

- appropriate level of linguistic complexity
- appropriate theme
- length
- richness and transparency of stylistic features
- familiarity of content and context
- extent of deviation from the standard language
- probability of student interest
- opportunity for students themselves to choose texts
- exploitability for language learning or theme exploration

Rosenkjar (2006) also recommends that the lesson planner perform a thorough analysis of the chosen poem to identify linguistic features suitable for task objectives and to arrive at a reasonable interpretation based on those features. Having done this, the lesson planner is well equipped to create interesting tasks that ask students to find and interpret the features.

A second point is that the earlier tasks focusing on specific grammar points, in addition to their usefulness for interpreting the poem, also offer a way for students to focus on grammatical accuracy. In contrast, the later tasks focusing on interpretation are a potential means for developing oral fluency. Throughout the task sequence, there is an underlying dimension of individual, pair, or group planning time in the activities, followed by a more general reporting of task outcomes to the class. Thus, the task conditions may support development of both accuracy and fluency.

The stylistic approach is useful for teachers because focus on linguistic features as a means of interpreting poems provides a definite direction for lesson planning, and it is highly motivating to be able to construct lesson plans with clear goals. In addition, the task-based dimension puts the learning burden on students while allowing them to generate their own ideas and interpretations within the constraint of adhering to the textual evidence. Undergraduate students seem to find the approach refreshing and useful, as one expressed in response to a question about how she liked the stylistic approach: "I learned how to read and understand poetry in this course, and now I know that poetry is enjoyable" (quoted in Rosenkjar, 2006, p. 128). Moreover, in terms of student language development, although there was no formal investigation into the L2 progress of the undergraduate students taking Introduction to Poetry, comparison of writing that they did at the beginning and end of the term reveals greater accuracy and complexity of sentences at semester's end as well as much improved discourse organization.

Finally, this lesson and the reactions of actual students and practicing teachers who participated in it point to the potentially transformative effect of good literature combined with effective student-centered, task-based pedagogy. I hope that readers of this chapter will be inspired to try the task-based stylistic approach in their own classrooms. Teachers planning to use this approach are specifically advised to choose their poems carefully, perform a thorough stylistic analysis of the chosen poem for themselves before planning the lesson, choose linguistic features that students can easily find and interpret, and fashion creative communicative tasks based on those features.

Patrick Rosenkjar has an EdD from Temple University and has been a faculty member of Temple University, Japan Campus, for more than 20 years. He has taught English for academic purposes in the United States, Malaysia, Japan, and China and is a past member of the editorial board and reviews editor of JALT Journal.

CHAPTER 7

Task-Based Templates for Multilevel Classes

Jennifer M. Herrin

English to speakers of other languages (ESOL) programs often reflect tremendous diversity with regard to age, amount of formal education, language background, and cultural beliefs. For a number of reasons, such as placement testing, funding limitations, or simple lack of space, "multilevel" students are often grouped together in the same English language class, which adds yet another element of diversity. For the teacher, the responsibility of setting up interaction, keeping motivation high, providing appropriate input, and instilling learner independence is daunting. Fortunately, well-designed task-based activities can address all of these important elements of learning language. Task-based activities naturally provide opportunities for learning, but students can also practice socially appropriate language and engage in language focus activities that are "contextualized through the task itself" (J. Willis, 1996, p. 40).

Many teachers are eager to set up task-based activities in their classrooms, but it may seem difficult to find starting points. Activity templates can serve as the basis for routines in the classroom, and even when repeated the templates can seem like completely different activities when reused with different subject matter or a different task. As Woodward (2001) states, "most teachers have elements of repetition in their teaching. . . . Routines free you up from worrying about classroom mechanics and allow you time to consider higher order concerns such as how much people are learning" (p. 194).

This chapter describes three activity templates that can successfully engage students in speaking, reading, writing, and listening. In addition, in these activities "the learners' principal focus is on exchanging and understanding meanings, rather than on practice of form or pre-specified forms or patterns" (J. Willis, 2005, p. 3). All of the activities require interaction, which is paramount because "there is a principle underlying current ELT [English language teaching] practice that interaction pushes learners to produce more accurate and appropriate language, which itself provides input for other students" (Hedge, 2000, p. 13).

The templates included here—the matrix, the dictogloss, and the survey—provide interaction opportunities for students of different levels in the same classroom, integrate polite language, improve motivation, and create a heightened awareness of independent learning. In addition, the templates can be adapted for different themes, levels of difficulty, and areas of language focus.

CONTEXT

Having worked at a community-based adult ESOL program in Arizona and in a large community college English as a second language (ESL) program in New Mexico, one of the best ways I found to involve all class members in collaborating, communicating, and learning is through task-based instruction (TBI). In addition, as an English as a foreign language (EFL) teacher trainer in Ukraine, I discovered that the same templates were attractive to EFL teachers, who viewed the interaction that the templates inspired as dynamic, involving all students regardless of level. Teachers found that the templates did not take much time to prepare, could be copied from the blackboard, were easy to adapt, and put the teacher in the position of facilitator. Also, the activities integrate student-generated and teacher-generated input as well as other authentic material such as short articles. Students build self-confidence and learn to become more comfortable taking risks, which are two affective elements of language learning (Brown, 2001).

CURRICULUM, TASKS, MATERIALS

The Matrix

The matrix is simply a type of graphic organizer that includes a list of questions or opinion statements with a "yes/no" column, "agree/disagree" column, and so on, indicating items to be checked off according to students' answers (see Appendix A). Students first fill out the graphic organizer with their own personal responses to the questions or statements. Next, they interview another student and record his or her answers on the other half of the matrix. Students are encouraged to use English to complete the task by not only focusing their attention on the matrix questions, but also using the following types of phrases:

- How do you spell that?

- How about you?

- It's your turn.

Awareness of these target language utterances needs to be raised for effective task interactions, especially in monolingual classes (Hobbs, 2005). Once students have filled out the matrix, the teacher can ask them to change partners in order to retell information about themselves and their original partners. They can also exchange matrices to report on another student. These matrices can be used for extension activities involving comparing and reporting the data by writing individually and in pairs or groups.

Procedure

First, any new terms necessary for the activity can be reviewed, brainstormed, and presented. The continuum of adverbs of frequency is reviewed by drawing a long line on the board and putting *always* at one end with 100% and *never* at the other with 0%. After making three tick marks throughout the line, the teacher asks, "Where should we put *sometimes*?" To which the students might call out, "In the middle!" The process goes on until the continuum is complete with the words that are needed for the activity.

Next, each student individually checks off how often he or she does each activity, using only the left side of the matrix.

Then students are put into pairs to interview one another. The teacher can set up chairs in rows facing each other so that the activity more closely resembles an interview. One row starts first, which enables the teacher to monitor how fast each pair is progressing through the questions.

When one student finishes the interview, the partners swap roles; the interviewer becomes the interviewee.

When students are almost finished, the teacher gives a signal for students to stop speaking.

The teacher collects all papers (while students are still with their partners) and then passes each pair's papers to a different pair.

The teacher demonstrates how to read the papers, saying, for example, "Tran hardly ever speaks English at home," stressing the third-person singular "s" sound. Students are not required to ask questions but merely report the information.

Then the second student in the pair reads the routine activities of the other student on the matrix.

Options

Because the tasks are completed in English, it is useful to preteach phrases like "Could you please repeat that?" and "Could you please speak more slowly?" Also, while students are listening to their partner report information, they could be encouraged to use body language and utterances to show active listening (e.g., "Really?" "Wow!" "Interesting!") while nodding to show interest.

Practice for other topics can be based on this matrix format. Another easy matrix to make includes a list of materials needed for the class. On the second day of class, students can check off which ones they have and then ask their partners, "Do you have . . . ?", checking off the other half of the matrix. Higher

81

level students can practice "Have you gotten . . . ?" or "Did you buy . . . ?" and possibly "Why not?"

How to Make This Activity More Challenging

More capable students can be encouraged to answer in complete sentences. When the teacher hears short answers, he or she can use a gesture, miming the pulling out of an imaginary tape measure, implying that students should try to answer in complete sentences. If a pair ends up finishing more quickly than the others, they can be asked to turn their papers over and try to repeat the task without looking.

If students finish quickly during the second half of the activity (reporting another pair's information), they can be asked to repeat the activity, this time incorporating questions and asking them in any order (e.g., "How often does Tran watch the news at night?"). Also, the *they* form can be practiced by looking at another pair's matrix and identifying the items for which the partners gave the same answer.

How to Make This Activity Less Challenging

Teachers may opt to allow lower level students to complete the left side of the matrix for homework before the lesson. This allows students to take more time, visit the tutoring center, and look up unfamiliar words.

During the first phase of the activity, the teacher may notice that one pair is making their way through the interview especially slowly. To make sure that both partners get a chance to speak, the teacher can encourage this pair to take turns asking and answering each question as opposed to trying to get through all the questions first before changing roles. Furthermore, if a student is unable to form the questions, the other partner can start the questioning and the lower level student can answer with one word, for example, "sometimes." Then the lower level student can return the question by asking, "And you?"

If lower level students do not finish all of the questions or check marks, they can still participate. It is not necessary for every student to have the matrix completely filled out; each one will have enough data to continue with the extension activities.

Extensions

The data generated from this activity can easily be incorporated into individual, group, or pair writing activities. Higher level students can be asked to write a paragraph comparing information on their matrices (e.g., "I always speak English at home, but Tran hardly ever speaks it at home"). Intermediate students can write 10 complete sentences on the matrix, half about themselves and half about their partner. Lower level students can write 5 sentences about themselves.

Through a journal writing assignment that asks students to write about their daily routine, higher level students can be encouraged to write without the matrix (see Appendix A, Student Sample 2) and intermediate students can write using the matrix as a reference (see Appendix A, Student Sample 3). Lower level learners can participate by copying directly from the matrix, making sentences such as "I sometimes speak English at home," "I always speak English in class," and "I always watch TV in English."

How Is This Activity Task Based?

This matrix activity can easily fit into the task-based model presented by J. Willis (1996) because it has a pretask phase in which students brainstorm or review the vocabulary and phrases that they will need. Also task based is the phase in which students complete the check marks on their papers and plan which piece of information they want to say publicly in class or what they are going to write. The reporting stage is reflected when students tell each other about other students or when they read the sentences they have written from the data. A language focus activity can easily be included by asking students to circle the base verbs on the matrix, underline the present tense in their writing, or write three questions that can be used for "he," "she," and "you."

The Dictogloss

The dictogloss is a type of dictation in which the original text is read twice at a rate that is slightly faster than the traditional dictation. Students are not expected to catch every word, and they only listen during the first reading of the passage. In an attempt to overcome the fact that language learners' notes can include "numerous structure words (e.g., articles and prepositions)" (Dunkel, 1988, p. 270), students are shown how to write in an abbreviated form. During the second reading of the text, students take notes. Then they get into groups to reformulate the text in writing (see Appendix B). Groups then read their versions to the class, and stages of self- and peer-correction are applied. The original text is shared with students to serve as a basis for extension tasks. The student samples presented in Appendix B are based on an adaptation of an authentic text from a local U.S. news station's web site.

Procedure

At the start of the activity, students preview the subject matter of the dictogloss. Because the sample dictogloss task used here is based on the theme of the New Mexico State Fair, students are first asked what they know about a fair. Then they call out related words and the teacher provides clarification.

The teacher gives some key vocabulary that he or she anticipates will be challenging for the students. In the State Fair example, students guess the meanings of *crowds, plenty of, rides,* and *booths.* The teacher clarifies with examples and visuals.

The teacher asks students to put down their pencils and only listen. He or she reads a short article, which can be an authentic text, an adapted text, or a personal story. The State Fair article was approximately 100 words.

Then the students are given a short explanation of taking notes. The teacher repeats the first line from the story (e.g., "The New Mexico State Fair starts on Friday morning") and gives a demonstration of good note taking (e.g., "NM State Fair starts Fri. morn."). Thus students are more prepared to write quickly and catch what they can.

The students are asked to pick up their pencils and take notes. The teacher reads the story again, pausing slightly longer than natural speech between phrases and between sentences. Students don't have to catch every word, but they should catch the gist and key words. The teacher does not repeat phrases from the text.

In groups, students reformulate the story. The teacher explains how one student may have caught one fact (e.g., "two-week event") that is different from what another may have caught (e.g., "it ends September 23," "games, fun, and entertainment"). Working together, students are to compare notes and things that they remember. The structures can be different from the original, but the information should be the same.

Students can be divided into groups either randomly or by ability level. If they work in mixed-ability groups, the groups should be reminded to include everyone. If they work in same-ability groups, the tasks can be altered slightly to be more or less challenging.

The reformulations can be written by a group secretary on large poster paper or on an overhead transparency (see Appendix B). The teacher ends the writing phase when most groups are finished. The sentences for each group are then presented by a group representative. Peer-correction is encouraged, but some grammar points can be overlooked at the teacher's discretion because correcting every single error is not the objective. The goal is to make students feel successful and practice catching their own and each other's mistakes.

Finally, the original text is passed out and students take turns reading it to each other.

Options

While preteaching key vocabulary, the teacher can encourage students to ask, "What does *rides* mean?" or "What does that mean?" Also, the teacher can write the words on the board and ask students for ideas mirroring back the same structure, "What does this word mean?" Encouraging phrases like "That's right!" and "Not exactly, but you're close" can be used to keep the entire interaction in English. Phrases like "How about you?" and "What do you think?" can be pretaught to encourage higher level students to get input from lower level ones.

Other texts can easily be used as dictogloss material, reflecting authentic themes and personal stories. Even texts from textbooks can be introduced in this way; students are much more interested in reading the original after having first worked through a text via the dictogloss format.

How to Make This Activity More Challenging

Advanced groups can be asked to write a paragraph reconstructing as much of the story as they can. The Dictogloss Sample 1 in Appendix B shows how even though the task for the class was to try to write at least five sentences, one group decided to write more and in paragraph form. In other words, they self-selected a more challenging task.

For pairs that finish first during the stage in which students read the dictation to each other, they can be asked to turn the text over and try to retell the story to their partner from memory.

How to Make This Activity Less Challenging

Lower level groups can be asked to write words or draw pictures from what they remember of the story. If necessary, once all groups are on task, the teacher can return to a lower level group and quietly repeat the story, paraphrasing it in simpler terms. Alternatively, a simplified cloze activity of the story can be provided, with some of the key words either blanked out or put in a mixed-up word list below the text.

Student Sample 2 in Appendix B shows how members of a lower level group were unable to write all complete sentences, but they were able to write some key phrases and vocabulary. In the reporting stage, peers could help expand the fragments into sentences.

Extensions

The original text can be used as a model for students to write about a similar topic. In the State Fair example, students could work in groups, pairs, or individually to write about an event that takes place in their country, such as Carnival. Higher level students can write without a model; lower level students can be encouraged to use the model text. In addition, students can be given follow-up readings that expand on the theme of the State Fair as the work that they do with the dictogloss can create schema for subsequent texts.

How Is This Activity Task Based?

In the dictogloss activity, not only are all four skills being engaged, but there are clear stages of J. Willis's (1996) task-based learning model. The activity includes a pretask stage, during which the topic is introduced and vocabulary is previewed. There is a task stage, when students listen and take notes. Then comes a planning stage, when students discuss what information they have and how they will write their sentences. During a reporting stage, students read their versions of the story. Finally, the language focus stage occurs when students call out self- and peer-corrections when the reformulations are being reviewed.

The Survey

The last template involves using yet another graphic organizer for each student to ask questions on a certain topic to many students in the class and record their answers. Whereas the matrix is more like an interview with one other person, the survey involves asking many people questions. The repetition involved in asking the same questions to many students serves as a kind of drill. As Bygate (1996) suggests, repeating a task may help students become more aware of formulating language and may help improve fluency.

The survey can be designed so that students give and record information on any topic such as likes and dislikes, personality traits, or monthly expenditures. The sample survey in Appendix C shows information collected by students that was based on a previous exercise in which each student had made plans to attend the New Mexico State Fair with another student. The data from the surveys can be extended to include writing, retelling information or reporting speech, and analyzing the data to design other graphic organizers such as bar graphs.

Procedure

Before students begin, the teacher models the procedure, handing out a survey to each student and saying, "Could you please ask me these questions?" After a student calls out a question, the teacher answers. This demonstration procedure continues until the students get the idea that they are supposed to write the name of the person to whom they are addressing their questions. Then the teacher asks them to fill in their answers on the survey sheet. Incomplete sentences or notes are encouraged—only the information has to be correct, not the grammar. Extending the information into complete sentences can come later in the task sequence.

Note: It is important that students already know the information they are going to share with each other. In the sample survey (see Appendix C), pairs of students had previously read a list of events offered at the State Fair, and they had decided what they would see, why, and when.

The teacher can briefly address confusion regarding issues such as prepositions for dates and days (e.g., *on* Saturday, *on* September 23, *at* 3 p.m., *around* 3 p.m.). Questions about this type of information can be answered without long explanations, which can be helpful to students.

Students set off on their own to interview classmates, writing down answers according to their level and ability.

Students are encouraged to speak to as many fellow students as possible, concentrating on getting the names and information down as correctly as they can.

Options

Because students speak with so many other students in this activity, it is important for them to ask, "What is your name?" and "Could you spell that?" It is also important for them to be able to ask, "Could you repeat that?" and "Could you please speak more slowly?"

When classes are smaller, and the survey questions more general, it often works well to ask another teacher if your students can come in and survey his or her students. It builds confidence for students to be around unfamiliar people and manage talking with them, asking their names and a few simple questions. Surveying a class of native speakers is ideal, but surveying another English language class can be productive too—for both classes!

Surveys can be designed to collect any type of information that may be related to the curriculum. For example, recording phone numbers and learning to say e-mail addresses with the *at, dot,* and *com* can be helpful, not to mention that students then have a record of their classmates' names and contact information.

How to Make This Activity More Challenging

Higher level students can be encouraged to ask the questions from the handout the first few times. Then they should fold over the top of their paper to hide the questions. From the other answers, they can be prompted to create the correct form of the questions, peeking at the written questions if necessary. More advanced students tend to naturally want to concentrate on spelling, and teachers should encourage them to ask for clarification and to answer in complete sentences, especially if they are capable and seem to be zipping through the survey quickly.

How to Make This Activity Less Challenging

Lower level students can write one-word answers, and they do not have to finish the whole survey. For a lower level student, it can be helpful to fill out a row with his or her own name and answers to the questions so that when another student asks the questions, the student can read his or her own answers instead of freezing up and forgetting them due to nervousness. Also, prompts of the correct question and answer forms can be written on the board to support these students. Remind others that if they can ask and answer correctly without looking at the board, it is better.

Extensions

Once the survey sheet has some data, it can be used for drills and further speaking practice. Students can get in pairs. The first student transforms the first line of information into sentences (e.g., "Tran is going to see the Bear Show. He is going with Mario. They want to see it because they like animals and it will be interesting. They are going to see it on Saturday at 3 p.m."). Then the other student chooses a different person from his or her list and transforms the data into sentences. Lower level students can face the board where the model sentences are written. Higher level students can turn their backs on the models and try to form the structures themselves.

Another task the students can do in pairs is to ask and answer about the entries on the survey. For example, "Who is the first person on your survey?" "What is he going to see?" "Who is he going with?" and "When is he going?" can be answered with real information. Again, supporting lower level students with the prompts and encouraging the higher level students to make the transformation is helpful.

Similar to the matrix, the survey can be used as a basis for different writing activities. Groups can analyze their data to write sentences using *nobody, a few people, some people, most people,* and *everybody.* For instance, they can create sentences like, "Nobody is going to stay home," "Everyone is going to the fair," and "A few people are going to see the Bear Show." Then group representatives can report the sentences to the class. Individually, students can write sentences, paragraphs reporting information, or paragraphs comparing information. Lower level students can make a calendar according to the dates and times, and write who is going to the fair on which date and at which time. Students can also work together to make bar graphs or pie charts to show how many or what percentage of the students are going to the various activities.

How Is This Activity Task Based?

The pretask is the discussion in pairs, in which students decide what they are going to see, why, and when. Also, the review of prepositions of time is conducted before the task. The task of speaking to many students in order to record answers to the questions creates a high-energy situation in which students are speaking English. Although the environment is dynamic, students tend to think (or plan) before they answer, knowing that their answers will be recorded. This is demonstrated by the little notes students write to themselves in light pencil on their papers (in Appendix C, you can see the "on" and "at" written in the When column). This effort to correctly produce the structure is evidence that independent monitoring is taking place. Also, before the writing tasks, students plan what information they want to include.

The reporting stage involves reading what they wrote or presenting the graphs they designed. Because the sample survey described here involves asking questions about plans, follow-up language activities that focus on using the affirmative and interrogative forms of *going to* can be covered, for example. So, in pairs, students write three more questions in the future tense that they would like to ask someone. In addition, some language that was pointed out before the students set off to conduct their survey (e.g., *on* and *at* as prepositions of time) can be considered part of focusing on form in meaningful context because the noticing was initiated by a student.

REFLECTIONS

Designing and conducting task-based activities is exciting because I find that the approach sets students up for success. Once they understand the task itself, they become engrossed with speaking as much English as they can, recording information, and helping each other.

I have seen how students become highly motivated, start taking risks, and build their self-confidence. I once had a student who was unable to take notes during the dictogloss because his writing skills were quite low. Once he was placed in a group to reformulate, however, I was surprised to find that he became actively involved in offering information from the story because his listening and memory skills were exceptional. As he was retelling what he remembered, the other students in the group wrote what he said, and they collaboratively completed the task. I have also seen students who were afraid to speak lose their fear and engage with higher level students to complete the survey. The confidence of lower level students also rises significantly when they fill an entire page in their writing journal by expanding on data from their matrix. At the same time, higher level students push each other to write more sentences in their dictoglosses, try to complete every row in the survey, and enjoy the challenge of trying to repeat questions from the matrix without prompts.

Teachers who have implemented these techniques in their classrooms have said that their students become very involved and more interested in their English lessons, even staying after class to complete an activity. Teachers have commented that they feel reassured knowing that the grammar or language focus can still be present in the context of a task. Also, in the role of facilitator, instructors are better able to observe progress in their students.

Task-based activities have become staples in my teaching. Students of varying ages, education levels, language backgrounds, and proficiency levels become genuinely interested in the lessons when they are engaged in a task and interacting in English. They become much more adept at figuring things out for themselves, more comfortable experimenting with language, and better able to notice forms and grammar patterns. I feel that these skills make them better prepared for real-world English language tasks.

These three activity templates—the matrix, the dictogloss, and the survey—not only fit nicely into J. Willis's (1996) task-based model, providing opportunities for pretask, task, reporting, and language focus stages, but also challenge and stimulate multilevel groups of students. The templates offer structure but give teachers freedom in choosing an appropriate topic and level of difficulty. Likewise, they give students flexibility in manipulating real data and an authentic text, progressing at their own pace. Through this approach, students get feedback, primarily from each other, which allows them to develop fluency, use pragmatic language, integrate the four skills, and most important, build confidence.

Jennifer M. Herrin teaches ESL at Central New Mexico Community College, in Albuquerque, New Mexico, in the United States. She has taught in Latin America, Eastern Europe, Asia, Australia, and the United States and has served as a Fulbright Scholar and a Senior English Language Fellow/Specialist with the U.S. State Department, conducting teacher training in task-based methodologies.

APPENDIX A: MATRIX AND JOURNAL WRITING STUDENT SAMPLES

Student Sample 1 (Matrix)

Adverbs of Frequency: Put a check ☑ in the correct box

How often do you .....?   How often does he/she?

YOUR INFORMATION

	Always	Usually*	Sometimes*	Hardly Ever	Never
Speak English at home			X		
Speak English in class	X				
Watch TV in English	X				
Talk on the phone in English			X		
Read magazines in English	X				
Drive to school					X
Drink coffee in the morning	X				
Drink beer on the weekend			X		
Exercise during the week				X	
Cook dinner at night	X				
Go out on the weekends		X			
Watch the news at night				X	
Eat food from my/your country			X		
Eat lunch after class	X				
Do my homework/your	X				
Attend class	X				
Say "hello" to everybody in class			X		
Come to class on time	X				

YOUR PARTNER'S INFORMATION

	Always	Usually*	Sometimes*	Hardly Ever	Never
Speak English at home		✓			
Speak English in class	✓				
Watch TV in English			✓		
Talk on the phone in English			✓		
Read magazines in English			✓		
Drive to school	✓				
Drink coffee in the morning	✓				
Drink beer on the weekend					✓
Exercise during the week		✓			
Cook dinner at night			✓		
Go out on the weekends			✓		
Watch the news at night	✓				
Eat food from your country			✓		
Eat lunch after class			✓		
Do my homework	✓				
Attend class	✓				
Say "hello" to everybody in class		✓			
Come to class on time	✓				

*You can use "usually" and "sometimes" at the beginning of the sentence.

Student Sample 2 (Journal Entry)

My schedule is the follow:

I get up between 5:30 and 5:45 am.
I take a shower. I go take breakfast
at 6:50 am. I leave my house between
7:00 and 7:05 am.. I arive my
work from 7:30 to 7:35 am.
I begin work at 8:00 am. I take
my lunch at 11:30 am. I finish my
work in the Monday, Wednesday and
friday between 2:15 and 2:30 pm.
a the tuesday and thursday I finesh
my work between 3:00 and 3:10 pm.

I go my house, I a little relax.

I go my class in the CNM, Tuesday
and thursday between 5:30 and 7:20pm.
come back my house, I made at the
cook dinner, I finesh the dinner more
o lest from 9:30 to 10:00 pm I go
to sleep between 10:15 and 10:30 pm.

My weekends, I clean the house and
Sometimes go to the movies I call
my family everyday. too the weekends
made the homework.. The weekends
I go to the walmart for the food.

Student Sample 3 (Journal Entry)

In the morning from 6 to 8 I usually go raning
from 8 to 9 I Alway drive car
to work
from 9 to 12 I Alway work

In the afternoon from 12 to 1 I Alway eat lunch
from 1 to 7 I usualty finish work
In the evening from 7 to 9 I Alway eat dinner

At night from 9 to 10 : Alway watch TV

APPENDIX B: DICTOGLOSS

Student Sample 1

> Two weeksevents will give crowds. games Fun. and ENTERtainment you can find best in NM ARTIST Over 100 animals and plenty of rides. There are alu music ART coming to this Fair. THe Fair has contest all Kinds cooKing. rides ArTisTs From around states seTup booths To sales. LAST year The Fair Th brought 3,500 THe lasT day will be 9/23/2007.

Student Sample 2

> ① 2007 NM State Fair open friday morning
> ② There are plenty of food. fun, entertainment
> ③ one hundred animals, plenty of rides on fairground
> ④ you can find some of best artist
> ⑤ contest all kind of competition cooking, raising best pig

APPENDIX C: SURVEY (STUDENT SAMPLE)

Name: _____

Making plans using "future" questions:

New Mexico State Fair: *What are you going to see?*

What is your name?	What are you going to see?	Who are you going with?	Why do you want to see it? (two reasons)		When are you going to see it?	
Jennifer	Big bear show	Alex	because bears are cute	I love animals	**Day:** on Saturday	**Time:** at 2:00
Malik	brait lights	daughters	I like the lights	I like the food	on Sunday	at 5:00
Anastacia	Great American Duck Race	Ali	I enjoy animals	I will be interesting	on Saturday	at 4:00
Alex	big bear show	Rosa	bear is cute	I want to see the bear	Saturday	5:00
Le	Actors	friends	enjoy to watch the people	listen to sing	on Sunday	at 4:00
Ali	Great American Duck Race	Anastacia	enjoy animal	interesting	Saturday	at 4:00
Rogelio	back yard circus	Jasmin	want to see costumes	see animals	on Saturday	at 4:30
Sun	back yard circus	Jorge	funny	interesting	on Friday	at 5:00
Jorge	back yard circus	Sun	will be interesting	funny	on Friday	at 7:00
Jasmin	back yard circus	Rogelio	costumes	see animals	Saturday	4:30

Technology

CHAPTER 8

Multitasked Student Video Recording

Tim Murphey and Jodie Sakaguchi

In longitudinal self-evaluated video recording (LSEV), students are periodically recorded as they perform in speaking activities such as conversations, debates, and presentations in their second language (L2). The metatask of preparing and performing for a video recording entails a host of subtasks regularly used in task-based teaching, such as telling a story, discussing issues, and arguing one's point of view (convincing another). Students might carry out additional tasks as they watch the videos of themselves and sometimes their peers speaking, such as listening in order to transcribe and correct, listening for understanding, or counting (noticing) the use of conversational strategies or nonverbal cues. Later, they might write a letter to their partner, giving feedback both on the content and the delivery of the presentation. Note that many of these subtasks might shift from those one can prepare for (e.g., telling a story) to those for which one needs to use speech more spontaneously (e.g., respond politely with slightly alternative proposals to whatever your partner proposes). These examples show how the procedures of LSEV provide an open platform for a variety of task-based learning activities through collaborative and experiential learning as well as student-centered pedagogy.

We find that, psychologically, the video recording offers great opportunities for students to identify themselves as users of the language, which in turn can greatly motivate them to prepare and study even more and engage in more effective language learning tasks. In second language acquisition (SLA) terms, students have multiple extended conversational opportunities (Murphey, 2009) to hear a variety of focused input at their approximate level and to produce an approximately equal amount of output, to negotiate meaning, and to display a wide range of functions (Chaudron, 1988; Hall & Walsh, 2002). We contend that, similar to the benefits of extensive reading, extensive talking in extended conversations of 4 or more minutes pushes the learning of students.

Tasks involving the exchange of personal experiences, ideas, and opinions are for many students inherently motivating. Whereas at first they may feel shy and find it difficult to continue talking in English with their partner for even a few minutes, they soon gain confidence as they realize that they can make themselves understood and that they can understand their partner. Viewing themselves on video after the speaking event allows students to step back and reflect on their own language use and speaking ability from a different position. These capacities for detachment and critical reflection are characteristic of autonomous learners (Little, 1991). Their motivation and confidence increase rapidly as they watch their videos and show them to classmates and family members and receive feedback from them. Because of the undeniable evidence from their own watching and from viewers' feedback, students begin to identify themselves as users of the language.

CONTEXT

Between 2005 and 2008, we both taught English as a foreign language at a mid-level private Japanese university near Tokyo, Japan, and used LSEV. Our students were mostly Japanese nationals aged 18 to 22 years old, and the average class consisted of approximately 25 students. Although we taught in the same university, our contexts were different in that Tim taught students who were majoring in English, whereas Jodie taught non-English majors. Tim had collected student-produced data for more than 10 years and explored a variety of activities stemming from the video recording as well as doing the video recording to various degrees with students. Jodie presents a newcomer's view to LSEV and proposes even more options and choices for the procedures. We explain our respective contexts, curricula, tasks, and materials in more detail in the next section of the chapter.

Tim taught undergraduates mainly in the English department, most of whom elected to take his courses knowing they would be video recorded and would need to talk quite a bit. About a fifth of his students spent a year or more abroad. Jodie, on the other hand, taught undergraduate students in the French, German, Law, and Economics departments, each of which required students to take a number of credits of English classes and offered various compulsory and elective courses. Compulsory classes were usually organized by major, year, and score on the Test of English for International Communication (TOEIC). Elective classes, on the other hand, were not as tightly controlled. Students with a wide range of TOEIC scores from all departments and all years were mixed in these classes. Jodie used LSEV with great success with first- and second-year compulsory listening/speaking classes as well as elective speaking classes.

CURRICULUM, TASKS, MATERIALS

We regularly record students having short conversations and present them with a variety of associated tasks to perform over time (e.g., writing transcriptions of their conversations, showing their videos to others for feedback, reviewing a class-mate's video and advising, writing papers comparing their first and last record-ing and saying how they have improved), which allows them to become more autonomous directors of their own development. The procedures also encourage individual goal setting and self-reflection on actual performances using personal artifacts of performance (their videos).

Numerous smaller level tasks are involved in the video recording process. We have found it useful to think of them in three time periods (pre-, during, and postvideo recording). In Table 1 we describe these time periods, and after each task or activity, we list research correlates that support doing the tasks. Note that we do not do all these tasks all the time, but select and focus on a few at a time in hopes that students will adopt them within their autonomous repertoires.

Table 1. Three Periods of Longitudinal Self-Evaluated Video Recording

Prevideo Recording	
Student Tasks and Learning Concepts	*Supporting Research*
Watch videos of previous students' work	Create intent to participate (Rogoff, Paradise, Arauz, Correa-Chavez, & Angelillo, 2003)
Plan content and language material to be used	Planning (Ortega, 2005)
Learner training	O'Malley & Chamot, 1990; Wenden & Rubin, 1987
Facilitative anxiety	Alpert & Haber, 1960
Choose and practice communication strategies	Strategy training (e.g., shadowing, summarizing, rejoinders, double questions, asking questions; Murphey, 2006; Oxford, 1990)
Visualize the type of desired performance	Intent participation (Rogoff et al., 2003; Vasquez & Buehler, 2007)
Practice output and use a great deal of self-talk	Output hypothesis (Swain, 1995)
Rehearse and recycle language	Bygate & Samuda, 2005
Build relationships and try to help others	Group dynamics (Dörnyei & Murphey, 2003)
Encourage responsibility	Skehan, 1998
Make goals	Nunan, 1997

Continued on p. 100

Table 1 (continued). Three Periods of Longitudinal Self-Evaluated Video Recording

Video Day	
Student Tasks	*Supporting Research*
Have multiple, fluent, extended conversations with diverse peers who challenge your abilities	Pushed output (Swain, 1995), performance events (Murphey, 1996)
Video record a conversation with a partner or make a short presentation	Facilitative anxiety (Alpert & Haber, 1960)
Learn items from partners	Cooperative learning (Jacobs, Power, & Inn, 2002)
Do your best to try to understand your partner and make yourself understood	Negotiate meaning (Yule & Macdonald, 1990)
Notice what you are and are not doing and learning	Noticing (Ellis, 1994; Ortega, 2007; Schmidt & Frota, 1986), awareness (Flavell, 1979)
Postvideo Recording	
Student Tasks	*Supporting Research*
Watch video and transcribe; identify strong and weak points	Noticing (Ellis, 1994; Ortega, 2007; Schmidt & Frota, 1986), awareness (Flavell, 1979)
Identify communication strategies used	Reflection with an artifact from the classroom (Oxford, 1990; Swain, 2000)
Write self-progress report comparing clips	Swain, 2000
Notice your own and your partner's mistakes and suggest corrections within the zone of proximal development (ZPD)	Focus on form (Vygotsky, 1934/1962; J. Williams, 1997)
Show the video to a friend or family member for feedback	Validation from others outside the class, identifying self as a user (Murphey, 2009)
Review partner's video and progress	Noticing others, near peer role modeling (Murphey & Arao, 2001)
Set goals for next time	ZPD (Vygotsky, 1934/1962)

In the following sections we present overviews of what we do in our respective classes and describe some of what we know of others using similar methods and technologies. The goal here is to show that LSEV can be done in a variety of ways, with a variety of tasks, with a variety of audiences.

Tim's Video Tasking

LSEV was originally supported technically by two video cameras, each attached to two VHS cassette decks (see Figure 1), so that two student pairs could be recorded at one time and all of them get a copy of their conversation immediately after it was over. While pairs are recording, in the same room the rest of the stu-

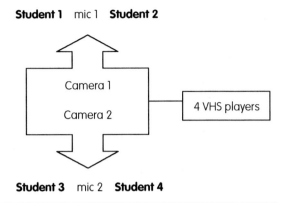

Student Conversation Area

Class of 20–32 students

Everybody changes partners every 5 minutes (having five to eight extended conversational opportunities, depending on the number of students), and one of the conversations is video recorded in a 90-minute class.

Figure 1. Tim's Classroom Setup

Note: VHS has been used since the mid 1990s, and the process is still reliable although antiquated. We have been experimenting with new technologies as Jodie describes in her section of this chapter.

dents in the class are also changing partners every 5 minutes and having multiple extended conversational opportunities.

Jodie's Video Tasking

Jodie uses video recording in elective speaking classes focusing on basic conversational skills and in compulsory first- and second-year listening/speaking classes that focus on academic speaking skills. In the elective classes, students' 3- to 5-minute conversations are recorded three or four times during a 12-week semester. Jodie often uses a similar video setup to Tim's; however, to decrease the amount of background noise on the video, if extra rooms are available, she sometimes does the video recording in a separate room (see Figure 2).

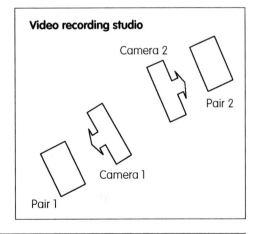

Rehearsal Room

Class of 20–30 students

Everybody changes partners every 5 minutes (having five to eight extended conversational opportunities, depending on the number of students), and one of the conversations is video recorded in a 90-minute class.

Video recording studio

Figure 2. Jodie's Alternative Classroom Setup for Recording Conversations

In the compulsory listening/speaking classes, students are recorded doing discussions, debates, or presentations two or three times a semester. To save time in recording presentations, the class can be split in half so that two presenters can be recorded simultaneously (as shown in Figure 3). This setup can also be adapted for recording debates and discussions.

For recording, Jodie uses video cameras that use digital video tapes or that can store video on an internal hard drive. The video files of students' conversations and presentations can be uploaded to password-protected web sites for students to view online, or they may be burned onto DVDs. When the videos are ready, students can complete associated post–video recording tasks such as identifying communication strategies and correcting mistakes (see Appendix).

In Tim's classes student conversations are recorded every lesson or every other lesson, and in Jodie's classes recordings are made three times during a semester. In both classes, students are told who their video recording partners will be at the beginning of class and told not to speak with them except on the video so that the conversation will be fresh and not rehearsed. Topics for conversations can be just about anything. Although we usually set the broad topics for conversation beforehand, the actual content is left to students to construct and rehearse partially before class and partially as they respond to the different people they talk to during the task. Notes are not allowed, and students respond to a partner whose reactions and questions cannot be known beforehand. Thus the conversations are semispontaneous and can be rehearsed in one's head beforehand, but reality usually creates a need for negotiation of meaning.

Shehadeh (2005) says that "if we want to promote fluency in the learner, we should get the learner engaged in meaning-oriented tasks; conversely, if we want to promote accuracy or complexity in the learner, we should get him/her involved in more form-focused tasks" (p. 23). The conversational video recording tasks that we do at first appear to be mainly aimed at meaningful fluency.

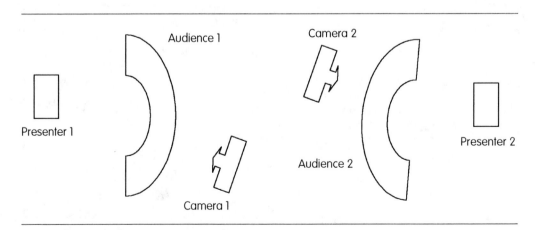

Figure 3. Jodie's Classroom Setup for Presentations

However, the fact that we have an artifact, a recording to look at and reflect on, means that students turn their attention to form as they transcribe their conversations and notice the gaps in their capabilities. We find that video recording affords them distinct times to focus on fluency and accuracy without sacrificing either. Here is what one student wrote at the end of the term when comparing her first and last transcriptions and video performances:

> Watching my videos, I noticed several differences between them. First in V1 [first video conversation], I didn't prepare anything to talk, so I haven't had any target words. And I didn't know much of shadowing, so my replies are often "Yeah" and "Oh!" When I saw this, I felt ashamed. Shadowing is much better. In V2 [second and last video conversation] I prepared for the video day (which is my custom). I practiced it the day before and arranged it shorter. . . . And I think I improved my shadowing and asking questions for comments. I am very happy. Second, in V1, I was very nervous. So I couldn't talk very much. But in V2, I was very relaxed. I laughed with my partner and had a good time. Relaxing is very important. I think I learned many things from video recording. I learned shadowing, target words, some reactions, etc. When I showed it to my friends they say "You are doing good job. You will improve your English very fast." I am a little bit proud!

Other Teachers' Variations and Innovations at Other Institutions

Sato and Takahashi (2008) report using an occasional video procedure with Japanese high school students of English and found that "students initially . . . had a conversation for 2 minutes at most. By the end . . . [they] had 4- to 5-minute conversations" (p. 217).

At Nagoya University of Foreign Studies, there are designated video rooms with enough booths equipped with cameras and VHS players to accommodate approximately 20 students at one sitting. Teachers can reserve the rooms for a 30-minute session, and thus three classes can use the facility in one 90-minute class period. A teaching assistant makes copies of the master tapes in the cameras after each class for the teacher.

The International University of Japan, in Niigata, probably has the most efficient high-tech system for copying and transferring video files and making them quickly accessible to students. Each student has his or her own online folder, which is password protected. After recording student presentations or conversations on cameras equipped with a hard disk drive, the cameras are connected to a computer using a USB port and the video files are transferred to the respective online folder in a matter of minutes. Once the files have been transferred, students can access their individual folders online and watch their videos.

From outside the field of language teaching, psychologist Peter Dowrick (1983), at the University of Hawai'i, has for many years researched what he calls *video futures,* enhanced performances that are recorded and that help one construct an ideal self (Dörnyei, 2005). Dowrick has worked with a variety of problems, recording participants succeeding in different tasks and then asking them to watch themselves regularly with the result that they actually come to see themselves as capable of doing the task and end up performing it. More recent research by Vasquez and Buehler (2007) explains the impact of this third person perspective and why watching ourselves on video could enhance our performances. Vasquez and Buehler "found that the third person perspective resulted in greater motivation to succeed at the task, especially when people imagined themselves performing well. The increased third person perspective appears to assign greater meaning to the task" ("Looking Into the Future," 2007, para. 3).

More recently, colleagues at Nanzan University are watching their students recording together with other teachers to evaluate students and to discuss what kinds of tasks and skills the students need in order to progress (Brad Deacon, personal communication, June 15, 2009). This is one example of the flexible extension of tasks for teachers and students involved in video recording student conversations. We think that there will be many more ways that we will find to benefit from this metarecording task.

REFLECTIONS

In closing we would like to first reflect on the many possibilities of using these tasks by looking at different continua. Then we highlight SLA and sociocultural theory support for the processes. Finally, we see how connecting the tasks to higher level student values enhances them and how scaffolding students' increasing agency and social capital through the tasks creates more effective autonomous learners.

Figure 4 captures for us different continua that help us conceptualize our choices and constraints in the video recording processes. Although we both use the same task of video recording student conversations, we use quite different technologies to record and distribute videos to students, and our students, curricula, and methods of assessment are quite different. Tim has a relatively mixed-technology approach, recording on VHS tapes for students. Jodie uses digital and Internet technology to copy and distribute video files. Tim teaches English majors, and Jodie teaches non-English majors. Tim's curriculum is largely built

Low tech . . . . High tech
English majors . . . . Non-English majors
Frequent video recording . . . . Occasional video recording
Fixed equipment . . . . Portable equipment
Curriculum built around tasks . . . . Curriculum built around textbook
Self- or peer-assessed . . . . Teacher assessed

Figure 4. Continua of Choices and Constraints

around video recording conversations, whereas Jodie's is based on a textbook. The video conversations are used mainly for self- and peer-assessment in Tim's classes. However, in Jodie's classes, in addition to being used for self-assessment, the video conversations are also evaluated by the teacher, with both the self-evaluated and the teacher-evaluated scores being included in the final grade.

We do not wish to claim that any particular technology or methodology is superior; rather, we believe that the task of video recording student conversations is flexible enough to be adapted to a variety of teaching contexts and teaching methodologies. We envision ourselves at different points along a variety of continua. We invite readers to reflect on their own teaching situations, add other continua as appropriate, and experiment with technologies and techniques that will allow them to video record student conversations in ways that fit their own teaching styles and contexts. We also wish to highlight that the video recording procedure is a wonderful way for researchers to collect data on how students actually perform a variety of tasks and how they might improve over time.

The multitasked video recording processes are supported by much of the literature on SLA, sociocultural theory, and the aspects of student agency and autonomy.

Ortega (2007) affirms that "L2 learning theories provide converging arguments for the central role that interactive practice among peers should play in formal L2 instruction, pointing at linguistic, psycholinguistic, and sociocognitive benefits that are thought to facilitate optimal L2 development" (p. 183). She further asserts that "all functional positions agree with the basic tenet that language is learned in and through performance" (p. 183). We find that this quite effectively describes our classes and why we record with video. More than a decade of practice and research concerned with LSEV (Murphey 2001, 2009; Murphey & Kenny, 1996, 1998; Murphey & Woo, 1998a, 1998b) has allowed us to explore a wide range of tasks, observe students' improvements, and learn a great deal from the agency and identity shifts of our students.

Although the SLA literature clearly points toward students performing more and teachers reducing their instruction time, Ellis (2003) states that "there are few courses that are organized entirely around tasks but many that utilize more traditional designs involving the presentation and practice of discrete linguistic features with tasks providing opportunities for their free production" (p. 320). Tim's video courses are indeed organized almost entirely around the metatask of recording weekly conversations in class, with a variety of preparatory and processing tasks, and their collection and reevaluation longitudinally. Jodie's courses incorporate video recording more as an occasional task and with alternative technology. Both of us feel that such video recording deepens students' personal reflections on their development, allowing them to notice (Ellis, 1994; Ortega, 2007; Schmidt & Frota, 1986) and self-correct as well as model the finer points of classmates (Murphey & Arao, 2001) and themselves. This task-based methodology is firmly framed in Dewey's (1997) perspective of experiential learning,

Wertsch's (1998) concept of appropriation (identification), Rogoff et al.'s (2003) intent participation, and Norton's (2000) concept of investment.

Also, we have found that students increase participation and investment in tasks, making them more effective, when it is shown how our pedagogical tasks relate to their own goals and values. As Marshall (2006) says,

> the nature and quality of our minds are powerfully shaped by the nature and quality of the learning environments in which they are immersed, activated and nurtured. How we are asked to learn matters profoundly. Mind shaping is world shaping. (p. xiii)

We try to tap into the life goals and values of students' natural socialization processes.

Finally, when learners are given more choices and control over the content, they build more agency and better group dynamics (Dörnyei & Murphey, 2003), which supports more autonomy. According to Littlewood (1997), equipping students with skills and strategies and building their confidence and motivation can enable them to become more autonomous as learners, as communicators, and as people in general. Through the task of talking with various partners, students' knowledge *about* English is turned into practical skills and strategies that they can use *in* English. This socializing also allows them to make friends and build networks of resources, also known as social capital (Bourdieu, 1977).

Tim Murphey has a PhD from the University of Neuchatel, in Switzerland, and is a professor at Kanda University of International Studies, in Japan. He is the editor of TESOL's Professional Development in Language Education series and co-author, with Zoltan Dörnyei, of Group Dynamics in the Language Classroom *(Cambridge University Press, 2003). He presently focuses on sociocultural hope and agency in learning through narrative inquiry.*

Jodie Sakaguchi has an MA in TESOL from Teachers College, Columbia University. She currently teaches undergraduate students in the Bilingual Business Leader Program at Rikkyo University, in Japan, and in-service teachers on the Diploma in Practical Teaching at the University of Chichester, in England. Her teaching and research center on autonomous learning and the role of reflection in learning.

APPENDIX: EXAMPLE OF AN ASSOCIATED TASK

Name: Partner's name:

Video Report

- Go to: http://www.dokkyo.net/~0000/
- Type in the ID and password that you received in class.
- Watch the video of your conversations. Write your answers on this paper. Answer every question.
- Submit this report by [insert date].

1. Questions

Which questions did you ask your partner?

A. Check ✓ the textbook questions that you asked.

B. Write the original questions that you asked.

Topic	Textbook Questions	Original Questions
Self-Introduction	Where do you live?	
	Do you have any hobbies?	
	What do you do in your free time?	
Family	How many people are in your family?	
	What does your _____ look like?	
	What is your _____ like?	
Sports	What sports do you play?	
	Do you belong to any sport club or sport circle?	
	What kind of sports do you like?	
Food	What food do you like?	
	What kind of _____ do you like?	
	Is there any food you don't like?	
Part-Time Jobs	Do you have a part-time job?	
	How much do you make an hour?	
	How often do you work every week?	

2. Hints

Which textbook hints (communication strategies) did you use?

A. Count how many times you said each hint. Write the number.

B. Write the total number of hints you used.

Hints	How many?		Hints	How many?	
	1	2		1	2
How 'bout you?			Oh, really?/Oh, yeah?		
Pardon me? Sorry? Excuse me?			Uh-huh./Mm-hmm.		
Shadowing (repeating what your partner said)			Sounds . . . nice/great/boring/interesting/ healthy/exciting.		
Hmm . . . let me see . . . Hmm . . . let me think . . .			Me, too!/I do, too!		
Me neither./I don't either.			Wow!/That's great! Congratulations! I'm happy to hear that!		
Really? I don't./Really? I do.			That's too bad!/You poor thing! Oh no! That's terrible! I'm sorry to hear that.		
It's okay./It's all right. It's not bad.			You're kidding!/You're lucky! I wish I were you! I didn't know that!		
			Total Hints		

3. Mistakes

Did you make any mistakes in your conversations?

A. Write your mistakes in the left column.

B. If you can, write the correct English in the right column.

Mistakes	Corrections
I said this . . .	I should have said . . .

4. Self-Evaluation

A. Good Points

What did you do well in these conversations?

Conversation 1 _____

_____

_____

_____

_____

Conversation 2 _____

_____

_____

_____

_____

B. Points to Improve

What didn't you do well in these conversations? What points do you want to improve next time?

Conversation 1 _____

_____

_____

_____

_____

Conversation 2 _____

_____

_____

_____

_____

C. Score

What score would you give yourself for these video conversations?

Write your score for yourself, and then write your reason.

Score

		Conversation 1	Conversation 2
a.	I had good eye contact.	___/ 1	___/ 1
b.	I didn't have any long silences.	___/ 1	___/ 1
c.	My partner and I both talked equally.	___/ 1	___/ 1
d.	I didn't use katakana English.	___/ 1	___/ 1
e.	My partner could understand my English well.	___/ 1	___/ 1
f.	I could understand my partner's English well.	___/ 1	___/ 1
g.	I used the textbook hints naturally.	___/ 2	___/ 2
h.	My English was smooth.	___/ 2	___/ 2
	Total	___/ 10	___/ 10

Reason

_____

_____

_____

_____

_____

CHAPTER 9

Learning Through CALLaborative Projects Using Web 2.0 Tools

Carla Arena and Erika Cruvinel

Recent shifts in the nature of the Internet have seen a move from a static web-based environment in which information and knowledge were available for students' exploration to a social sphere with a new generation of applications that can easily evolve into interactive content—what is known as Web 2.0. Because of this change, computer-mediated collaboration has also been redesigned in terms of its forms and possibilities in the language classroom. According to Siemens (2005), Web 2.0 "collaborative platforms are reshaping learning as a two-way process. Instead of presenting content/information/knowledge in a linear sequential manner, learners can be provided with a rich array of tools and information sources to use in creating their own learning pathways" ("Implications," para. 3).

The challenge for English language teachers within this new online environment, in which learners can easily be creators of content, is how to promote students' interaction in the target language through carefully designed major tasks that lead to meaningful connections. Once the process by which knowledge sharing will take place is established, learners will have the chance to use all their language resources to perform tasks, negotiate meaning in order to communicate in authentic settings, and be exposed to real language as well as develop cross-cultural awareness and tolerance.

CONTEXT

Web 2.0 presents educators with a wealth of online tools that can really make an impact on the way they teach. How can teachers effectively use these online spaces to engage learners in meaningful, cultural connections, having English as a tool for communication and learning? Our experience as English as a foreign language (EFL) teachers at Casa Thomas Jefferson, a Brazilian binational center where students of all ages and levels of proficiency come to learn English, has proved that collaborative projects can only flow in the right direction if the tasks devised for the exchanges are well designed and carried out in a way that motivates students, makes them reflect, and guides them in what Splitter (n.d.) calls a *dynamic of inquiry*:

> that which provides the energising or motive force which makes it possible to move forward (toward a solution, or at least a clearer understanding of the problem). This dynamic is a form of thinking, to be sure, but it is the thinking *of the community*, that is, dialogue. It is the reflective conversation of the community of inquiry, with all of its stops and restarts, "umms" and "aahs" and self-correction—but also with its palpable sense of movement—that provides a sense of structure to the thinking of its members. ("4. Philosophy," para. 10)

Besides, the process by which these dialogues are established fosters learners' understanding of the world from different perspectives and stimulates their senses with the goal of enhancing their language skills. As stated by Gitsaki and Taylor (2001),

> from a pedagogical point of view, web-assisted language learning satisfies the three "essential" conditions for language learning as these are outlined in the task-based framework for language learning, i.e. exposure, use and motivation. In order for anyone to learn a second or foreign language these three conditions must be met: learners must be exposed to rich input of the target language used in real life situations; they must be given opportunities to use the target language to communicate meaning; and they must be motivated. (p. 2)

With the variety of tools available online, the array of possibilities has widened for teachers to engage learners in the learning process through collaborative projects that promote authentic, contextualized, culturally rich, and motivating interactions. In this chapter, we describe a podcast project called SambaEFL, which was carried out with Brazilian students ranging from 16 to 45 years old. This conversation group met weekly for 100-minute classes and was not tied to any specific pedagogical material. In fact, the teacher had the freedom to choose the topics for the weekly encounter. To make this time spent practicing English together a meaningful experience, the teacher had an informal discussion with the students in the first class to find out about their interests and needs. Based on students' feedback about what they wanted to study for the semester, their main goal of enhancing their communication skills in English, and the fact that they would not have any formal assessment (they simply received a Certificate of Attendance if they were present at 75% of the classes), the teacher decided to take a project-based task-oriented approach. This approach would balance in-class tasks and the use of dynamic web-based services so as to enhance learners' ability to better express themselves in the target language while accomplishing the activities and interacting with peers to develop their final online product, a podcast (a downloadable audio file that can be listened to online or on a portable media device such as an iPod).

The idea behind the podcast project was that learners could visualize their skills in English through a tangible outcome, the result of their own collaboration and negotiation of meaning. Collective knowledge construction was the core of the podcast production. It is important to highlight that this was the teacher's first experience in producing a podcast with her students.

By describing the development of our SambaEFL podcast project, we hope to encourage other language educators to take the first steps toward engaging students in significant interactions that take place in technology-mediated environments. Observing the cooperation and dialogue taking place while learners work is a rewarding experience for any educator who wants to have an impact in some way on students' learning journey. If educators can tap into what students are really passionate about, the classroom lessons can have long-lasting effects on the learning process, even more so if the medium that they are using to produce content and learn the target language is the one that learners are used to (in this case, computers and the Internet).

CURRICULUM, TASKS, MATERIALS

Developing a CALLaborative Project

There is no formula for collaboration. The project can take many directions, shapes, and forms. However, after developing different CALLaborative (collaborative computer-assisted language learning) projects at Casa Thomas Jefferson, we observed that the steps listed in this section were vital to ensuring the continuous flow of collaboration and achieving the expected results. In delineating these steps, we explain our reasons for deciding on a collaborative effort that fits our language learning goals and suits our students' interests, keeping in mind that a project can be developed during a single class, can be ongoing, or can take place over a specific period of time—short term or long term. It all depends on your educational setting and the pedagogical needs and objectives of your classroom.

Step 1: Identify a Need and a Purpose

An effective way to start any successful endeavor is to identify the reasons for investing time and effort in a specific project and to define its pedagogical goals.

Step 2: Negotiate Meaningful Topics for and With Learners

Consider topics that will motivate students to do their best or make them want to explore by using the language they are learning. Consider the learners' interests and the way that you, as a teacher, can link what is being taught in the classroom to their preferences.

Step 3: Define a Concrete Result

It is important for learners to visualize their learning process in terms of a concrete outcome. This may take the form of an online video, a slideshow, a scrapbook, a blog, a wiki, a book, a podcast—whatever the group agrees on is the best possibility for the final result of the project.

Step 4: Choose the Right Tools

With the group of learners, decide which online tools they can use to make collaboration motivating, involving, and meaningful. The tools must be user-friendly for the group, easily accessible, and viable for developing the project according to the specific educational setting.

Step 5: Find and Invite Partners

Based on the project goals, you can keep it local or expand it to a national or international context. Think about possible ways to find and invite partners. You can announce the project in the communities of practice that you are part of, blog about the project and see who responds, contact other educators via e-mail, and so on. If you contact partners, you should make clear the kind of collaboration and interaction that you are looking for.

Step 6: Prepare a Schedule

Determining a timeframe is an important step in the process so that all teachers involved can visualize the time limits and restrictions to accomplish the project goals. Sometimes the school year is different for your partners, so defining deadlines ensures that all involved get to finish the final product of the collaboration and share it with each other in a timely manner.

Step 7: Plan the Tasks

Make sure to develop a task plan in which some of the activities are determined by the learners as they progress during the project. Be prepared to adjust and adapt the plan if so required by students or collaborators.

Step 8: Implement the Project

Think of the practical aspects of the project. Remember to address issues such as whether the tasks will be accomplished during class time or at home and whether the activities will be online and thus possibly require specific training for the learners to perform them.

Step 9: Aggregate the Artifacts

If you are producing online content (e.g., audio files, slideshows, stories, messages), plan the organization of the resources that will be produced during the collaboration. Think of the resources that are most adequate for aggregating this content. It could be a wiki, a blog, or a class page using any number of Web 2.0 tools (e.g., *Pageflakes*, n.d.; *Protopage*, n.d.).

Step 10: Evaluate the Project

Assess the process and the outcomes. One possibility is to make use of online surveys via *SurveyMonkey* (SurveyMonkey.com, 1999–2009) or *Quia* (Quia, 1998–2009). Another is to ask students to write a note or a post on the class blog discussing what worked, what they liked about the project, and what they would improve. Students could also make a video about their impression of the whole collaboration effort.

SambaEFL Class Podcast in Perspective

The purpose of the SambaEFL podcast was to give voice to students, to let them express themselves and use language to convey their message to an authentic, global audience. The podcast was always a final result of the discussions led on a specific theme in the conversation class. The students generated the content for their audio production with the facilitation of the instructor. There were three main podcasts in SambaEFL according to the topics discussed in the classroom: Stereotypes, How to Make a Chocolate Egg, and the Wonders of Brazil (cities to visit). All of these topics were comprehensively explored in the classroom in terms of reading and listening tasks, vocabulary building, and conversation practice. The Stereotypes and the Wonders of Brazil lessons took place over the course of three 100-minute classes, and the Chocolate Egg lesson took place during one 2-hour session.

Although the topics were diverse, the ideas behind producing a podcast and the steps for publishing it online were the same each time. The only variation in terms of production happened during the Chocolate Egg class. The lesson was conducted in the teachers' room, instead of the regular classroom, because students needed to use a microwave oven and refrigerator. Because of time constraints, we decided to conduct the entire lesson in one room, so students also recorded the podcast using a laptop in the teachers' room instead of doing it in the computer lab.

In class, activities played out in the following sequence:

- Students explored the topics through engaging vocabulary, reading, and discussion tasks (for a detailed plan and overview of the Stereotypes lesson, see Arena, 2006).

- The teacher divided the class into small groups that would collaboratively work together on podcasts. The teacher and the groups decided what aspect of the topic each team would focus on. For example, in the case of the Stereotypes podcast, the groups needed to define which stereotypes held by foreigners about Brazilians they wanted to demystify, whereas in the Wonders of Brazil podcast, they needed to choose a city in Brazil that they wanted to talk about, which characteristics of the city they would call attention to, and how they would collect the photos of the city.

- The teams then wrote their scripts for the podcast. At this point, there was constant negotiation of meaning in the groups to come up with a cohesive, well-structured text that would be the basis for the audio recording. The teacher was merely an observer of the collaboration taking place and occasionally would give students some advice on content, sequence of ideas and vocabulary, and how to improve their texts.

After these classroom activities were completed, the following took place in the computer lab:

- The teacher and the student groups worked on vocabulary, looked for synonyms in online dictionaries, and clarified pronunciation aspects of specific words to improve the script written in class and to increase students' confidence about recording their voices.

- Students practiced recording using Audacity (Version 1.2.6), free audio recording and editing software. In general, they were only satisfied with the audio quality and their pronunciation after recording for the third time.

- Students named and saved their files in a folder created for the project on the computer.

- While students were involved in the audio recording and editing, the teacher went around the room providing help whenever they requested it. Also, the teacher took pictures while the learners were recording their podcasts.

At this point the class was over, so the teacher uploaded the files to *PodOmatic* (PodOmatic, 2009), a podcast site where she had previously set up a free account. Photos were always added to the podcasts to enrich the audience's experience of the topic the students were talking about and the people who produced the show. In the case of the Wonders of Brazil podcast, there was an extra step in which the students collected their personal photos of the cities they were talking about and produced an online slideshow in Bubbleshare (no longer available) to go with their podcasts. The fact that they could include other elements such as slideshows added a dynamic visual element to their podcasts. Finally, the teacher invited online international partners to listen to the podcast and leave comments for students.

Benefits of SambaEFL

A podcast is an engaging way to bring voices to an online space with the possibility of having an authentic audience. During the preproduction stage of the podcast, when students were discussing what to include in their texts, there was a

116

true dialogue taking place naturally with the purpose of achieving a main goal: a well-written text that would become an online audio file available to an audience other than peers and their teacher.

The students wanted to excel. They had a concrete reason for using the language accurately, and they wanted to be understood. They questioned, analyzed possibilities, and decided how they wanted to explore a given topic. They were using all the language skills they had acquired throughout the years to generate content and enhance their learning, sometimes in unexpected and unpredictable ways, because they were the producers of their own show and wanted it to reflect their personal views and perspectives. They were building meaning and knowledge in a collaborative way using English to negotiate and communicate to achieve a tangible result: the production of clear, objective, content-rich audio. Indeed, to produce the podcast, they used all four skills of reading, writing, listening, and speaking in such a contextualized way that they did not even notice how much language practice and language learning were taking place.

Another language learning aspect of the process was that when students thought about different ways to demystify stereotypes that foreigners might have about Brazil, or when they discussed which information was relevant and attractive about each Brazilian city, they became more aware of their own culture and the image of their country that they wanted to advertise to the world. Besides all the language learning and collaboration going on, the important concepts of cultural awareness and tolerance were being internalized.

There is no doubt that by using tools that learners are used to (in this case, computers and the Internet) and by tapping into their specific interests, the teacher helped students present a quality product that was the result of enthusiastic engagement and careful attention to the language being used. Furthermore, as the international element (the audience) was added to the process, the experience of meaningful, contextualized learning fulfilled its own cycle of richness.

Weaknesses of SambaEFL

An essential feature that we learned about later with other Web 2.0 collaborative projects is the power of having international partners interact with our student groups from the beginning. In the case of SambaEFL, the international audience was added only when the final product was posted online. Our international partners left comments for students, praised their podcasts, and asked questions. However, at that point, we had to move on to other topics and did not really explore the true possibilities that the read/write nature of the web provides for engaging in online dialogue and promoting a network with which to cooperate, learn, and share.

The main aspects of Web 2.0 that are pertinent here are knowledge sharing and construction of a networked online space where people establish conversations and learn from each other. The situation is not like it was in the past, when the flow of online information was mainly unidirectional, with students browsing through sites to gather information. Nowadays, the web has evolved into constant possibilities for establishing meaningful interaction with people scattered all over the globe. What does that mean in a practical way for the podcast project? We could have had an international partner collaborating with our group on a specific topic (e.g., food, family traditions, music, favorite spots). Then, the partners could not only decide how the project would develop but also keep interacting through the comment feature of the podcast to further their understanding of the cultural differences and similarities among them. This interactivity aspect would have had an even greater impact on learners' ability to communicate in English and reflect on their own ideas and their comprehension of the world that surrounds them with its cultural subtleties and richness. Having carried out other projects since SambaEFL, we now understand the value of connecting to others and maintaining that connection to establish meaningful and contextualized conversations in online social spaces.

REFLECTIONS

To have a successful computer-mediated collaboration, a plan needs to be designed to guide the participants in the project. They need to know what their goals are within that collaborative effort, where they are heading, and how they will accomplish the tasks to achieve the stated goals. Of course, throughout the collaborative process there needs to be room for flexibility and change of plans when adjustments to the initial idea are necessary, especially if you consider the astounding speed of technological changes and students' creative ways to achieve an educational goal. As interactions progress, educators and learners will likely find interesting applications they had not thought of initially. Thus, they might consider adding some extra tools along the way to take the best advantage of the most suitable Web 2.0 alternatives within the language learning framework. With the guidelines set, everyone involved in the collaborative project needs to be comfortable with the tools they are going to use to build their own online artifacts, whether audio files, blog posts, or slideshows. In fact, information and computer literacy are key elements that should be dealt with when working with CALLaborative projects. As Herrington, Oliver, and Reeves (2003) suggest,

> as educators move to adopt learning settings that focus on student-centred rather than teacher-centred learning activities, the need for strategies to support and encourage learners in what are sometimes unfamiliar and discomforting activities becomes an important element in the design process. Support for students in the early weeks of immersion in student-centered learning environments is crucial. This is particularly important in online learning environments where isolation can be an additional mitigating factor against successful engagement with the course. ("Conclusion," para. 1)

In fact, the chances for a tech-based activity with a task-based approach to be successful depend directly on an educational design and practice that contemplates the use of different media in a purposeful way for the learners to accomplish the activities. Educators need to make sure that they are planning, remixing concepts, and using multiple online sources as means for engaging students in active learning and promoting language development. That is exactly the way in which project-based learning fits the concept of *learn by doing.*

As for technology, it works as an aggregator of content, an element of motivation for the participants of the project, and a collective intelligence harnesser. Our experience as teachers and as technology supporters for other teachers is that once a group starts working on a collaborative project using computers and Web 2.0 tools, there is this spark of interest that begins to flow, this collective willingness of having a well-elaborated final product that can be shared and cherished long after the project is completed.

Also, the multiplying effects that these projects have among the school community are just amazing. By observing how engaging the tasks can be and what the results are, more and more educators become eager to shift paradigms, to try what is new, to experiment with emerging technologies, and to learn with their students. At Casa Thomas Jefferson, that is exactly what happened after we advertised our podcast. More teachers felt compelled to test collaborative possibilities using technology, and we became the technology supporters of these new endeavors. From then on, more and more learners started to benefit from projects being developed in their classes due to this enthusiasm and the recognition that one does not need to be an expert to engage in CALL. Nowadays, with the read/write nature of the web, the possibilities are limited only by learners' and educators' imagination and engagement in a project.

The SambaEFL podcast project had an essential item that was crucial to the process of students becoming confident and competent in a second language. Because the final product would be exposed to the world on the Internet, students were not dealing with English merely to communicate among themselves. They had an external motivation, a real audience. They needed to accomplish various tasks in class and use different media to convey their message. The fact that they wanted to make their final product understandable made them more aware of the bits and pieces of the language and stimulated their attention to producing accurate English. Besides, due to the learners' self-consciousness about their own voices, they were undoubtedly more cognizant of their oral production, becoming more attentive to their pronunciation and realizing that they needed to work on their utterances, intonation, and pitch if they wanted to be understood.

Modified to meet specific needs, the SambaEFL podcast project could be part of any educational context, with students ranging from the lowest to highest levels of language proficiency capable of exploring a variety of exciting topics that interest them (see Appendix A for a project for young learners). The main requirement for success is shifting from a teacher-centered to a student-centered approach, for the beauty of it lies exactly in the fact that learners see that they have options and that they are able to find their way into creating meaning in the target language. This empowers students. Another important issue related to implementing the podcast idea in the classroom is the ability of those involved in the process to skillfully use technology to achieve the expected learning outcomes. Considering that the read/write web offers so many possibilities in a user-friendly mode for educators (see Appendix B), technological expertise should not be a hindering aspect of the CALLaborative classroom. Collaboration through computer and web-mediated environments has never been so accessible. It is just a matter of delving into this brave technological world.

Carla Arena is a Brazilian EFL teacher trainer and educational technology supervisor at Casa Thomas Jefferson, a binational center in Brasilia, Brazil. She has been delving into the infinite possibilities of new and emerging technologies in the classroom for the past decade and been involved in e-learning projects for 5 years.

Erika Cruvinel is a teacher, teacher trainer, and member of the Ed Tech team at Casa Thomas Jefferson, in Brasília, Brazil. She has given presentations, both in person and online, about the potential of technology integration into language learning and is especially interested in online teaching.

APPENDIX A: A PODCAST IDEA FOR YOUNGER LEARNERS

Each day we find ourselves experimenting with new tools and discovering ways to engage students in the language learning process through dynamic, student-centered, content-rich tasks and projects. Here you will find an example of a podcast idea for younger learners.

Following the same idea as the SambaEFL podcast project, a group of young learners from Casa Thomas Jefferson engaged in a podcast about pets (*Juvenile 3 Podcast*, n.d.). In a previous podcast activity, students recorded introductions and their teacher advertised the class podcast in an e-mail group. Other language teachers interested in international collaborative projects wrote comments to each student.

One of these commentators was Sharon Holdner, an ESL teacher living in Boston, in the United States, and she mentioned in a comment that she had a foster dog. Because fostering pets is unusual in Brazil, students were curious and wanted to know all about her pet and the fostering program. After meeting Sharon and her foster dog Holling (German Shepherd Rescue of New England, 2003–2008), students were touched by the fact that Holling was found on the street and was waiting for adoption. The teacher realized that the students were really motivated to talk about pets and were eager to keep exploring that topic, so she asked them to bring photos of their pets to class and to write sentences about their pets' habits using adverbs and expressions of frequency, which was the grammar point they were learning. At the computer lab, each student recorded his or her sentences using Audacity (Version 1.2.6), the same audio recording software used in the SambaEFL project. When the class was over the teacher uploaded the photos, the audio files, and students' written sentences to the class podcast. Sharon and these students kept interacting online until the end of the semester.

This podcast collaboration shows that educators should always be aware of students' interests and take advantage of these interests when the opportunity arises. Learners are much more committed when they play an active role in the learning process.

Also, considering the issue of Internet safety, an online activity about pets is entirely appropriate for young learners. By writing and talking about pets, kids do not provide any personal information to other Internet users. A podcast with young learners can also be the communication channel between school and home. In this case, students were eager to share their production with their friends and families, who could check out what the kids were producing in class.

APPENDIX B: POWERFUL WEB 2.0 IDEAS FOR ONLINE COLLABORATION AMONG EDUCATORS

- Use *Flickr* (Yahoo!, 2009) photos licensed under Creative Commons for your classroom projects. (For interesting suggestions, see Campbell, n.d.)

- Write a book collaboratively using *Mixbook* (Mixbook.com, 2006–2009), an online book creator. With *Mixbook*, different collaborators can work on the book, adding photos, text, and backgrounds. When the book is ready, the group can publish it online or order a hard copy. Also, a class can join the Open Book, in which they contribute to the creation of a book together with the Mixbookers community. (For more inspiring ideas, see Arena, 2007.)

- Use *Twitter* (Twitter, 2009) as a communicative tool for your classes. Microblogging can connect the class beyond its physical walls by presenting information that needs to be summarized in 140 words or less. (For ideas that might inspire class activities, see White, n.d.)

- Finally, we'd like to end with a comprehensive resource for digital storytelling called *The Fifty Tools* (Levine, 2007). You will certainly find an e-tool that will fit your educational goals and will create passionate English language learners connected to the world.

CHAPTER 10

The Harmonica Project: Task-Based Learning Beyond Words

Betty Litsinger

In a multilevel, mixed-grade, middle school English as a second language (ESL) classroom, and with students previously accustomed to teacher-centered, rote methods, creating effective task-based learning (TBL) opportunities can be a challenge. The Harmonica Project described in this chapter involved students in a nonlinguistic pursuit that resulted in language growth for each member of the group and improved classroom climate.

I wanted to design a series of tasks that would shift the language production focus from form to function and from self-conscious performance to authentic communication. It was, of course, important to promote the development of English proficiency in all four modalities and to reinforce focused tasks that the students had recently completed. Broadly speaking, a focused task requires the learner to produce or demonstrate understanding of a particular linguistic form in the performance of the task (for a full discussion of focused and unfocused tasks, see Ellis, 2003, pp. 16–17). The learning unit also needed to include unfocused, problem-solving tasks using academic skills that would transfer to assignments and interactions that students were encountering in their other classes.

Creating greater opportunity for self-initiated modification of output was an important goal (for discussion of the role of self-initiated modification of output in interlanguage growth, see Shehadeh, 2001). At the same time, I hoped to build social cohesion and positive group dynamics and minimize inequalities based on differences in age, culture, economic status, and previous educational experience. Finally, my intention was to incorporate a "fun factor" sufficient to engage students and motivate them to take the risks necessary to advance their communication skills.

I found that by centering students' attention on the nonlinguistic, extracurricular goal of learning to play the harmonica well enough to play at a school assembly, I was able to encourage them to embrace TBL activities. Because their goal did not demand any particular set of English proficiency skills, they were able to view their use of language as a communication tool rather than as a goal in itself. Academic tasks such as asking questions of their harmonica instructor, giving speeches on how to take care of a harmonica, and writing a practice journal were all viewed as subordinate skills needed to achieve the goal of learning to play their instruments.

Harmonica instruction was provided by a volunteer for 1 hour each week. Over the course of 1 month, students followed oral and written directions, completed web searches, and kept journals and practice charts. They gave speeches, wrote essays and reports, designed T-shirts, took notes, wrote outlines, created graphic organizers, and wrote song lyrics. In other words, they engaged in the typical, real-world tasks of adolescents in U.S. classrooms.

As the project progressed, I observed improvement in students' fluency, complexity, and accuracy in speaking and writing. They engaged in self-initiated repairs when they encountered difficulties. In addition, students more frequently relied on each other, rather than the instructor or teaching assistant, for explanations and clarification when working independently or in small groups. The unit culminated in the class playing as a harmonica ensemble for an audience of 1,200 people. The project resulted in increased self-confidence, greater sense of community, improved language and technology skills, and at least one continuing harmonica player. Employing a nonlinguistic activity to lower the affective filter (Krashen, 1982) and lend authenticity to TBL activities may be useful for other teachers.

CONTEXT

This sheltered instruction ESL language arts class was composed of 10 students, ages 11–15, in Grades 6–8. The class met for 90 minutes 5 days a week and served all ESL students in the school. Students spent the rest of the day in classes with the English-speaking population of the school. Depending on their proficiency level when they entered the class, students could be assigned to the class for all 3 years of their middle school careers. As a result, sibling classmates were a frequent occurrence. The group involved in the Harmonica Project included two sets of siblings and three students from one family. Native languages included Russian, Korean, and Spanish. Families included expatriates as well as immigrants and were socioeconomically diverse.

These social factors and the wide range of English proficiency, from low beginning to advanced, presented many obstacles to effective, task-based, group instruction. During the first weeks of school, in August, beginning-level students tended to wait for advanced-level students to take the lead or provide models. Siblings were quick to correct each other, leaving little opportunity for self-initiated modification of output. Newcomers expected teacher-modeled responses, grammar drills, and memorization activities. In addition, some of the students had little or no previous experience using computers.

Equal access to the resources of the larger school community was also an area of concern. Although the real world of the adolescent in a U.S. school revolves around the social situations of the school environment and the pedagogical tasks of the classroom, these are often the greatest sources of anxiety for the middle school ESL student. When other content area teachers assigned the ESL students to work in groups and dyads with native-English-speaking students, the ESL students often reported not having a significant role in projects and being marginalized by group members. They were often socially isolated as well. The native-English-speaking students, not knowing how to initiate conversations during the school day, simply ignored them or quickly abandoned their efforts when communication broke down. The ESL students' access to afterschool extracurricular activities and sports was limited not only by language proficiency issues but often by lack of required transportation and health insurance. These cultural, economic, and language proficiency differences constituted barriers to learning and threatened to raise the anxiety level, affecting language acquisition, which Krashen (1982) has termed the affective filter.

By September I knew that the ESL students needed to participate in cooperative, team-building activities that would minimize the effects of high diversity and lower the affective filter. In October we began our quest to learn to play the harmonica. By introducing a task at which everyone, including the teacher, was a complete novice, I hoped to redefine my role for the newcomers as the "guide on the side" rather than the "sage on the stage." I also welcomed the opportunity to observe students' efforts to negotiate meaning with the harmonica instructor, who did not preemptively engage in what Ellis (2003) refers to as teacher talk, anticipating and avoiding complexity that might cause difficulty for students.

Before beginning this project, the class had just completed a focused task in which they learned to use *wh-* question words and used them to conduct a series of interviews, first with their classmates and next with various adults in the school. They then wrote biographical sketches of the interviewees. With their courage to speak and their question-asking abilities at a new high, it was an opportune time to stretch those skills with some less focused tasks.

CURRICULUM, TASKS, MATERIALS

I met with Ron Beer of the Gateway Harmonica Club to plan the lessons. He adapted lessons from *First Step Harmonica Course* (Gateway Harmonica Club, 1993) to fit into the 4-week time period. Some of these materials originated from the Society for the Preservation and Advancement of the Harmonica (1995), which gives permission to reprint their materials without charge. These materials are simply written, in a playful tone, and are exceptionally appropriate for ESL students. Mr. Beer also obtained Hohner Bluesband harmonicas for each student from a local music store for $2.50 each. It was important to me to introduce an activity that any of the students, regardless of socioeconomic status, could continue to enjoy if they chose, so the harmonica suited my purposes well. As Sullivan (2000) and others have noted, students are more open to TBL when the lesson involves an element of fun, and the harmonica lessons fostered a spirit of play and stress-free experimentation.

Language activities were designed to produce opportunities for participants in three broadly defined proficiency groups (beginning, intermediate, and advanced) to contribute equally but differently to class sessions. The tasks were chosen to give practice in the procedures and skills the students needed to use in their other classes. Students were asked to complete five tasks:

1. Follow oral instructions and ask clarifying questions during the harmonica lessons.

2. Practice the harmonica for 10 minutes a day, keeping a practice chart and explaining their practice habits to the teacher.

3. Keep a journal of their thoughts and feelings about the project.

4. Research and share information: giving a speech using notes they had prepared on the parts of the harmonica or how to care for a harmonica (beginner group), researching and writing a report on a famous harmonica player or the history of the harmonica (intermediate group), or composing an essay comparing and contrasting the harmonica with another instrument (advanced group).

5. Write song lyrics and sing as the class played, or find a harmonica tune on the Internet and teach it to the class.

A T-shirt design activity was also included as an option, but because it was not defined clearly enough, the products did not result in the accomplishment of significant linguistic tasks. Assessment was based on successful completion of the tasks as specified in written instructions that students received at the beginning of the project.

My instructions to the students for the project and for each task are included as Figures 1–6 and are accompanied by explanation of the purposes of the assignments.

The first task (Figure 2), interacting during the music lesson, gave all students the opportunity to test their understanding of English in a nonthreatening way. They knew they had misunderstood a direction when the sounds from their instruments were different from those modeled by the instructor or produced by the rest of the group. Because we were all making many mistakes and students were more interested in correcting their playing than their English, they did not pay attention to the English errors made by others. In addition, because the harmonica instructor was not a professional language teacher, there were more

---

The Harmonica Project

In this project you will practice writing from personal experience (The Harmonica Diaries). You will also use research skills to prepare written and oral reports (Harmonica Facts). In addition, you will have a chance to use English as you write songs and design T-shirts (Playing Around With the Harmonica). At the same time you will be improving your skills in English communication. And best of all, you will have fun learning something new with your classmates. You will learn to play the harmonica!

Figure 1. Project Introduction

misunderstandings and incomplete interchanges. These were useful in eliciting requests for clarification that fostered language growth.

During the lesson, I tried to maintain my role as fellow music student, refraining from serving as interlanguage interpreter unless absolutely necessary. As a result, students engaged in more self-initiated modification of output when their attempts to ask clarifying questions were not immediately understood. Sometimes this self-correction process developed over the course of the week between lessons. For example, when a student's request that the instructor modify the lesson to allow time for students to play the song they had practiced was not understood, the student did not immediately attempt to rephrase his question and did not achieve his goal. However, by the next lesson, he had prepared alternate ways of making the request and was successful in expressing his desire to have the group show what they had accomplished before moving on to the next lesson.

The practice chart requirement referenced in Figure 3 could not really be considered a linguistic task because it merely involved placing stickers on the chart, but it was a useful self-motivation technique that students could transfer to other study activities requiring rehearsal. In addition, when my teaching assistant and I

Task 1: Harmonica Lessons (50 points)

Listen carefully to the information and instructions that Mr. Beer gives. Take notes. Ask questions when you do not understand. Take good care of your harmonica.

Figure 2. Behavioral Expectations

Task 2: Harmonica Practice (50 points)

Practice playing the harmonica at least 10 minutes a day. Place a sticker on your chart each time you complete a practice session.

Figure 3. Practice Assignment

checked the charts, we engaged students in one-to-one conversations about how their practice was going. (Making excuses is an essential speech act in a middle school student's repertoire.)

The Harmonica Diaries (see Figure 4) were primarily a tool for developing fluency. Students could write any reflections they had about their experience learning to play the harmonica, or they could choose a topic from a list. The amount of writing required varied among the three proficiency groups. Although my instructions specified a minimum number of sentences that students should write, as the weeks progressed I found that students were experimenting with sentence structure, sometimes writing fewer but more complex sentences. It appeared that they were dwelling less on meeting the requirement and more on telling their

---

Task 3: The Harmonica Diaries (60 points)

You must write in your diary 15 times. You may make only one entry per day. Use your best English (spelling, grammar, punctuation).

      Group 1: two sentences or more

      Group 2: three sentences or more

      Group 3: five sentences or more

You may use the following questions or think up your own topics. You may answer a question more than once.

1. Describe how you feel about the Harmonica Project today.
2. Who would you like to teach to play the harmonica? Why?
3. Think of something that was hard for you to learn. Is playing the harmonica easier or harder than the thing you thought of?
4. Do you think you will continue to play the harmonica? Why?
5. What did you think when Ms. Litsinger told you that you were going to learn to play the harmonica?
6. Tell about other instruments you or other people in your family can play.
7. If you could learn to play any musical instrument, what would you choose?
8. Why is the harmonica a great instrument to play?
9. What does your family think about your harmonica playing?
10. "Practice makes perfect" is a common saying. What do you think it means?
11. Would you rather play the harmonica alone or with friends? Why?
12. What question would you like to ask Mr. Beer? Why?
13. How do you think it would sound if everyone in the school played the harmonica together?
14. Playing an instrument is one kind of hobby. What is your hobby, and why do you like it?
15. Do you think you could learn to play the harmonica without a teacher? How would you do it?

Figure 4. Journaling Assignment

stories. They chose to interpret the assignment as requiring a certain number of ideas rather than a minimum number of grammatical forms. Because students could answer the same question more than once, they were encouraged to find new ways to talk about the same topic.

The research and report tasks, Harmonica Facts (see Figure 5), allowed students to work on language development as well as the study skills that they would be expected to use in other classes. As Pica (2005) points out, in sheltered and regular classrooms, the emphasis on content can easily push aside attention to syntax, morphology, and semantics. By differentiating these tasks for the three groups and providing ample time for rehearsal in student pairs and with the teaching assistant, it was possible to directly address the language development needs of each proficiency group.

The beginner group read about and took notes on harmonica care and the parts of the harmonica. They then gave short demonstration speeches. These "How To" speeches provided an opportunity to use present-tense verbs, short imperative sentences, and concrete vocabulary appropriate to the beginning-level students' language competency. The intermediate group used the Internet to find information on the history of the harmonica and famous harmonica players. They prepared written reports and made oral presentations. Reporting on historical events and biographical information necessitated using past-tense verbs, the sequence of tenses, prepositions of time and place, and transition words; locating and evaluating sources; and prioritizing facts. The advanced group created graphic organizers and wrote essays comparing and contrasting the harmonica

---

Task 4: Harmonica Facts (50 points)

Group 1: Read the handouts you received during your lesson and search the Internet for more information. Write notes or an outline. Describe to the class one of the following:

    A. how to care for your harmonica

    B. the parts of the harmonica

Group 2: Use library and Internet sources to research one of the following; write a report and present it orally to the class.

    A. the history of the harmonica

    B. a famous harmonica player

Group 3: Read about the harmonica and one other instrument. Compare and contrast the two instruments in as many ways as you can. Make a graphic organizer. Then write an essay describing the most interesting similarities and differences, and telling which you would recommend to someone who wants to learn to play an instrument.

Figure 5. Integrated Academic Skills Assignment

with another instrument. These tasks allowed them to practice the writing process as it is taught in U.S. schools and to use a variety of linguistic forms, such as conditional verbs and comparative adjectives, to synthesize information and express inferences and predictions. In addition, all of the Harmonica Facts tasks engaged students in learning to use the computer for word-processing and Internet searches.

The creative task, Playing Around With the Harmonica (see Figure 6), gave students the opportunity to use English in novel ways. Some students wrote lyrics to be sung to one of the tunes they had learned to play and then sang their songs while the class accompanied them on harmonica. Others used the Internet to find a new tune, learned to play it, and then taught it to the class. By taking on the role of teacher at this point, near the end of the project, students were able to use all of the language production skills they had acquired through observation, repeated exposure, and experimentation. Two students enhanced their presentations with a culture lesson by choosing to write lyrics for traditional tunes from their countries.

The culminating activity was a school assembly at which the group played "My Country 'Tis of Thee" (which is the same tune as "God Save the Queen") for the entire school community. There was much nervousness surrounding this event. After the performance, the applause was thunderous and the ESL students were ecstatic. They were proud of themselves for having the courage to stand in front of 1,200 people. Beginning-level students, who would have been too self-conscious to speak English in such a setting, gained visibility in the school through their musical accomplishment. In the days following the assembly, fellow students recognized them and approached them in the halls congratulating them on their performance.

Task 5: Playing Around With the Harmonica (40–60 points)

Choose two or more of the following activities:

A.   Write lyrics (words) to go with one of the tunes we learned to play. Sing your song while the class plays the tune.

B.   Compose (write) a tune, or find a tune we haven't learned in a book or on the Internet. Teach the class to play it.

C.   Design a T-shirt for the Harmonica Project. Your shirt must include words. It may include pictures if you like.

Figure 6. Creative Expression Assignment

REFLECTIONS

Directing the learner's attention to a nonacademic, high-interest activity proved fruitful in that, in addition to providing motivation to successfully communicate, the activity was interesting enough to distract students from correcting each other's language. This allowed both the time and the opportunity for self-initiated repair, which research has shown to be an important component in expanding learners' interlanguage (Shehadeh, 2001).

Because the subject matter was limited in scope, the redundancy provided by Internet sources, written materials, and oral instructions during the harmonica lessons permitted even beginning-level students to master the vocabulary and grammatical structures necessary to complete real-world tasks. For example, one newcomer, who had been in a silent and often tearful period at the beginning of the year, was able to prepare and deliver an authoritative talk on how to care for a harmonica. The need to communicate this information to his classmates gave him a reason not only to overcome his hesitancy to speak, but also to rehearse and modify his output. Near the end of the project, when students taught each other to play or sing a song, they were able to draw on 4 weeks of modeled language by the harmonica teacher, as well as their own recent experience in understanding and misunderstanding instructions, in order to anticipate and avoid communication difficulties. Their language choices and repairs were undertaken in the service of accomplishing a teaching task, and in all cases they were successful in communicating their meaning.

The large amount of time dedicated to the project was efficiently used because it made it possible for me to introduce curricular skills to all three grade levels. I was aware of the academic tasks students needed to perform in other classes and was able to incorporate component skills into the project. For instance, in preparing their written reports, intermediate-level students constructed timelines, a product required in the world history and U.S. history classes they were taking. Similarly, advanced-level students used Venn diagrams as a prewriting tool to show similarities and differences. Use of this graphic organizer was included in the school's curriculum in all core subjects. Students in the United States begin using such visual representations of thought early in elementary school, so it was important that the ESL students master them early in their middle school careers and understand that they are not content area–specific tools. By choosing which graphic organizers to introduce in each language proficiency group, I was able to indirectly guide the practice of language skills. For example, intermediate-level students explaining their biographical timelines naturally made use of such grammar features as irregular past-tense verbs and prepositions of time and place.

As class discussion and journal entries reflected, students maintained a high level of commitment and interest throughout the month-long project. They sometimes reported practicing for an hour or more beyond the required

10 minutes a day, and there were stories of parents begging their children to stop playing for a while. I believe that it was particularly helpful that students were involved in an activity during which it was impossible to talk in any language, thus reducing language production anxiety. The choice of an instrument that produces tolerably harmonious sounds even when inexpertly played also sustained motivation to continue practicing.

Each morning, as they entered the classroom, students were eager not only to demonstrate but to talk about the progress resulting from their practice. This enthusiasm produced a naturally occurring conversation time at the beginning of the school day, which served as an excellent warm-up activity, increasing oral participation during the rest of the morning. The speech acts of negotiation, requests for clarification, and instruction giving that students attempted were spontaneous and progressively less timidly delivered as students realized that their speech was not being monitored for error by their classmates and siblings.

A skilled teaching assistant and an enthusiastic volunteer harmonica instructor were keys to the success of the project. Their work was especially valuable in allowing me to take on the role of music student during lessons. This made it possible for students to see me as a fellow learner, taking risks, making mistakes, and correcting them. The small number of students in the class was also an advantage; a larger group might have become too chaotic and loud. The excellent materials from the Society for the Preservation and Advancement of the Harmonica required no modification for English language learners. The 90-minute class period made it possible to allot 3 hours of class time, including the 1-hour music lesson each week, for 4 weeks to complete the project.

As might be expected, not every aspect of the project was successful. Although students enjoyed doing it, the T-shirt task did not result in the kind of language use I had anticipated. I had hoped that the more advanced students would come up with clever slogans or names for the group; however, the shirt designs mostly featured pictures of flowers, rainbows, and harmonicas and the words "Harmonica Project" or "Harmonica Club." I would not include this activity again. I would also add class sessions in which we could hear recordings, watch DVDs, or invite guest performers to enhance students' appreciation of the performance range of the harmonica and its place in U.S. and world music.

This unit could be modified or extended to include other readily available or inexpensive and easy-to-learn musical instruments such as electronic keyboards, recorders, or student-made percussion. If instructors in several instruments are available, it would be possible to form a mixed ensemble. My classes have also made CDs on which students sing to prerecorded music and for which they design CD covers and compose liner notes introducing themselves. This idea could be combined with learning to play an instrument to result in an entirely student-created recording project. For schools that do not have the advantage of 90-minute block-scheduled classes, such a project could be the basis of an after-school conversation club.

This project met students' academic and social needs by creating a level of comfort and camaraderie in the classroom that encouraged language development. There was much laughter and, particularly on lesson days, a great deal of excitement among all the students. They were not only proud of their own achievements, but genuinely helpful toward and happy for each other as their playing improved week by week. Because I initiated the project partly to prevent the students from being self-conscious and overly critical of one another, I was pleased with the results. The transition from asking teacher-modeled questions, concentrating on word order and pronunciation, to asking sincere questions to satisfy real curiosity and authentic need for information was rewarding for students to achieve and teacher to observe. Using this or another enjoyable nonlinguistic activity may prove helpful to teachers who are seeking to create bridges between the language classroom and the real world of the adolescent.

Two pieces of advice from the Society for the Preservation and Advancement of the Harmonica (1995) illustrate the parallels between second language acquisition and the acquisition of music skills:

- *Don't worry if you make mistakes.* The only way to learn how to do something you've never done before is to try it. If you've never done it before, you have to make mistakes on the way to mastering it.

- *Keep trying.* Sometimes you may feel like you're not getting any better even though you're practicing. Whatever it is you're working on, one day it will suddenly happen as long as you don't give up.

For my students, these and other positive lessons gained from playing the harmonica made this project worthwhile.

Betty Litsinger has an MA in TESOL from Southeast Missouri State University and is currently an English language support coordinator and adjunct professor at Arcadia University, in the United States. She teaches writing courses for nonnative English speakers at Arcadia and at Bryn Mawr College. She has taught ESL in a variety of settings and at every level from prekindergarten to adult.

Evaluation, Testing, and Assessment

I Can! Bringing Self-Evaluation to a Task-Based Syllabus for Language Learning Success

Jan Edwards Dormer

"But I've already done book two!" exclaimed an enrolling student, in her native language of Portuguese, upon hearing the result of her placement test. She had transferred to our school from another that used the same course book series that we were using, and proudly showed me her very much completed book two. Yes indeed, she had "done" book two. Knowing that placement tests are fallible, and knowing that book two covered the present perfect tense, I tried to elicit this same statement from her in English. But the best she could come up with, haltingly, was "I do this book before." Then and there I made my final decision: We would change our program. I wanted a system in which students would gauge their learning on communicative ability, not on the completion of a book.

As director of a new English language school in southern Brazil, this was not the first time that I had encountered a vast discrepancy between the language supposedly "covered" in the course book and the language that learners could actually use in real communication. I was aware that this age-old dilemma was sparking some interest in the new task-based approach, both in Brazil (see Lopes, 2004; Passos de Oliveira, 2004) and elsewhere, and I was actively trying to discover how this approach might be applicable in our context.

The student in question went on to enroll in our level two, and within 6 months she was among the first group of students to be taught from our newly created task-based, topical syllabus. She learned to take responsibility for her own learning as we teamed task-based learning with self-evaluation. She learned how to monitor her own language acquisition as she pursued a relevant goal: effective communication.

CONTEXT

I have been privileged to work as an English as a foreign language (EFL) private school program developer in both Brazil and Indonesia. I initiated the task-based system discussed here in Brazil, in which foreign as well as local teachers provided invaluable feedback throughout its implementation. After 5 years in Brazil, I moved to Indonesia and began using the same system in a school there, again working alongside local teachers whose expertise made possible adaptations for a new context.

Brazil and Indonesia are on opposite sides of the world and seem to have little in common where culture is concerned. But they are similar environments in terms of EFL. In both countries, English is not a majority first language, but it is a highly valued foreign language. In both countries, English is a required subject in school, and private English schools abound. However, both countries also seem to have a large number of people who have studied English for years and yet have not developed the ability to communicate in English.

The student highlighted in the opening of this chapter is one example of many that I encountered in Brazil and Indonesia. Many English language learners in these countries have experienced traditional, teacher-centered, textbook-mediated learning environments. Yet many are frustrated that their hours spent in English classes have not achieved the result that they wanted: the ability to speak English effectively and naturally. However, few students have considered that the approaches used in their classrooms may be to blame. Most feel that they are "not good language learners" or that they "do not study enough."

It was into this learning context that the task-based, self-evaluated approach explained here was introduced, first in Brazil and later in Indonesia. Its implementation was not without bumps and setbacks in both countries, and my colleagues and I learned that a significant orientation and adjustment period was required to help learners overcome their distrust in an approach that was so radically different from what they had previously experienced. Still, the final outcome has been extremely positive, with increased language acquisition and much greater student responsibility for learning.

CURRICULUM, TASKS, MATERIALS

The Task Framework

Tasks can be understood as anything from "things people will tell you they do" (Long, 1985, p. 89) to "pedagogical tasks intended to reach [language] goals" (Brown, 2001, p. 243) to "activities that call for primarily meaning-focused language use" (Ellis, 2003, p. 3). Our school goal in Brazil was to ensure that students in our program were able to accomplish basic communicative tasks on a variety of topics using all four language skills. Thus, we envisioned tasks from a functional perspective as what our students want to be able to do in English. Our listing of such tasks amounted to a needs identification for our student group, which Richard-Amato (2003) proposes as the first step in the development of a task-based syllabus.

Ours were also real-world tasks (Brown, 2001; Ellis, 2003; Widdowson, 1987), rather than pedagogic ones, in that we wanted students to engage in activities in English that adults are likely to do outside of the classroom. We did not forgo tasks simply because they would not normally be found in the real EFL world. Rather, we tied our new syllabus to our preexisting school motto: "We bring the world to you." We justified tasks that might not normally be part of the life of an English speaker in Brazil on the basis of our endeavor to create an English-speaking enclave on our campus and our goal of preparing students for travel abroad. This perspective assisted us in appropriate task selection. We included activities such as shopping, even though one would rarely use English while shopping in Brazil, while excluding tasks that our students would probably never encounter in English, such as opening a bank account.

We further sought to develop real-world tasks that would help students make long-distance connections to the English-speaking world. We included many writing tasks and sought e-mail buddies from the English-speaking world. We included authentic materials from free Internet sources, exploiting the vast potential for English input from the web.

Our Thematic Syllabus

After developing a general understanding of *task* for our purposes, we sought a scheme for selecting and ordering appropriate tasks. We discovered that grading tasks according to linguistic content is extremely complex (Nunan, 1989; M. Williams & Burden, 1997) and that even after spending considerable time and energy on carefully designed tasks, there is no guarantee that particular language forms will be used or learned. As Van den Branden (2006a) states, "task designers can ask, demand or invite the learner to do meaningful things with language and meanwhile pay attention to particular forms, but they cannot force the learner into anything" (p. 10). Van den Branden goes on to suggest that learning may well result more from the interaction provided through tasks than by the task design itself.

Ellis (2003) explains that tasks are "not designed with a specific form in mind" (p. 16) and that "no attempt is made to specify what the learners will learn, only how they will learn" (p. 31). Further support for a broader and non-language-specific task design comes from J. R. Willis's (2004) concept of the internal syllabus:

> Learners acquire language according to their own inbuilt internal syllabus, regardless of the order in which they are exposed to particular structures and regardless of mother-tongue influences. In other words, it is unlikely that learners will acquire a

new pattern unless they are developmentally ready for it, no matter how many times they practice it. (p. 5)

With these issues in mind, we opted to base our task design on broad themes rather than on linguistic content. We did provide students with separate sequenced grammar study drawn from a popular text. But though we made some cursory efforts to line up grammar structures covered with those we anticipated would be used in certain tasks, this was by no means a comprehensive selection process, and thus the grammar studied often had no correlation with the language used in tasks.

We chose themes for each level, sequencing the themes from most concrete and familiar to most abstract (see Table 1). We reasoned that this thematic selection itself would likely result in a progression from simpler to more complex language forms.

For each theme, eight 2-week units were developed. Each unit includes five to seven tasks and one vocabulary acquisition goal. Our tasks are not complex, but rather are reminiscent of activities found in many English language learning materials, such as "take a phone message" and "read an article about health." All were selected to provide interaction on topics of interest and value, in the four skill areas, within our selected themes.

The final step was to provide the input for task completion, "the data that form the point of departure for the task" (Nunan, 1989, p. 53). The selection of input involved the use of authentic materials wherever possible, but with appropriate adaptations for various levels. We discovered that many of the games and activities that we were already using in our classes could be called tasks. What became different for us was the absence of other agendas along with the tasks. We envisioned a simple goal for learners: develop the ability to do these things in English. The task was not the means to an end; the task was the end.

Table 1. Theme and Content for Each Level

Level	Theme	Content
1	Introduction to English	Letters, numbers, colors, food, body, clothing, school, personal information
2	Home and Family	Introductions, descriptions, jobs, home life, family, house, schedules, habits
3	Community	The neighborhood, stores, services, directions, professions
4	The World	Culture, customs, holidays, geography, countries
5	Personal Development	Relationships, traditions, beliefs, worldview, problems and solutions, change, the future

Evaluation

I was excited about our new syllabus. Eager to put it into practice, I realized that our system was not yet fully developed when one of the teachers asked, "How will we test them?" I wanted to forcefully assert that we did not need tests. I envisioned that our task-based syllabus would naturally lend itself to student-centered, ongoing, formative assessment whereby students could simply enjoy language acquisition without the threat of evaluation. But I knew that such a concept would be difficult to sell on several fronts. First, it would not have validity in the eyes of learners who had only experienced traditional paper-based tests. It would not seem like a responsible approach, as has already been noted by Passos de Oliveira (2004) within the Brazilian context. Second, teachers would be hard-pressed to quickly develop the skills needed for such ongoing assessment, when they had never experienced it before. Finally, even I had to admit that a school of more than a hundred students needed some practical and clear-cut means for monitoring student learning and assuring progression through the various levels.

Student-Centered Assessment

I began to explore the possibilities of involving learners in their own assessment. M. Williams and Burden (1997) urge that "increasing the involvement of the learners in all aspects of the learning process should be encouraged at every opportunity" (p. 75). They point to fostering the ability to self-evaluate as essential in the formation of autonomous learners. We had based our task selection on learner needs, and we were in good company believing that our assessment procedures could focus on learner involvement as well.

The benefits of including learners in their own assessment are well documented. Brindley (1994) outlines four positive outcomes: Students view language as a tool for communication, assessment is integrated with learning, students receive ample feedback, and results are easily understood by learners. Dickinson (1987) reminds us that if language learners are to achieve high levels of proficiency, much of their learning will be in their own hands, because classroom time accounts for only a small portion of language learning. Learners who are able to self-assess will naturally be better equipped to go forward with their own learning. By the same token, Dörnyei (2001) points to the motivational benefits of involving learners in assessment: "Self-assessment raises the learners' awareness about the mistakes and successes of their own learning, and gives them a concrete sense of participation in the learning process" (p. 94).

Our Assessment Design

Assured of the value of student-centered assessment, we developed a system that placed our task-based syllabus at the center of the learning process, but that also included portfolio and teacher evaluation elements as additional support in the assessment process.

M. Williams and Burden (1997) state that "teachers should see one of their primary functions as encouraging a positive self-image, self-esteem, self-confidence; a feeling of 'I can', or 'I am capable of doing this'" (p. 72). So we began by rephrasing the tasks as "I can" statements, as in Figure 1. Thus the task, "take a phone message" became "I can take a phone message." The key action required was put in italics. We wanted students to fully grasp the true goals of their language learning program: to be able to *use* all skills in the English language for a variety of communicative purposes on a variety of topics. We placed boxes next to each "I can" statement for students to check off as tangible evidence of their progress in language learning.

The list of tasks, organized in eight units, was given to students as their Ability Checklist at the beginning of each level. Classes then consisted of teachers orchestrating materials and activities so that learners would acquire the skills needed to complete the tasks. Figure 2 provides a sample teaching guide utilizing various types of input for some of the tasks in Figure 1. At the end of each 2-week unit, the list of tasks was revisited. For oral tasks, teachers often provided additional opportunities at this point to engage in the tasks again, this time for the purpose of assessment: having the student decide whether he or she was successful in completing the task.

To accompany the checklist, students kept samples of their class activities in loose-leaf binders. These served as a type of portfolio demonstrating students' accomplishments. The value of portfolios in assessment has been well documented. For example, D. H. Graves (1992) says that "the portfolio movement promises one of the best opportunities for students to learn how to examine their own work and participate in the entire literacy/learning process" (p. 4). O'Malley and Valdez Pierce (1996) extend this to second language learning and add that "the key to using portfolios successfully in classrooms is engaging students in self-assessment" (p. 38).

Responsibilities in a Community

- ❏ I can *discuss* civic responsibilities and *tell* about my involvement.
- ❏ I can *understand* and *fill out* an Internet volunteer registration form.
- ❏ I can *read* a story about volunteering and *take notes*.
- ❏ I can *read* about a volunteer opportunity.
- ❏ I can *write* a letter applying for a volunteer position and *answer* questions in an interview.
- ❏ I can *compare* volunteering in the United States and Indonesia in a *discussion*.
- ❏ I can *give a report* about a local volunteer project and *answer* questions.
- ❏ I can *create* an advertisement for a volunteer project.
- ❏ **Vocabulary:** I know words related to civic duties and volunteering.

Figure 1. Sample Unit of Tasks: Level 3, Module 8

❏ I can *discuss* civic responsibilities and *tell* about my involvement.
  - Brainstorm: What are civic duties (or responsibilities)?
       Voting?
       Supporting local businesses?
       Giving food to the poor?
       Volunteering at your child's school?
  - In small groups, have students tell about their involvement in their community.

❏ I can *understand* and *fill out* an Internet volunteer registration form.
  - Use the Volunteer Match form (from the Internet) to give students experience in signing up to volunteer and filling out an Internet form.

❏ I can *read* a story about volunteering and *take notes.*

❏ I can *create* an advertisement for a volunteer project.
  - Have students read a story (from the Internet) about volunteering.
  - Have them take notes on what the volunteer in the article does.
  - Have students share their notes with each other and create an advertisement for this kind of volunteer work, including what qualities the volunteer should possess and what he or she would be expected to do.

Figure 2. Sample Teacher Input for Tasks

In our system, students would not only have a check beside the task "I can take a phone message," but should also have in their binders actual phone messages taken in or out of class. The binder served as concrete evidence of learning for tasks that could be documented in some way.

Simply having the checklists and binders, however, was not enough for some students. There also needed to be some form of accountability—some day of reckoning when checklists and binders were officially reviewed. For this purpose, we instituted mid- and end-of-term evaluation meetings. During these meetings, teachers had individual conferences with students. Both student and teacher filled out evaluation forms prior to the meeting. The forms asked each of them to comment on the student's effort, Ability Checklist, binder (portfolio), and overall development in the four skill areas. Though simple, these forms provided a valuable basis for student–teacher dialogue. At the end of the midterm meeting, both teacher and student were to determine actions that they would take to further the student's learning. These commitments were key to helping learners grow in taking responsibility for their own learning and helping teachers develop their role as facilitators of language learning.

At the end-of-term evaluation meeting, the teacher and the student discussed whether the student had truly achieved success in the majority of tasks and whether he or she was ready to move to the next level. Our program tried to create a climate in which moving on was not required and retaking a level did not involve shame. Admittedly, though, old perceptions regarding slow language acquisition as failure were hard to overcome.

Interconnected Tools for Self-Assessment

The three elements of our assessment design are shown in Figure 3 as interlocking gears. Traditional evaluation focuses on an assessment event such as a test. In our system this focus shifted to teacher–student individual evaluation meetings, which were seen as the "evaluation" in our program, represented by the largest gear in the diagram. However, it is actually the Ability Checklist that works in conjunction with both the evaluation and the binder/portfolio that drives the system. It is this skills checklist against which students measure their success. It is a tool that students keep and refer to and that places the system in the category of student-centered evaluation.

REFLECTIONS

Difficulties

Student Reluctance to Self-Assess

When we began asking students to check off tasks as they were able to do them, many of them responded, "How can I do that? I do not know if my language is good or not." Though Dickinson (1987) deals with the issue of students rating

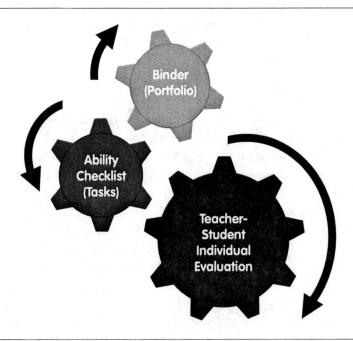

Figure 3. Relationship of Assessment Components

themselves more highly than they ought, our problem was the opposite: The majority of students were reluctant to state that they could actually accomplish a certain task in English. The nagging question, voiced by teachers and students alike, was always "How good does the language need to be to check off the task?" Of course, the setting of appropriate goals and appropriate parameters has always been a complexity of language teaching and testing, respectively. But it was made painfully real to students when they had to make judgment calls concerning their own performance.

We handled this issue in part by encouraging students to set their own individualized language learning goals and then evaluate themselves on that basis. Students who desired a high level of accuracy were encouraged to pursue that goal, and students who were content with basic success in communication were also affirmed in checking off the task as achieved, even if their accuracy was not as high as we would have liked. Although Passos de Oliveira (2004) suggests that when discussing task-based assessment in Brazil "a fully formative assessment system may fail to achieve the level of commitment needed on the part of both young and adult learners" (p. 253), our experience was the opposite. We found that learners became highly committed to realizing their own goals, an outcome supported by M. Williams and Burden (1997): Learners who "set their own goals in any learning activity are more likely to achieve those goals than ones that are set for them" (p. 74).

We doubted at times whether students could be trusted with their own assessment. However, in time we discovered that students and teachers were much more likely to agree on assessments than not and that in the majority of cases students demonstrated a fairly accurate understanding of their effectiveness in communication.

The good news was that students showed remarkably increased comfort levels with both the activity and validity of self-evaluation after they had been in our program for a semester. Nearly always when I checked back in with teachers regarding students who had complained throughout their first evaluation, the story was much different the second and third time around. Those who were skeptical at first often became staunch advocates of self-assessment.

Fluency and Accuracy

I alluded to the question of fluency earlier and the question, "How good is good enough?" We discovered a problem early on in using our task-based syllabus: Teachers did not know how much emphasis to place on accuracy. Some ended up focusing almost entirely on communication, not stopping to explain needed grammatical forms or to correct students' usage. Others went too far the other way, turning tasks into grammar lessons, a problem that Lopes (2004) has also identified in the Brazilian context.

It was necessary to spend considerable teacher discussion time on the issues of fluency, accuracy, and communication. I did not want to set out specific teacher guidelines for each lesson, detailing exactly how instruction should proceed. Rather, I wanted teachers to develop their own internal monitoring guidelines aimed at achieving a middle ground somewhere between the two extremes. I felt that this eventually happened for the majority of teachers.

Student Lack of Organizational Ability

As shown in Figure 3, the binder is a key form of input that is central to self-assessment in this system. However, many students had difficulty keeping their materials organized and available for learning. I surmised that this was because they had been used to course books, and our system utilizing many handouts and self-created lists and documents was new to them.

I also felt that for some students, organization was of cognitive importance: They would simply learn best with their materials in the right places and easily accessible. My personal penchant for orderliness was also no doubt a contributor to this requirement, but I did see tangible evidence that students who learned to organize materials used those materials more often in more appropriate ways and indeed became better language learners.

To help students learn organizational skills, we began each new term with a new student orientation: a 2-hour session that included specifics on how to organize the binder, the importance of keeping and referring to materials, and the significant place that the binder would have as a portfolio in their evaluation. Even with this orientation, helping some students become organized was an ongoing battle. Invariably, some would come to midterm evaluations with little documentation, and it was these cases that caused the most frustration in evaluation. Often the teacher had also kept records, and students who had obviously achieved the tasks were usually passed on despite the fact that they did not meet the portfolio requirement.

Over time we realized that a key to using this type of assessment effectively was frequent looks at the Ability Checklist and the binder within the classroom setting. In classrooms where the teacher set aside a weekly time for students to check their checklists and compile their binders, with the teacher available to provide informal input, students acquired better skills in monitoring and documenting their own progress.

Teacher Desire to Evaluate

The teachers in this program had largely experienced traditional forms of education in which testing figured prominently. Some felt they could not teach effectively unless they could give tests. Others did not mind not having traditional pencil-and-paper tests, but nevertheless felt that they should be doing some sort of evaluation. Our mid- and end-of-term individual evaluation meetings did provide teachers with an opportunity to give feedback on broad aspects of student learning. But for some teachers this was difficult. They had little confidence in their subjective evaluation, much preferring "concrete evidence" on which to base their statements.

We compromised by allowing occasional formative quizzes because teachers felt they were necessary. In addition, some teachers kept simple checklists or anecdotal notes as they watched students engage in the tasks and were then able to complete their portion of the evaluation with more confidence in their assessments.

In time, the majority of teachers became more focused on the actual language learning that was taking place than the assessment of that learning. They also grew more comfortable with encouraging students to take the lead in evaluation, relying less on the teacher's opinion.

Benefits

Increased Student Language Acquisition

My main goal in switching to a task-based system was to increase language learning. Teachers and students alike felt that this goal was realized in our program. As the focus of learners and teachers shifted away from going through a book and toward using language for real communication, it was as if we all suddenly realized, "Yes! This is why we're here!"

Increased Student Autonomy in Learning

Although the main motive for a task-based syllabus was language learning, the impetus for coupling task-based learning with student self-assessment was largely a desire to see students take greater responsibility for their learning. We have already seen the positive effects of student involvement in assessment in terms of increased motivation (Dörnyei, 2001), and it may well be that higher levels of intrinsic motivation account for increased responsibility for learning. Some of the signs that students became more autonomous included the following:

- greater interest in setting personal language learning goals, as opposed to passively accepting teacher or program goals

- greater willingness to repeat coursework and levels when learning had not been achieved

- fewer complaints from students regarding teachers, texts, and activities; the self-evaluation system seemed to help many students realize that language learning was more about what they did in class

Enhanced Teacher–Student Collaboration

The greatest joy for me has been seeing teachers take a more collaborative role with students, as facilitators of their learning. During evaluations, teachers and students make commitments as needed to enhance learning. As students take more responsibility, teachers can shed some of the traditional teacher image and work with students more as mentors and facilitators. This fosters more enjoyment in working together for all.

Further Development

Teacher Preparation

The teachers I have worked with sometimes struggled to develop a learner-centered perspective in their teaching. They were required not only to switch from a transmission role to a facilitation role, but also to learn to embrace student initiative in the classroom. When students took a task in a different direction than the teacher had planned, it sometimes left teachers unsure of how to proceed and unclear in their roles.

In many teacher preparation programs in EFL settings, teachers have not seen modeled or even heard much about task-based instruction or student-centered learning, let alone extending that theory into the realm of evaluation. In addition, few teachers have been trained to act as facilitators and to foster student autonomy. It is hoped that teacher education programs in EFL contexts will embrace new ways of educating adult learners and begin preparing teachers for these new roles.

Research

The evidence presented here is anecdotal in nature and cannot provide conclusive answers to important questions such as these:

1. How might traditional testing systems hinder or even defeat the purposes of task-based instruction?

2. Are there any ways in which learning is hindered when there is no "objective" measurement of what has been learned?

3. What actually is the correlation between what students think they can do with the language and what they can really do?

Task-based instruction is just beginning to take its place as a legitimate choice for course programming and syllabus design. What type of evaluation is most appropriate for such systems is still in question. But until definitive answers are found, the students in these programs will continue to say "I can . . ." as they feel they are able, progressing through the system as they determine.

Jan Edwards Dormer has a doctorate in education from the University of Toronto and currently teaches at Anderson University, in Indiana, in the United States. For 14 years, she worked internationally in program development and teacher education. Her publications focus on task-based and authentic learning and native/nonnative teacher issues in TESOL.

CHAPTER 12

Knowing Who's in Your Audience: Task-Based Testing of Audience Awareness

Betty Lanteigne

Task-based language performance assessment uses assessment tasks to measure not only students' use of English but also how well they actually accomplish the given tasks. Bachman (2002) and B. K. Lynch and McNamara (1998) have raised concerns about construct validity in task-based assessment. Messick (1996) points to construct underrepresentation and construct-irrelevant variance as the major threats to validity, and Bachman particularly says that construct underrepresentation is a problematic issue in task-based assessment because since "performance assessment tasks themselves are of greater richness, the domains to which our task-based inferences about language ability extrapolate become potentially more restricted" (p. 5). These concerns are valid, especially for high-stakes assessment of general language proficiency, but they are not insurmountable. Indeed, Bachman encourages language test developers and researchers to identify language performance tasks that do in fact represent the construct in question.

However, in formative classroom assessment, the situation is different when measuring students' ability to accomplish the tasks presented in a particular unit of study. Sheehan (2005) says that "the task, in class, parallels a 'real-world' activity . . . while retaining an authentic goal within the language classroom" (p. 53). Because task-based assessment directly measures student performance on specific tasks, it is well suited to measure the content addressed in a class project. For example, in my English-medium public speaking course, one of the learning outcomes is for students to develop and analyze results from audience analysis surveys and then use those results to prepare and deliver informative speeches, which are explanatory rather than persuasive. Such a task-based learning outcome reflects real-world language use in that it is not uncommon for public speakers (in business, politics, or academia) to investigate their audiences' knowledge of their topic, sometimes informally and sometimes formally through audience analysis surveys.

In the project described here, content-related evidence of validity (Brown, 2004) was high because students were directly measured on how well they had implemented what they had been taught about audience analysis, including questionnaire content and form as well as use of the audience analysis results in their informative speeches (course content). Also, because the construct being directly measured was the real-world target language use task (Bachman & Palmer, 1996) of preparing and implementing an audience analysis survey and using its results to adapt a speech to the audience surveyed, construct validity was high as well.

CONTEXT

This task-based teaching and assessment project took place in an undergraduate-level public speaking course at an English-medium university in the Middle East. The students were from Africa, Asia, the Middle East, and Europe and spoke a variety of first languages (e.g., Arabic, Hindi, Urdu, Farsi, Swahili, Telagu, Tagalog), reflecting their countries of origin. Many students were multilingual, speaking two or more languages. Their majors were in a wide variety of disciplines in business, engineering, architecture, physical sciences, and humanities.

The students' English levels varied, which reflected the fact that the criteria for university admission had been gradually raised each year from an initial paper-based Test of English as a Foreign Language (TOEFL) score of 500 in 1997 to 530 (or 71 on the Internet-based TOEFL or 197 on the computer-based TOEFL) for incoming freshmen in 2007. In this course, the students were sophomores, juniors, and seniors, which added variations in academic maturity as well as English language ability. Some students were near-native English speakers who had lived in and attended school in English-speaking countries, whereas others had only attended Arabic-medium schools in the Middle East with English taught as one course, and they had not spent time in an English-speaking country.

A common characteristic of many of the students was that their English speaking ability was greater than their English writing ability. In the large cities in this region (e.g., Dubai, Abu-Dhabi, Riyadh, Doha, Kuwait City), English is used as the language of wider communication for interaction in restaurants, businesses, and stores, resulting in many people who are able to use spoken English for such real-world communication but who have less developed written English skills. There was thus a great need to integrate instruction and assessment of written as well as verbal skills in this speaking course, which was particularly manifested in the audience analysis project, which involved students in preparing the questionnaire (writing), reporting their analysis of survey results (writing), and using the survey results to adapt their speech to their audience (speaking).

The public speaking course in which this audience analysis project took place fulfills the speech communications requirement for some majors and is also an English or humanities elective. The textbook used was *The Art of Public Speaking* (Lucas, 2007). The course included weekly practice speeches, a 6- to 8-minute informative speech and portfolio for the midterm, debates on hot topics, and a final exam consisting of a 7- to 9-minute persuasive speech and portfolio.

CURRICULUM, TASKS, MATERIALS

The Project

The audience awareness project was part of the effort to prepare students for their midterm speech, which was their first opportunity to speak for longer than the 1–2 minutes of their preceding practice speeches. The project was multistaged, including cycles of instruction and assessment. First, students studied the importance of audience awareness in public speaking and subsequently adapting speech content to communicate more effectively with the audience. Next, after receiving training in how to write survey questions, they developed audience analysis surveys containing two or more fixed-alternative questions, two open-ended questions, and two or more scaled questions, with the requirement that there be no more than ten questions and that the survey be only one page. Fixed-alternative questions provide multiple options for respondents to choose from (e.g., the seasons—spring, summer, fall, winter), whereas scaled questions give options that are ranges (e.g., extent of agreement—strongly agree, agree, neutral, disagree, strongly disagree). Open-ended questions give opportunity for respondents to explain an issue in their own words.

The surveys were assessed for form, content, and language structure. After receiving their graded surveys with instructor feedback, students revised and distributed them to each other. They then analyzed the results of the surveys and used those results to prepare their informative speeches, which were evaluated for effectiveness in relating to the audience as well as speech organization and delivery. Finally, students wrote a paragraph in which they discussed the results of their surveys and how they used those results to prepare their speeches. The survey results paragraph was evaluated for both language structure and content (explanation of the survey results and how they affected speech preparation).

Throughout this process, students gained an increased appreciation of audience awareness and how they could make their speeches more effective by adapting them according to the audience's background. They also learned how to write appropriate questions for the audience analysis surveys, both in terms of question form (open-ended, fixed-alternative, scaled) and syntax and mechanics. The real-world communication nature of the audience analysis task emphasized to students the importance of accuracy in vocabulary, syntax, and mechanics because mistakes in these areas resulted in respondents misunderstanding the intent of the questions and thus the surveys failing to obtain the needed information.

Audience Awareness

Sociolinguistic studies point out that speech variations occur in response to the interlocutors, setting, and domain (Boxer, 2002; Saville-Troike, 2003). People change the way they speak depending on the formality of the situation, their relationships with their audience, and their purpose in speaking. Such accommodations are a result of what Lucas (2007) refers to as audience awareness, being alert to the audience's background knowledge of and attitudes toward the topic presented in the speech. Because the students in this public speaking course differed in nationality, ethnicity, religion, and academic major, it was crucial for students to develop audience awareness in order to effectively present their speeches to this diverse audience. Callison and Lamb (2004) point to the importance of audience awareness in speaking and writing:

> Audience analysis involves the process of gathering and interpreting information about the recipients of oral, written, or visual communication. Audience awareness involves the conceptions of the writer, speaker, or performer concerning the recipients of his or her communication. Regardless of whether the author is sharing an oral history, debating an issue, or writing an editorial, the writer or speaker must be aware of the needs, interests, and expectations of his or her audience. (p. 34)

Practice Speeches

To educate them about the importance of audience awareness, students were given the opportunity to practice giving speeches (1–2 minutes) in which they explained technical subjects in their various majors, adapting the content to present the specialized topics to a mixed audience of students from various disciplines. For example, business majors, when speaking about marketing strategies to engineering, architecture, and physics majors, needed to give more background information about marketing, use less specialized vocabulary or explain technical terms, and present their ideas using examples that would be understood by people outside of their discipline. These practice speeches increased students' awareness of the need to accommodate audience background while preparing for and presenting speeches.

From the beginning of the semester, students had been giving weekly speeches. Evaluation of these practice speeches initially began simply (focusing on introducing the topic and not saying "that's it" at the end), and then with each speech more elements were added to the assessment (see Appendix A). Ultimately, the speech before the midterm was assessed using the full speech evaluation form in the teacher's manual, addressing speech format (introduction, body, conclusion with appropriate transitions), language skill and use of transitions, speech delivery, timing, and audience awareness.

Class Discussions

We also held class discussions about audience analysis surveys, and I showed students a customer satisfaction survey from one of the restaurants in the Student Center, a survey with which they were all familiar. This survey consisted of two open-ended questions, two fixed-alternative questions, and two scaled questions.

We talked about what it was like to fill out a survey (from the respondent's perspective), and the students observed that if the survey took too long to fill out, people simply would not complete it. They noticed that the survey was only one page, and I reinforced the importance of limiting the survey to one page, telling them of a previous student whose survey had one question on the back of the page, a very important one in terms of audience analysis, but a question that most of the respondents did not answer, very likely because they did not look on the back of the page. Another point that the students commented on was that open-ended questions took longer to answer and respondents very likely would not answer open-ended questions that required too much thought or explanation. They all agreed that, although open-ended questions could give valuable information about the audience's view of the topics, there was always the chance that the respondents would leave the questions blank if they took too long to answer. Limiting the number of open-ended questions to only two, as done in the restaurant survey, seemed feasible.

Training in Writing Questions

The students then learned how to develop audience analysis surveys, including fixed-alternative, open-ended, and scaled questions. This written portion of the audience analysis unit consisted of in-class demonstrations and writing assignments. Training students in how to write these various types of questions involved explaining the characteristics of each type, looking at examples of each type, and practicing writing survey questions in class. The students readily understood what open-ended questions were, but more explanation was needed about the difference between fixed-alternative and scaled questions.

In the class discussions and question-writing activities, I emphasized the importance of clarity and accuracy in grammar, spelling, punctuation, and word choice. If students were to obtain helpful feedback from their audience, they had to write clear and unambiguous questions. Seemingly small errors in grammar, spelling, and punctuation could change their intended meaning, resulting in audience feedback that was not what they intended to elicit. As a result, this authentic task reinforced to students the relevance of language structure and mechanics in real-world communication. Their survey questions had to be accurate for them to find out about the audience's knowledge of or attitude toward their topic.

Writing the Audience Analysis Surveys

Next, students developed audience analysis surveys containing two or more fixed-alternative questions, two open-ended questions, and two or more scaled questions, with the requirement that there be no more than ten questions and that the survey be only one page. The survey drafts were assessed for question form (as described previously), content (seeking useful information about the audience's knowledge of the topic), and language structure (grammar, spelling, vocabulary, punctuation). Their revisions allowed them to improve their surveys so that they could effectively communicate what it was that they wished to discover from their audience members. The revised surveys were also graded using the same criteria, giving both evaluation of survey effectiveness and feedback about how to further improve the surveys in order to make them more useful in surveying the audience.

After revising their graded surveys, students distributed them to each other. In earlier semesters, I had tried having students e-mail the surveys to each other, but not everyone responded, e-mail glitches resulted in some of the completed surveys being lost, and e-mailed responses meant the identity of each respondent was revealed. Thus in subsequent semesters I required each student to bring hard-copy surveys to class, which were then distributed to the other students. Students handed in the completed surveys during the next class session, which made it possible for me to tell if and when someone did not complete them. The surveys were then collated and returned to each respective student. However, collating was time-consuming, either requiring teacher or assistant time outside of class or student time in class, and as a result this method was not used again.

The third method that I tried in terms of handling the surveys was the use of Discussion Board, an online group communication feature of Blackboard (the university's online course management system), which proved to be the most efficient and is what I used for the project described in this chapter. I created a Discussion Board entry that allowed students to post their surveys, and then their classmates and I responded to each survey by copying the questionnaire, entering our answers, and pasting the results in a new posting. As with previous e-mail attempts, however, there was still the challenge of maintaining anonymity of respondents. Ease of access was more important to the students, though, so we used the Discussion Board because they were able to post their surveys and get classmates' responses within 2 days.

Informative Speech and Portfolio

The students then analyzed the results of the surveys and used them to prepare informative speeches, which were evaluated for effectiveness in relating to the audience as well as speech organization and delivery. I used three measures to assess how well the speakers accommodated their audience:

1. audience feedback

2. my observation of the speeches

3. students' self-reporting in their audience survey analysis included in their portfolios

All semester long, students had been giving each other feedback on the aspects of each speech targeted by the specific speech assignment. However, with the 6- to 8-minute informative speech, I used the full speech evaluation form from the textbook, which would have been challenging for the students to complete in its entirety. Therefore, I assigned groups of students to give their classmates feedback about specific aspects of the speeches: the introduction, including attention getter, introduction of the topic, and preview of the main points; supporting detail in the body of the speech, including citation of authoritative sources, speech delivery (e.g., eye contact, vocal variety), and timeliness; and the conclusion, including restatement and ending comment. Students were required to give one positive comment and one suggestion for improvement. This peer feedback was given to me after the day's speeches were completed, and I then reviewed the students' comments.

In evaluating the effectiveness of a speech as a whole, I used both student feedback and my observations. In particular, when evaluating the speaker's audience awareness during the speech, I watched and listened to see if I understood the concepts and information presented in the speech (often on a topic unfamiliar to me). Also, I considered whether the students' audience feedback comments indicated understanding of the ideas explained in the speech. For example, if an architecture major presented a speech about the dynamics of space integration to an audience of business and engineering majors, was this specialized topic presented in terms that were understood by his or her (non-architecture-major) classmates and teacher? Did peer comments indicate that the speech was confusing (indicating poor audience awareness) or clearly explained (indicating effective audience awareness)?

Finally, the third aspect of evaluating students' audience awareness was having the students write a paragraph in which they discussed the results of their surveys and how they used those results to prepare their speeches. The survey results paragraphs were evaluated for content (explanation of the results and how they affected speech preparation) as well as language structure. Although all I required was explanation of the survey results and discussion of how those results made a difference in the speech content, many students created elaborate presentations with graphs and charts to illustrate the responses of their fellow classmates, and then they went on to explain how they adapted their speeches based on the survey results. Some students used the chart feature in Microsoft Word to create visual representations of their audience feedback, with the most common forms chosen being pie graphs for each question and bar graphs indicating the different responses to the survey questions. Other students simply wrote a paragraph about each question's responses.

After looking at the responses to each question, students wrote a paragraph about what they observed from the surveys. Their observations about the feedback from the surveys can be categorized into two groups: Either they found that their audience had very little knowledge of the topic, or they realized that the audience was well informed about the topic. If the audience did not know much about the topic, then the speaker had to simplify the speech, explaining technical concepts and terms. If the audience indicated that the topic was familiar to them, then the speaker needed to give more information from a unique perspective.

REFLECTIONS

This audience awareness project used a three-tiered task-based assessment: writing and analyzing the audience analysis surveys, preparing and delivering the speeches, and writing reports on using the results of the surveys to prepare the speeches. The primary goal of the project was to improve students' public speaking ability by increasing their awareness of the importance of adapting their speech to fit their audience. Students gained an increased appreciation of audience awareness and how they could make their speeches more effective by adapting them according to the audience's background understanding of their topics. Through the process of writing the surveys, they also learned how to write effective questions to elicit the information that they needed (indicated through improvement in the surveys through multiple drafts). In addition, this project helped students understand that part of public speaking involves the development of written materials and that accuracy of survey questions is crucial to obtaining the desired feedback from members of their target audience.

One challenge of this project was logistics: having students survey each other (and the instructor) without taking up class time to do so while making sure that all students responded to each other's surveys. The most effective solution to this dilemma was to use Blackboard's Discussion Board feature, which enabled students to post their own surveys and then respond to each other's surveys online.

This course, Public Speaking, focuses on a specific aspect of language skill—the ability to give effective presentations—which is a skill that students need both in courses at the university and in their future professional lives if and when they are called on to present information, ideas, plans, programs, and so on to the organizations they will work for after graduation. Through increased awareness of their audience's background, students in this project demonstrated improved presentation skills in adapting speech content to their audience's level of knowledge of the topic and relating their topic to the audience's experience. They also learned how to write questionnaires using scaled, fixed-alternative, and open-ended questions, which is a writing skill needed in research (both in university courses and professionally, particularly in vocational fields such as marketing).

Although the English proficiency level of students in my class was high compared to English language learners in some K–12 or university settings, this audience analysis project can be adapted for use in other contexts, primarily through simplifying the tasks and providing more structure. Instead of having students give 6- to 8-minute speeches, teachers could require shorter speeches (e.g., limiting them to 1- to 2-minute speeches, not having a time limit at all). Also, the number of audience analysis questions could be lessened, and the scaled questions could be eliminated, thus limiting the surveys to open-ended and fixed-alternative questions, which are easier to write. Structured activities that teach students about writing survey questions also could be included (see Appendix B).

For me, as a teacher, this task-based teaching and assessment experience was overwhelmingly positive. The students learned how to use audience analysis surveys to adapt their speeches through audience awareness, a highly valuable public speaking skill, and saw its potential for enhancing speech preparation. In fact, some students, of their own initiative, prepared audience analysis surveys for their final persuasive speeches (which they were not required to do). All in all, this project was a positive task-based teaching and learning venture. I plan on using this type of project again in future public speaking classes, not just because it is a required learning outcome for the course but because it gives students a public speaking skill that they can use in classroom presentations for university courses and in professional presentations throughout their careers.

Betty Lanteigne has taught ESL and EFL in the United States and Middle East for 15 years. She currently teaches language assessment in the MA TESOL program at the American University of Sharjah, in the United Arab Emirates. A member of Phi Kappa Phi, Pi Lambda Theta, the International Association of Language Testers, and TESOL, she is also a former English Teaching Fellow and Fulbright Dissertation Fellow.

APPENDIX A: PRACTICE SPEECH FORMS

ENG 208 Speech #1

Name _____

	Clear	Somewhat Clear	Vague	Missing
Telling the topic	4	3	2	1
Concluding sentence	4	3	2	1

Total_____

ENG 208 Speech #3

Name _____

	Clear	Somewhat Clear	Vague	Missing
Telling the topic	4	3	2	1
Preview of main points	4	3	2	1
Concluding sentence	4	3	2	1
Time	1–2 min.	+/− 15 sec.	+/− 30 sec.	+/− 1 min.

Total_____

ENG 208 Speech #5

Name _____

	Clear	Somewhat Clear	Vague	Missing
Introduction	4	3	2	1
Specific purpose statement	4	3	2	1
Preview of main points	4	3	2	1
Citation of sources	4	3	2	1
Concluding sentence	4	3	2	1
Time	1–2 min.	+/− 15 sec.	+/− 30 sec.	+/− 1 min.

Total_____

APPENDIX B: EXERCISES FOR WRITING SURVEY QUESTIONS

Fixed-Alternative Questions

With these questions, you give your friends several choices, and they have to choose just one. For example, you might want to find out what their favorite color is, what month their birthday is in, or how many brothers and sisters they have.

EXAMPLE OF A FIXED-ALTERNATIVE QUESTION ABOUT COLOR:

What is your favorite color? (Check one.)

____ red   ____ yellow   ____ blue   ____ green   ____ purple

____ brown   ____ black   ____ white   ____ orange

Write a fixed-alternative question about cars.

1. _____

_____

_____ ? (Check one.)

List the alternatives you want your friends to choose from.

____ _____

____ _____

____ _____

____ _____

____ _____

____ _____

Scaled-Alternative Questions

This kind of question asks your friends "how much" they like something, "how many" they have of something, or "how much time" something takes.

EXAMPLE OF A SCALED-ALTERNATIVE QUESTION
ABOUT THE COLOR RED:

How often do you wear red? (Check one answer.)

_____ every day

_____ two to three times a week

_____ once every week or two

_____ once a month

_____ never

Write a scaled-alternative question about cars.

2. _____

_____

_____ ? (Check one.)

List the alternatives you want your friends to choose from.

_____ _____

_____ _____

_____ _____

_____ _____

_____ _____

_____ _____

Open-Ended Questions

Open-ended questions cannot be answered with just "yes" or "no." Your friends have to write what they think and not just check an answer. "Why" questions make good open-ended questions.

EXAMPLE OF AN OPEN-ENDED QUESTION ABOUT COLOR:

Why do you think sports cars are often red?

_____

_____

_____

Write an open-ended question about cars.

3. _____

_____

_____

(Space for their answers.)

_____

_____

_____

CHAPTER 13

Assessing Task-Based Activity in a Speech Training Class

Aiden Yeh

In speech or oral training courses, students are introduced to the fundamental skills needed for the successful delivery of speeches. Students are expected to perform. However, for many English as a foreign language (EFL) learners, speaking in public can be a nerve-wracking experience. Some students even compare speech presentations to life-threatening events. Difficulty in breathing, forgetting what to say, sweaty palms, butterflies in the stomach, and dry mouth are some of the most common physical conditions that students experience during oral presentations. How can teachers make such presentations less stressful? In these tasks, can students really gain language skills? How can teachers know when learning takes place, and how do they assess it?

In this chapter, I discuss a blended or hybrid learning task-based activity designed for intermediate- to advanced-level students in speech or oral training classes. In addition, I describe the pedagogical framework and the assessment tools used in evaluating student performance. Finally, I share the results and analysis of a class survey. Although I used the tasks and ideas contained in this chapter in an EFL context, they are appropriate to English as a second language contexts as well.

CONTEXT

At this university in Taiwan, Speech Training courses are offered to third-year students majoring in English. Although English is considered a foreign language in Taiwan, the majority of students have been learning it for years. However, due to limited exposure to the target language (English), many of them find it extremely difficult to compose, produce, and perform oral speeches.

In my speech class, students learn the basic skills and concepts needed for effective oral presentations. Topic selection, organization of ideas, delivery skills, audience analysis, creation of visual aids, methods of persuasion, and constructive critiquing are some of the learning content that students need to cover. Examples of well-crafted speeches are shared with students to give them a better understanding of how the speech elements (introduction, supporting ideas and examples, and conclusion) come together to present the speaker's main message clearly and coherently. By looking at speech examples, students have a model to help them create their own speech outlines and drafts. In doing so, they develop their critical thinking skills as they look for similar forms of language use. They exercise careful judgment of their own work, revising and editing their speech draft until they successfully meet the criteria for a given speech task. Pronunciation and oral skills guidelines are also provided to help students enhance their oral proficiency, which is a major factor that influences the outcome of any speech presentation. In this course, students also carry out various speech presentations ranging from self-introductions to informative and persuasive speeches to speeches for special occasions.

Aside from traditional in-class lectures and discussions, multimedia and online tools are integrated into the curriculum to maximize students' learning by using different formats. Also referred to as *flexible learning, e-learning,* or *hybrid learning,* blended learning allows the mixing of such tools with a face-to-face course, thereby offering multimodal forms of learning and teaching (Yeh, 2007a). With blended learning, teachers and students are not limited to the constraints of physical space. Learner content (e.g., syllabus, lessons) and learner support (e.g., task guidelines) are provided using our class group on *Yahoo! Groups* (Yahoo!, 2008), a free online learning environment. I create folders in the Files area and upload learning materials and other documents, which students can peruse whenever and wherever they want. Submission of written assignments (e.g., speech drafts) is also done online; students upload their documents in the Files area under a specified folder. Once uploaded, a list of file names and the name of the person who uploaded a file is automatically updated, indicating the time and date the file was uploaded. This also serves as a tracking device that provides evidence of successful assignment submissions, which leads to increased accountability. Other features of *Yahoo! Groups* (e.g., e-mail-based messages, chat), can increase the level of rapport and interaction among group (class) members. For classes that meet only once a week, an online learning environment can offer many benefits.

In addition to using *Yahoo! Groups,* I created a class blog using *Blogger* (Google, 1999–2009). More accurately, this is a video blog (vlog), or a web site where I post videos of students' presentations. The videos and PowerPoint slides from their in-class presentations that are shared on the vlog are used for self-assessments and peer feedback purposes. According to Tsutsui (2004), video recording of students' speeches can significantly enhance postperformance feedback and offer advantages where the traditional method of providing feedback in a face-to-face class falls short. The time, money, and effort spent on CDs or DVDs to copy, transfer files, and distribute videos to each student is largely reduced with the use of vlogs. They make it possible for students to access the videos anytime, anywhere (Yeh, 2007b). And the comments area of the class vlog allows students to post their presentation self-evaluations.

Aside from in-class presentations, students are also given tasks that can be done outside the classroom. Such tasks involve audio or voice recording of short speeches in which they get the chance to practice their oral skills. Listening to and analyzing the audio posted on the vlog for self-evaluation and peer feedback purposes also enhance students' aural skills. There are several tools that offer free online audio/video recording over the Internet, including *PodOmatic* (PodOmatic, 2009), *Voxopop* (Voxopop/Chinswing, 2007–2009), and *VoiceThread* (VoiceThread, 2007–2009). The selection and application of the tools mentioned in this section are necessary for creating an optimal learning environment for the Speech Training class (Yeh, 2006). However, how they are utilized to meet students' learning needs is what enhances their effectiveness.

CURRICULUM, TASKS, MATERIALS

In this section, I discuss the theoretical and pedagogical underpinnings of a collaborative task-based activity that involves two speech presentations (presentation of an award and acceptance speech) and illustrate the phases involved in implementing a task-based activity as suggested by J. Willis (1996).

Theoretical and Pedagogical Framework

The presentation and acceptance speeches task is based on constructivist principles because the task allows students to make use of the target language in an authentic and meaningful way (see Grabe & Grabe, 2000). Tasks that support constructivist views focus on students' active roles that involve crafting solutions to a problem and creative personal adaptation of a text, topic, or theme. This highly corresponds to the principles of task-based teaching, which stress the need for the creation of tasks that give learners more chances to "use the language for themselves" (D. Willis & Willis, 2007, p. 1).

The setting created for this task simulates an awards presentation event that provides students with an opportunity to work on their public speaking skills as they team up and take on make-believe roles as presenters and award recipients. Students interact with one another and attempt to understand and appreciate each other's personal abilities and characteristics. The simulation of a real awards event requires the application of various skills that make study and fun work together, thus making topics more interesting. This task, therefore, meets the definition of a language learning task, which, according to Shehadeh (2005), is an activity that has "a clear outcome," "uses the four language skills" to complete the task, and "reflects real-world language use" (p. 19). Ornstein (1990) argues that in a simulated task the teacher's role changes as he or she takes a back seat while students engage in active learning. Although the teacher plays a minimal role while students present their speeches, it is important that task guidelines and instructions should be set up as clearly as possible to help students successfully meet the requirements. Joyce, Weil, and Calhoun (2003) state that students "must develop concepts and skills necessary for performance" (p. 348). These concepts and skills must be thoroughly discussed and explained before the task is set.

Phases Involved in Implementing a Task-Based Activity

This section outlines the various phases of the presentation and acceptance speeches task based on J. Willis's (1996) task-based learning framework, which blends meaning, form, analysis, and practice. The framework follows this basic outline: pretask (introduction to topic and task), task (task-planning-report), and posttask (analysis and practice). J. Willis argues that learners engaged in a task-based activity are able to apply their language skills and the acquired knowledge necessary to carry out the task fully. The process of doing the task itself, from planning to execution (presentation), is also a means for oral expression.

The task employed here calls for back-to-back presentations: one for recording and posting online and the other for presenting in the classroom. Students first have to present the awards, then the recipients express their gratitude. Students are given 1 week to prepare drafts and practice them. Preparation time can be extended to 2 weeks depending on time availability. During this stage, I conduct teacher–student conferences in which students present their outlines or drafts to me and I give them feedback on content and organization of ideas to guide their revisions.

Pretask

Pretask activities involve in-class lectures and discussion of speech samples, task guidelines, and criteria for assessing the task. One class period is devoted to discussing the essential parts of presentation and acceptance speeches. Another period is spent reviewing and discussing speech samples and criteria.

The main purpose of a presentation speech is to present an award, gift, or recognition. It is necessary for the speaker to refer to the occasion (e.g., Special Awards Night) and briefly state why it is a special event. It is also important to recognize the recipient's achievements in relation to the award being bestowed in a way that is meaningful to the audience (Lucas, 2007).

On the other hand, the purpose of an acceptance speech is to give thanks to the person, organization, or group of people who bestowed the award and others who deserve credit (Lucas, 2007). According to Busey (2005), "a good acceptance speech is marked by three traits: brevity, humility, and graciousness" (p. 138). These traits are included in the evaluation criteria that are used in assessing this speech presentation.

Aside from the lecture, I also ask students to discuss in groups and analyze sample speech drafts. The analysis requires the use of their critical thinking skills, taking into account how the elements found in the drafts relate to and meet the evaluation criteria for presentation speeches (Arter & McTighe, 2001).

I distribute copies of the rubric as soon as the task assignment is given, and I also upload it to the Files area of our Yahoo! Group for archival purposes. The same evaluation criteria are used for self-assessment and peer feedback. By specifying particular criteria, I let students know what to expect, which helps them assess their own progress. The use of evaluation criteria also provides substantial objective information about students' skills and development, and serves as a checklist to help them when preparing their speeches.

In addition to the analysis of written examples of speeches, reviewing video recordings of experienced speakers is also ideal for enhancing students' cognitive skills. Videos of successful speeches can model or demonstrate specific skills that they need in their own presentations (see MacEvoy, 1998). Zhao, Zhang, Wang, and Chen (2005) posit that "modeling is generally the first step in instructional scaffolding" (p. 3). Scaffolding is a kind of support or assistance given to students as they acquire and develop their skills to help them achieve the task at hand (Jonassen, 1999).

The following criteria and guidelines for presentation speeches were adapted from Lucas (2007, pp. 467–468):

1. State the purpose of the award.

2. Acknowledge the achievements of the recipient (the person receiving the award).

3. Tell the audience why the recipient is receiving the award.

4. Point out his or her contributions, achievements, and so on.

5. Focus on the achievements related to the award.

6. Discuss the recipient's achievements in a way that makes them meaningful to the audience.

The evaluation criteria for the acceptance speech are as follows:

1. Give thanks for the award.

2. Offer brief remarks about the award.

3. Humbly accept the award.

4. Show graciousness.

These criteria focus on the desired contents of each type of speech. Standards for organization (introduction, body, and conclusion), delivery (voice, body language, eye contact, etc.), and overall evaluation of the speech (meeting the task requirements and time limit, etc.) were also included in the rubric.

Task

The presentation speech task is given as an out-of-class assignment. Students create a voice or video recording of their 1- to 2-minute speech in which they give an award to their partner. They need to answer the question: "If you were to give your partner an award, what would the award be and why?" There is no right answer to this question, but students are encouraged to think carefully, look at the positive attributes of their partner, and try to match these qualities with an award that would most likely exemplify these features. The following is a partial list of the awards that have been presented by students in my classes:

- Miss Taiwan

- Most Excellent Youth Representative Award of Wenzao Ursuline College

- Miss Sports

- Humane Society Award of Wenzao Ursuline College

- The Excellent Youth of Wenzao Ursuline College

- Drummer of the Year

- Top Speaker of World Debate 2007

- The Best Smile of the Year

The different categories range from mundane awards (e.g., Ms. Taiwan) to distinctive awards that carry meaning (e.g., Humane Society Award of Wenzao Ursuline College). Other award classifications bear the recognition factor that highlights the recipient's talents, which conveys more relevance and importance.

The task is also announced on the class vlog and Yahoo! Group, which involves a step-by-step process to guide students in creating and submitting their audio recording. The voice recording can be created using a computer and a microphone and can be done online or offline (using digital voice recording software such as WavePad [Version 4.26] or Audacity [Version 1.2.6]). The audio files are sent to me as e-mail attachments, which are also archived and retrievable from my mail account. This archive gives a full account of students who submitted their assignments. Each file sent to me has a corresponding embedded code (html) and a link code (URL), which can be copied and pasted to a blog or web site. This makes the publication and sharing of files on different web platforms easy for teachers who are less technologically savvy.

In face-to-face class, the time students spend on oral exercise to sharpen their public speaking skills is simply not enough. This task breaks down the traditional barriers of a physical learning environment. It extends the scope of learning possibilities, allowing the application of multiple skills from preparation and practice to doing the actual task of recording speeches—all carried through to completion outside the classroom. Audio recording tasks can also enhance vocal improvement. Booher (2003) argues that speech slipups (e.g., fast speech rate, monotone, fillers) are more discernible when listening to one's audio recording. Listening to recording playbacks also improves students' auditory skills because they can listen to a continuous flow of verbal expressions. Repetitive listening allows students to engage in auditory self-monitoring, deciding on the appropriate tone needed for presentation speeches. This exercise can even strengthen a novice speaker's confidence, which can be truly beneficial even in everyday situations.

In the acceptance speeches, student awardees acknowledge the award, prize, or honor and give thanks to the people who helped them gain the recognition. The award, prize, or honor of being acknowledged in this task must be exactly the same as the one that was presented during the coordinating presentation speech. Students are not allowed to change the type of award because that would defeat the purpose of doing the task.

Keeping documented evaluation records for many classroom oral presentations is difficult because the assessment is done in class, and evaluation and observation are done simultaneously as the students give their speeches. Marks are given based on the teacher's immediate reactions to student presentations using a (scoring) rubric with assessment criteria (see Figure 1). Without any evidence to support the teacher's claims (aside from what he or she can remember about a student's presentation), any dispute concerning students' grades would be difficult to settle. It is because of this that all in-class presentations are video recorded.

A video recording combined with peer feedback and the teacher's evaluation can provide valuable data for student progress (or lack thereof). Hence, it is made clear to students that the video recording of presentations is necessary to gauge how much their presentation skills have improved and is a vital instrument for assessing their work. Students have the option of not being recorded, without grade deduction; however, it is also made clear to them that the lack of visual evidence to document their improvements could influence the outcomes of other learning tasks.

Posttask

The posttask stage begins as soon as all student presentations are completed. Evaluations are based on the criteria indicated in the scoring rubric (Figure 1). Personal assessment of their performance and peer feedback are based on watching playback of the videos of their presentations posted on the class vlog. These videos are great tools for monitoring student progress because the feedback based on video playback helps determine students' good and bad speaking habits. According to Brownlie, Feniak, and McCarthy (2004), "video recording contains more useful information than a set of notes since the context of learning is present. In addition, progress in oral-language development over a term is demonstrated, and goals for further growth are evident" (p. 46).

Speech of Presentation Evaluation Rubric Excellent Good Average Fair Poor

Criteria	E	G	A	F	P	Comments
Speech adapted to the audience and occasion	E	G	A	F	P	
Acknowledged the achievement/contributions of the recipient related to the award	E	G	A	F	P	
Praised the losers (for awards won in competition)	E	G	A	F	P	
Remarks about the award Briefly described what the award was for	E	G	A	F	P	
Delivery Maintained strong eye contact	E	G	A	F	P	
Avoided distracting mannerisms	E	G	A	F	P	
Articulated words clearly	E	G	A	F	P	
Used vocal variety to add impact	E	G	A	F	P	
Met assignment	E	G	A	F	P	
Speech completed within time limit	E	G	A	F	P	
Level of Enthusiasm	E	G	A	F	P	

Other comments:

Speech of Acceptance Evaluation Rubric Excellent Good Average Fair Poor

Criteria	E	G	A	F	P	Comments
Gave thanks for an award	E	G	A	F	P	
Thanked the people bestowing the award	E	G	A	F	P	
Thanked people who helped in gaining the award	E	G	A	F	P	
Remarks about the award Briefly described what the award was for	E	G	A	F	P	
Humility Humbly accepted the award	E	G	A	F	P	
Graciousness	E	G	A	F	P	
Delivery Maintained strong eye contact	E	G	A	F	P	
Avoided distracting mannerisms	E	G	A	F	P	
Articulated words clearly	E	G	A	F	P	
Used vocal variety to add impact	E	G	A	F	P	
Met assignment	E	G	A	F	P	
Speech completed within time limit	E	G	A	F	P	
Level of Enthusiasm	E	G	A	F	P	

Other comments:

Figure 1. Full Scoring Rubric

Class Survey, Analysis, and Results

A class survey using *SurveyMonkey* (SurveyMonkey.com, 1999–2009; an online survey tool) is conducted at the end of the semester to gauge students' learning and language skills gained in the task. The survey results also indicate their assessment of their own performance. Of the 26 students enrolled in my speech class one semester, 30% believed that their presentation speech performance was good, and 48% felt that it was average. Regarding the in-class presentation of acceptance speeches, 26% perceived theirs as good, and 52% felt they were acceptable. When asked about the suitability of the award given to them, whether it suited their character and personality, 22% felt that it was highly suitable, 74% felt that it was suitable, and only one (4%) felt that the award given was not a match. In terms of preparing their speech drafts, 18% felt that they did an excellent job, and 37% thought that they did a good job. The majority of the students felt that they successfully followed the guidelines given for this task: 64% gave a good rating, 18% average, and 14% excellent. The role of video playback in self-reflection and assessment garnered positive reviews from students: 55% deemed it good, and 23% excellent. Regarding the language skills gained in this task, 36% percent felt that they showed improvements in presenting acceptance speeches. The data reveal the positive outcomes of this task related to the achievement of the set task goals. One comment from a student sums up the usefulness of having engaged in this task: "I think this activity is quite helpful and practical in the future. This activity will improve our skill of giving and receiving awards, presents, or knowing how to express our thanks to others."

Some students expressed concerns about their pronunciation, body language, facial expression, and enthusiasm. It is apparent to them that they have to persevere in order to see significant progress in their development. As one student put it, "I must work hard and improve my weaknesses and then I will do better." The evaluative questions used in this survey allowed students to assess their own strengths and weaknesses. In doing so, the questions raised awareness of student potential while at the same time helping students improve.

Pitfalls of the Task

Three students' comments about this task represent pitfalls present in the collaborative aspects of task implementation.

- "I didn't know what kind of award I should give to [name of partner]. He is good at raising fish, but he said that I can't give this kind of award to him, not related to the audience."

- "The award given was inappropriate."

- "It's kind of hard to present someone an award, and it's also hard to give an acceptance speech under the condition that I already know I'll receive an award."

Students had the option to choose any award they saw fit, provided that it was not too outrageous and did not make a mockery of the task. The student who commented about not knowing what award to give raised a valid point about relating the topic to the audience. He could have still kept to his original idea. He could have given his partner an award associated with his passion for raising fish and relate this topic to the audience by briefly mentioning the importance of having the tenacity and ardent interest in pursuing something you love. In the end, this student presented his partner an award for environmental protection advocacy.

The student who complained about the inappropriate award was in fact the recipient of this environmental protection advocacy award. He did not feel strongly about this award, so he refused to accept it. Refusing an award also happens in real life, and when that happens there is usually a feeling of discomfort in the air. The refusal of an award is a personal and subjective action. However, in this student's case, his refusal to accept the award put the presenter (his partner) in an embarrassing situation.

Because the presentation for acceptance speeches was slated 2 weeks after the presentation speeches were given, students already knew what they would be receiving. In a way, the student who made the comment about the difficulty of accepting an award you know is coming has a valid point. Two ways to retain the suspense and excitement of awards presentations is to do both parts of the task on the same day and to make sure that the award to be given is not disclosed prior to the event.

In designing a similar task, it is important to address students' comments and concerns during the early stages as they provide invaluable feedback about the extent to which they understand the task criteria. During the pretask stage, time could be allotted for a question-and-answer session to address any questions students may have. Student–teacher meetings can also be conducted to follow up on students' speech preparation status. The class Yahoo! Group can also be used to post any comments or questions pertaining to the task. Identifying problems early can help avoid consequences that might negatively affect the overall outcome of students' presentations.

REFLECTIONS

There is no doubt that speaking in public can make even the most seasoned professional high strung. For EFL students, this fear can escalate and make or break a presentation, which could have detrimental effects on student motivation to learn. Enrolling in a speech course can help boost speaking skills. However, once the basic concepts of successful speech presentations have been laid out, it boils down to doing what was learned: practicing for presentations, again and again. With good planning and a proper approach to addressing the task requirements and guidelines, students have a better chance to not only make the grade, but also experience productive learning outcomes. Tasks assigned in speech and oral training courses should assess students' knowledge and achievements, but most important, they should provide students with the opportunity to learn and grow. If their presentation videos are available on a class vlog, students have easy access to them for evaluating their own presentations as well as those of their peers. The online collection of students' artifacts also serves as an online portfolio containing evidence of live presentations, audio recordings, and other materials that support their learning.

The presentation and acceptance speeches task is an enjoyable learning activity that employs both online technology and instruction in a traditional classroom setting. To perform the task successfully, students need to know and understand their partners as human beings with skills and talents worthy of respect and appreciation. The speech guidelines and criteria provide not only the key points to help students gain the language skills needed to meet the task requirements, but also the groundwork for constructing the assessment rubric used in evaluating their performance. Successful language learning is possible when it is done in a meaningful way. In the end, the ability to effectively speak in front of an audience can be a powerful way to build language ability as well as students' confidence and self-esteem.

Aiden Yeh has a master's degree in English language teaching management from Surrey University and is a PhD student at the University of Birmingham, in England. She lectures in the Department of English at Wenzao Ursuline College of Foreign Languages, in Taiwan. She is the chair (2009–2010) of TESOL's Nonnative English Speakers in TESOL Interest Section.

CHAPTER 14

Using Online Tasks for Formative Language Assessment

Paula M. Winke

Teachers often wonder how to use technology to develop online language learning tasks. Computer labs, Internet connections, and video cameras are enticing, but it can be challenging to use them to develop meaningful tasks that reveal students' development without spending too much time or money.

In this chapter I explain how to use online tasks for formative assessment. Online tasks can be created with course management systems (CMSs) and rich Internet applications (RIAs). I give specific instructions for accessing and using freely available RIAs so that any language teacher located anywhere in the world can use a computer, a microphone, and an Internet connection to start making online tasks for formative language assessment for his or her students.

Before discussing specific software, I explain how I use the terms *tasks* and *formative language assessment* and what I mean by *online tasks*. I also outline useful and cost-effective tools that can be used to put tasks online.

Task-based language instruction requires that students use the target language in meaningful contexts. Doing so improves language acquisition and motivates students (Dörnyei, 2002; Swain & Lapkin, 2001). Numerous publications have defined the term *task* over the years (in particular, see Bygate, Skehan, & Swain, 2001; Shehadeh, 2005; Van den Branden, 2006b; J. R. Willis, 2004). Most definitions mention that tasks give students specific objectives. Every task thus has a point at which it is complete (Nunan, 1989) and results in a product or outcome for evaluation (Ellis, 2003, p. 16).

Formative Language Assessment

Formative assessment is defined as classroom assessment that is used in "evaluating students in the process of 'forming' their competencies and skills" (Brown, 2004, p. 6). According to Poehner and Lantolf (2005), this type of assessment fits within the realm of dynamic assessment and enables teachers to evaluate students' strengths and weaknesses in obtaining course objectives. Student progress is regularly monitored based on work conducted in class. Formative assessment provides continuous feedback to the teacher and learners (Bachman, 1990), which can be used for making decisions about ongoing instructional procedures and classroom tasks. Part of the goal of formative assessment is to have the teacher and students reflect on the actual learning that has taken place during tasks. This type of assessment takes into account the student's ability to develop *during* task-based performance. In contrast to static assessment (Sternberg & Grigorenko, 2002), dynamic formative assessment allows students to demonstrate their ability to modify their performance in response to authentic feedback from others, the way they do in the real world.

Researchers have argued that language programs that use a task-based syllabus ought to use task-based assessment (Chalhoub-Deville, 2001; de Oliveira, 2004). In formative assessment, task outcomes are collected for the purposes of reflection and evaluation. To make formative assessment more formal, concrete task outcomes can be collected into a course portfolio that is assembled by the student and commented on by the teacher and other students (Stefani, Mason, & Pegler, 2007). Students document and reflect on how they completed tasks and how the tasks worked within the social dynamics of the classroom. The course portfolio can be used as all or part of the overall course assessment.

Online Tasks

Task outcomes can be difficult to document. Student interactions cannot be evaluated after the fact unless they are recorded. Using tape or digital voice recorders to document classroom interaction during tasks is cumbersome and impractical. A more efficient way is to conduct tasks online. A certain number of tasks during the course can be done online, during class in a language lab, or outside of class on home or lab computers, and those tasks can be the basis for student portfolios for formative assessment, which in this case would be an electronic or e-portfolio.

Several tools can be used to develop online tasks for formative language assessment. Teachers and students can use a CMS for recording synchronous (real-time) and asynchronous (disjointed time) conversations and for storing and managing multimedia applications related to tasks. Commonly used CMSs are presented in Table 1.

Teachers can also use stand-alone Internet-based programs for building tasks without needing to download software. Such programs allow for the recording, use, and storage of audio and video files, something that many CMSs are still not able to do without significant added costs. One such suite of programs was designed and is currently hosted by the Center for Language Education and Research (CLEAR) at Michigan State University (MSU) in East Lansing, Michigan, in the United States. The web-based *Rich Internet Applications for Language Learning* (Michigan State University Board of Trustees, n.d.) can be accessed and

Table 1. Commonly Used Course Management Systems

	Course Management System	URL
Fee-based	ANGEL	http://angellearning.com/
	Blackboard	http://blackboard.com/
	Desire2Learn	http://www.desire2learn.com/
Free	Moodle	http://moodle.org/
	OLAT	http://www.olat.org/

used without programming knowledge. The five RIAs at MSU that were used in the workshop described in this chapter are listed in Table 2, along with explanations of their features. (Additional features have been added since.)

To design tasks with any of the CLEAR RIAs, you first need the relevant computer hardware (a computer, a microphone, and a webcam or video recorder). Then you can create a free RIA account by clicking on New User toward the top of the *Rich Internet Applications for Language Learning* page. By creating one account, you have access to all five RIAs. Detailed documentation of how to use any one RIA can be downloaded as a PDF from its specific homepage.

One shortcoming of CMSs is that they usually lack an easy way to collect audio or video samples of student speech. However, one can use free Internet-based programs, like the CLEAR RIAs, to design online tasks that collect such samples. These programs do not require any software downloading or web hosting. Although the RIAs at CLEAR were made with language acquisition theory in mind, it is still up to the teacher to devise tasks with them that adhere to sound principles of language acquisition theory.

CONTEXT

At MSU, CLEAR offers summer workshops on second language acquisition and computer-assisted language learning theory and practice. The workshops, sponsored by the U.S. Department of Education, are for pre- and in-service language teachers. In the summer of 2007, Dennie Hoopingarner (CLEAR's associate director for technology implementation and a developer of the RIAs outlined in Table 2) and I presented a 3-day workshop for language teachers who wanted to learn to use technology for formative assessment. The workshop modeled a language learning class with online tasks used for formative assessment. The 13 workshop participants, who were high school and university language teachers, gained hands-on experience in designing and using online tasks and conducting online assessment activities with their students. They also compiled an online language learning portfolio as a sample type of formative assessment.

Table 2. Free Rich Internet Applications (RIAs) Developed and Hosted by Michigan State University

RIA	Function
ViewPoint	Similar to *YouTube* (YouTube, 2009), this video-hosting site allows you to upload, download, and record live video and add subtitles to your videos. You may embed ViewPoint videos into other web pages or link to them from any web page. In ViewPoint, there is no length restriction on the videos, as there is with *YouTube* and other such sites.
SMILE	SMILE allows you to design interactive, language practice exercises. You can create a database of items organized by type (multiple-choice, multiple-select, true/false, drag-and-drop, sentence mix, paragraph mix, cloze) and then group selected items together into SMILE "activities." Items designed in SMILE can be set to provide feedback after each answer choice.
Audio Dropboxes	This audio collection tool can be put on or embedded into any web page. Students record themselves and then can preview, re-record, or submit their files directly to their teacher. The audio files are organized into the teacher's Dropbox for listening, responding to, and scoring.
Mashups	A mashup is a web page that combines media from several sources, be they other rich Internet applications or media or text from other web pages. Teachers or students can create mashups and share them via their URLs.
Conversations	This audio collection tool allows the teacher to create a series of audio or video prompts that can be formed as one end of an asynchronous conversation. Students can access the questions and respond to them in practice (with preview and re-record capabilities) or real-time mode.

Note: All rich Internet applications are free; see Michigan State University Board of Trustees, n.d.

Our general goal for the workshop was to learn what difficulties these language teachers had experienced in implementing online tasks for formative language assessment. Were the difficulties based more on insufficient technical knowledge or on insufficient access to technology? We also wanted to know how the participants would react to the concept of using online tasks for formative language assessment. All participants were interested in the content of the workshop and were already open to using online tasks for formative language assessment. But we still wanted to know what personal and logistical problems they were likely to have implementing such a plan.

In the next section, I review three examples of specific tasks made with a CMS chat room and CLEAR RIAs. I also present a template that students can use to design their own e-portfolios for formative assessment.

CURRICULUM, TASKS, MATERIALS

The curriculum required the participants to pretend that they were language learners while they designed online language learning tasks for formative assessment. Each of the three tasks described in this section was performed on a different day of the workshop. The participants did other tasks as well, but these three exemplify the variety of tasks that can be used for formative assessment.

Task 1: Learning About East Lansing and East Lansing Web Sites

On the first day, the participants got to know each other and East Lansing by working together in groups on a web-enhanced information gap task. This first task demonstrated to them how working together to find web sites can be a task that is interactive (learners interact with each other and not just the computer) and has an end goal. The task also created a log of student language use that could be included in a language learning portfolio for formative assessment.

Part A

After discussing as a group what they knew about life in East Lansing, the participants were put into pairs. Each pair sat at adjoining computers in a computer lab and received Worksheets A and B (see the Appendix). Together, Worksheets A and B presented an information gap activity. Each person in the pair completed the top half of his or her worksheet by visiting local web sites to find events in East Lansing over the weekend. When both partners were done, they discussed in person the information they found by answering the rest of the questions on the worksheets.

Part B

I instructed the participants to log onto the CMS, which had a specific page set up for the workshop. Each pair from Part A was matched with a second pair from Part A. The four individuals logged onto a synchronous chat room and were instructed to discuss what they could do together over the weekend in East Lansing. They were told that their goal was to plan to get together at least once over the weekend and decide ahead of time what they would do. They needed to plan when and where they would meet and what they should bring with them when they met.

Part C

Each group presented their plans to the class.

Part D

I provided all of the participants with a copy of their group's transcript from the chat room. As homework, they were asked to highlight their own language use in the chat room and write a one-paragraph summary of how they felt the chat room had worked. (Was the chat room talk meaningful? Was it fun? In the transcript was there any indication that new language forms were learned by any of the group members? If so, what were the forms?)

Task 2: Learning How to Design Tasks in Conversations

On the second day of the workshop, after reviewing what they had done the day before, the participants learned to use Conversations, one of the CLEAR RIAs. This task demonstrated how students can use the target language to design their own tasks, which they then have their classmates complete. This type of ownership and engagement in task work is a form of co-constructed motivation, which has been shown to aid in task performance (Dörnyei, 2002). This task also resulted in a record of language use, this time oral, which could be reflected on and used for formative assessment.

Part A

Each participant was seated at a computer. Participants were instructed to open a web browser and go to the CLEAR RIA web site to create an account on the Conversations homepage. They were instructed to join a Conversation that I had made, which contained video clips of me asking a series of questions about the prior evening (see Figure 1). The learners were taught how to use the webcams attached to their computers to record video-based answers to my questions.

Part B

Participants were given paper documentation on how to create their own Conversations. I demonstrated using Conversations to create a series of prompts that mimicked a real-time conversation. Participants then recorded their own series of three to five questions using their webcams. They were told to record questions asking their peers what they had done the night before. After they finished designing their conversations, they were told to share them with three other people in the class. Each person responded to three other people's Conversation tasks. At the end, I asked the participants to discuss whose evening seemed the most interesting.

Task 3: Designing Items in SMILE That Can Be Put Into a Mashup

On the third day of the workshop, participants learned to use ViewPoint, SMILE, Mashups, and Audio Dropbox. This part of the workshop continued to show that students in class can create essential task components. Doing so helps them feel ownership over their learning and allows them to practice their language skills while creating tasks. Like the previous two workshop tasks, this one showed how student work can be documented for formative assessment.

Part A

The participants watched a ViewPoint video about a week in the life of an East Lansing family (which was actually my family). They were then instructed to write down three multiple-choice questions related to the video.

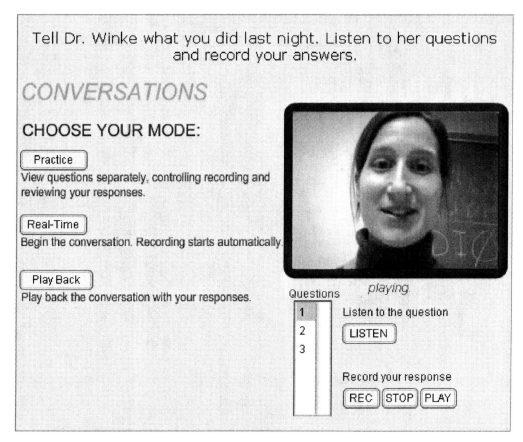

Figure 1. Online Task 2: Using Conversations to Answer Questions

Part B

The participants were given paper documentation on how to create items in SMILE. After a demonstration, they logged into SMILE using the same login and password they used for Conversations. They put their multiple-choice items into SMILE. I showed them how to share (forward copies of) those questions with others. I then asked each participant to share with me his or her best multiple-choice item.

Part C

I entered a selection of the participants' multiple-choice items into a Mashup that already contained a set of directions, the ViewPoint video about the East Lansing family, and an Audio Dropbox. Participants were given the URL of the Mashup (see Figure 2) and asked to respond to the items that their fellow participants had written. They were then instructed to record an oral response to the questions by using the Audio Dropbox embedded in the Web page.

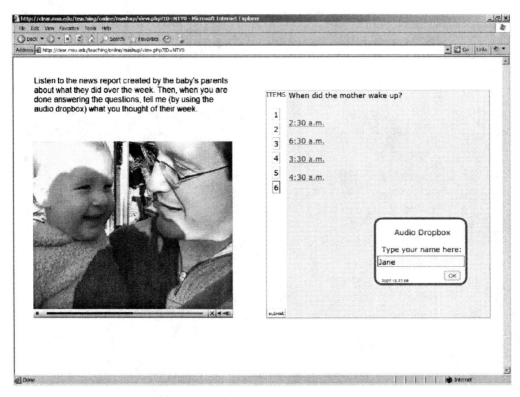

Figure 2. Using Mashups to Design Multimedia Tasks

Part D

I handed out and reviewed with participants a sheet with guidelines for making multiple-choice items. Participants were instructed to get into groups of four to review the multiple-choice items they had made. They then revised their multiple-choice items online based on their group members' feedback.

Part E

I taught participants how to use Mashups and Audio Dropbox to replicate the Mashup, SMILE, and Audio Dropbox item I had created. They first found a short and interesting video on ViewPoint, *YouTube,* or *TeacherTube* (TeacherTube, 2009) and then learned how to embed the video into a Mashup using the embed code on the page (ViewPoint, *YouTube,* and *TeacherTube* all provide the same type of embed code in the same area of the page). They created three SMILE multiple-choice comprehension items based on the video clip they had selected and entered those into the Mashup as well. Finally, they were taught how to make their own Audio Dropbox and entered one into the Mashup. They shared their multiple-choice Mashup items with each other by sharing the URL of the Mashup.

Throughout the course of the workshop, participants had performed a variety of online tasks and learned how to teach their students how to perform similar tasks. At the end of each online task, there was an outcome that was appropriate for formative evaluation. For the first task, the participants had an electronic version of their chat room transcript from the CMS and their written reflection on the chat. For the second task, they had their own Conversation, which they had shared with several of their classmates. For the third task, they had their own Mashup with SMILE questions and an Audio Dropbox, on which they had also received and given peer feedback. By the end of the workshop, participants had participated in four chat room tasks and created two ViewPoint videos (one with captions), four Mashups, and four Conversations. They had also written two drafts of an English teaching philosophy statement, the first of which was reviewed by their peers with Microsoft Word's Track Changes feature.

As a brief formative assessment, each participant recorded his or her various task outcomes and accomplishments in a personal folder on the CMS, which served as the shell for his or her e-portfolio. Participants uploaded their essays, chat room transcripts, and papers into their folders. A document within each folder listed the participant's RIA products and their Web locations by providing his or her URLs and access codes. By the end of the workshop, each participant had to highlight within the e-portfolio one of each task type to exemplify his or her best work. All e-portfolios were open for viewing by any participant or me. On the last day of the workshop, each participant was randomly assigned to review one other person's e-portfolio and provide that person and me with a one-paragraph review of the person's accomplishments. The workshop ended with me giving comments on each participant's portfolio, sharing highlights, and assigning mock grades based on the e-portfolios.

REFLECTIONS

By the end of the workshop, I realized that the participants' previous difficulties in implementing online tasks for formative assessment tended to be more related to lack of software access than anything else. Once they had learned how to access and use available software, most of their difficulties in implementation dissipated. However, time constraints still posed problems for them. Even though creating online tasks for formative language assessment using free software is relatively cheap (only computer hardware and an Internet connection is required), it is still time-consuming. Many of the participants noted that they wished the workshop were longer so that they could have time to fully develop an online portfolio plan for their specific language programs.

The participants stated that the most useful RIAs were Conversations and Audio Dropboxes, programs that could help them leave behind the world of assessment via CDs, cassette tapes, and recorded telephone calls. Knowing about these programs is a tremendous benefit for students and teachers alike. Teaching the participants how to use them was straightforward, but some mentioned that they especially appreciated the hands-on nature of the workshop because relying solely on a manual to learn how to create activities with programs like SMILE does not work very well. They said that the key is to try out applications with others and see how they work.

I also wanted to know how participants would react to the idea of using online tasks for formative language assessment. At the end of the workshop, I asked them how they planned to apply what they had learned to their teaching (and if they could not, why not). One participant mentioned that she would use them for "OPI-like" testing, but on the computer. She was referring to the American Council on the Teaching of Foreign Languages Oral Proficiency Interview (OPI), which is an oral language assessment format in which the learner is interviewed face to face by an instructor or language expert to assess the learner's oral proficiency. (For more information on the OPI, see Malone, 2003.) The OPI is also sometimes adapted and administered via cassette tape (Simulated Oral Proficiency Interview) or computer (Computerized Oral Proficiency Interview). The participant commented that she would like to use RIAs to administer oral proficiency test items of this type via computer to learners using Audio Dropboxes, Conversations, or both.

The following are a few more comments from the participants:

- "I will definitely use Conversations and ViewPoint. I would like to get a video camera to use for ViewPoint. I would like to try portfolios this year and also do writing assignments in groups."

- "I will use SMILE and Mashups for weekly homework projects; ViewPoint to have students upload video projects and add subtitles; Track Changes in MS [Microsoft] Word for writings tests; Conversations for speaking/listening tests."

- "I love the Conversations feature and want to use that throughout the year. ViewPoint and Mashups would be great too—I just need to find the time to get started."

- "I will absolutely use the Conversations application in my ESL [English as a second language] testing. I can now replace my cassettes!"

These selected comments reveal that participants found the tools to make online tasks extremely useful and that they will use them for assessment and formative assessment. But the comments also indicate that time is a critical constraint. Thus, teachers need sufficient time not only to learn the programs, but to fully develop an assessment program that can be integrated into the curriculum. In the future, we plan to lengthen the CLEAR workshop on online formative assessment, giving participants twice as much time to work on developing their own tasks.

Two of the workshop participants were nonnative speakers of English. I asked them how they felt their English had progressed by participating in the workshop tasks. They replied that while doing the tasks they had not thought that they were developing their language skills per se. However, after reviewing the chat room logs and listening to their own audio recordings, they concluded that performing the tasks had in fact improved their English language skills. Not only did they learn computer literacy skills and associated English vocabulary through the tasks, but they also gained information on their immediate surroundings, got to know their fellow participants, established a sense of community, and learned about daily life and culture in Michigan. Tasks are supposed to do those things, and I was pleased to hear that they had succeeded. These two participants also mentioned that they liked the tasks for formative assessment because after having done them, they had "something to take home"—concrete, positive evidence of their individualized learning.

Based on the outcomes of the workshop, I believe the following issues should be taken into consideration when creating online tasks for formative assessment in other contexts:

- Teachers make the best use of computers for language learning when they encourage students to perform authentic tasks on the computer (Warschauer, 2004).

- When learners are familiar with the logistics of a task, they can focus better on achieving the task goals and will be able to pay more attention to linguistic accuracy (T. Lynch & Maclean, 2000; Pica, 2008).

- Task-based language assessment in a social context presents a more authentic, practical, and valid method of measuring students' actual use of the target language (Bachman, 2004; Roever, 2006).

Therefore, when designing online tasks for formative assessment, teachers should (a) develop tasks that directly address students' needs in target-language computer literacy; (b) repeat tasks or use a task template with which students become familiar; and (c) create tasks that have students interact not just with their computer, but with each other and the teacher via the computer. I believe that the three tasks showcased in this chapter adhered to these principles. Nonetheless, technology in the classroom affects learning in the same way that any other learning tool does. You want to use the tool effectively in a way that is pedagogically sound. Whether you succeed will depend on how you use the technology and what you use it for.

Paula M. Winke has a PhD from Georgetown University and is an assistant professor at Michigan State University, in the United States, where she teaches MA TESOL and second language studies courses. A former Peace Corps volunteer and researcher at the Center for Applied Linguistics, she now publishes on assessment, individual differences, computer-assisted language learning, and language teaching methods.

APPENDIX: WORKSHEETS USED FOR PART A OF TASK 1

Name: _____

WORKSHEET A

Your partner: _____

Internet Search: Outdoor Things to Do in East Lansing, July 12–14

Directions: Work in pairs to find out what you can do outside in East Lansing during your free time over the next 3 days. Go to the web site indicated to find the appropriate information. Fill in the information where asked.

Part A. Outdoor Entertainment

There is a Moonlight Film Festival in East Lansing on Thursday nights. Read about it at the following web site and answer the questions below.

@ http://www.cityofeastlansing.com/; click on Moonlight Film Festival.

1. Where is the movie playing? _____

2. What movie is playing on July 12? _____

3. When does the movie start? _____

4. What happens before the movie?_____

   Do you think you will go to see the film? Think about why or why not.

   ☐ Yes ☐ No

   _____

Your partner found out some information on a Fountain Summer Concert Series in East Lansing on Friday nights. Ask your partner about the concert.

5. Where is the concert? _____

6. Who is playing on July 13? _____

7. At what time do they start? _____

8. What does your partner think of the concert? Will he or she go?

   _____

   _____

   _____

Name: _____

WORKSHEET B

Your partner: _____

Internet Search: Outdoor Things to Do in East Lansing, July 12–14

Directions: Work in pairs to find out what you can do outside in East Lansing during your free time over the next 3 days. Go to the web site indicated to find the appropriate information. Fill in the information where asked.

Part A. Outdoor Entertainment

There is a Fountain Summer Concert Series in East Lansing on Friday nights. Read about it at the following Web site and answer the questions below.

@ http://www.cityofeastlansing.com/; click on Summer Concert Series and Fountain Square Concert Series.

1. Where is the concert? _____

2. Who is playing on July 13? _____

3. At what time do they start? _____

   Do you think you will go to hear the concert?
   Think about why or why not.

   ☐ Yes ☐ No

   _____

Your partner found out some information on a Moonlight Film Festival in East Lansing on Thursday nights. Ask your partner about the film.

4. Where is the movie playing? _____

5. What movie is playing on July 12? _____

6. When does the movie start? _____

7. What happens before the movie? _____

8. What does your partner think of the film? Will he or she go?

   _____

   _____

   _____

References

Alpert, R., & Haber, R. (1960). Anxiety in academic achievement situations. *Journal of Abnormal and Social Psychology, 61*, 207–215.

Arena, C. (2006). *Stereotypes.* Retrieved from http://sambaefl.podomatic.com/entry/2006-05-16T10_47_23-07_00

Arena, C. (2007). *Reading treasures in the language classroom show.* Retrieved from http://explorations.bloxi.jp/a/reading-treasures-in-the-language-classroom-show/

Arter, J., & McTighe, J. (2001). *Scoring rubrics in the classroom: Using performance criteria for assessing and improving student performance.* Thousand Oaks, CA: Corwin.

Audacity (Version 1.2.6) [Computer software]. (2006). Retrieved from http://audacity.sourceforge.net/

Bachman, L. F. (1990). *Fundamental considerations in language testing.* Oxford, England: Oxford University Press.

Bachman, L. F. (2002). Alternative interpretations of alternative assessments: Some validity issues in educational performance assessments. *Educational Measurement: Issues and Practice, 21*(3), 5–18. doi:10.1111/j.1745-3992.2002.tb00095.x

Bachman, L. F. (2004). *Statistical analyses for language assessment.* Cambridge, England: Cambridge University Press.

Bachman, L. F., & Palmer, A. (1996). *Language testing in practice.* Oxford, England: Oxford University Press.

Booher, D. (2003). *Speak with confidence: Powerful presentations that inform, inspire and persuade.* New York, NY: McGraw-Hill.

Bourdieu, P. (1977). The economics of linguistic exchanges. *Social Science Information, 16*, 645–668.

Boxer, D. (2002). *Applying sociolinguistics: Domains and face-to-face interaction.* Amsterdam, Netherlands: John Benjamins.

Brindley, G. (1994). Task-centered assessment in language learning: The promise and the challenge. In N. Bird, P. Falvey, A. Tsui, D. Allison, & A. McNeill (Eds.), *Language and learning* (pp. 73–94). Hong Kong: Hong Kong Institute of Language in Education, Hong Kong Education Department.

Bronfenbrenner, U. (1979). *The ecology of human development experiments by nature and design.* Cambridge, MA: Harvard University Press.

Brown, H. D. (2000). *Principles of language learning and teaching* (4th ed.). New York, NY: Longman.

Brown, H. D. (2001). *Teaching by principles: An interactive approach to language pedagogy* (2nd ed.). White Plains, NY: Longman.

Brown, H. D. (2004). *Language assessment: Principles and classroom practice.* White Plains, NY: Longman.

Brown, H. D. (2007). *Teaching by principles: An interactive approach to language pedagogy* (3rd ed.). White Plains, NY: Pearson Education.

Brownlie, F., Feniak, C., & McCarthy, V. (2004). *Instruction and assessment of ESL learners: Promoting success in your classroom.* Winnipeg, Manitoba, Canada: Portage & Main Press.

Burns, A. (1999). *Collaborative action research for English language teachers.* Cambridge, England: Cambridge University Press.

Busey, B. (2005). *Stand out when you stand up: An A to Z guide to powerful presentations.* Charlotte, NC: Presentation Dynamics.

Bygate, M. (1987). *Speaking.* Oxford, England: Oxford University Press.

Bygate, M. (1996). Effects of task repetition: Appraising the developing language of learners. In J. Willis & D. Willis (Eds.), *Challenge and change in language teaching* (pp. 136–146). Oxford, England: Heinemann.

Bygate, M. (2001). Effects of task repetition on the structure and control of oral language. In M. Bygate, P. Skehan, & M. Swain (Eds.), *Researching pedagogic tasks: Second language learning and testing* (pp. 22–48). Harlow, England: Pearson Education.

Bygate, M., & Samuda, V. (2005). Integrative planning through the use of task repetition. In R. Ellis (Ed.), *Planning and task performance in a second language* (pp. 37–74). Amsterdam, Netherlands: John Benjamins.

Bygate, M., Skehan, P., & Swain, M. (Eds.). (2001). *Researching pedagogical tasks: Second language learning, teaching and testing.* Essex, England: Pearson Education.

Byram, M. (1997). *Teaching and assessing intercultural communicative competence.* Clevedon, England: Multilingual Matters.

California Distance Learning Project. (2005). *Adult learning activities.* Retrieved from http://www.cdlponline.org/

Callison, D., & Lamb, A. (2004). Key words in instruction: Audience analysis. *School Library Media Activities Monthly, 21*(1), 34–39.

Campbell, A. P. (n.d.). *Motivating language learners with Flickr.* Retrieved from http://e-poche.net/flickr/

Chalhoub-Deville, M. (2001). Task-based assessments: Characteristics and validity evidence. In M. Bygate, P. Skehan, & M. Swain (Eds.), *Researching pedagogic tasks* (pp. 210–228). Harlow, England: Pearson Education.

Chaudron, C. (1988). *Second language classrooms: Research on teaching and learning.* Cambridge, England: Cambridge University Press.

de Oliveira, C. P. (2004). Implementing task-based assessment in a TEFL environment. In B. L. Leaver & J. R. Willis (Eds.), *Task-based instruction in foreign language education: Practices and programs* (pp. 253–279). Washington, DC: Georgetown University Press.

Dewey, J. (1997). *Experience and education.* New York, NY: Touchstone.

Dickinson, L. (1987). *Self-instruction in language learning.* Cambridge, England: Cambridge University Press.

Dörnyei, Z. (2001). *Motivational strategies in the language classroom.* Cambridge, England: Cambridge University Press.

Dörnyei, Z. (2002). The motivational basis of language learning tasks. In P. Robinson (Ed.), *Individual differences and instructed language learning* (pp. 137–157). Amsterdam, Netherlands: John Benjamins.

Dörnyei, Z. (2005). *The psychology of the language learner: Individual differences in second language acquisition.* Mahwah, NJ: Lawrence Erlbaum.

Dörnyei, Z., & Murphey, T. (2003). *Group dynamics in the language classroom.* Cambridge, England: Cambridge University Press.

Dowrick, P. (1983). Self-modeling. In P. Dowrick & S. Biggs (Eds.), *Using video: Psychological and social applications* (pp. 105–124). New York, NY: Wiley.

Dunkel, P. (1988). The content of L1 and L2 students' lecture notes and its relation to test performance. *TESOL Quarterly, 22,* 259–282.

Edwards, C., & Willis, J. (Eds.). (2005). *Teachers exploring tasks in English language teaching.* London, England: Palgrave Macmillan.

Ellis, R. (1994). *The study of second language acquisition.* Oxford, England: Oxford University Press.

Ellis, R. (2000). Task-based research and language pedagogy. *Language Teaching Research, 4,* 193–220. doi:10.1177/136216880000400302

Ellis, R. (2003). *Task-based language learning and teaching.* Oxford, England: Oxford University Press.

Ellis, R. (2005a). *Instructed second language acquisition: A literature review.* Wellington, New Zealand: New Zealand Ministry of Education, Research Division. Retrieved from http://www.stanford.edu/~hakuta/Courses/Ed388%20Website/ Resources/Ellis%20Instructed-second-language%20-%20latest%20version.pdf

Ellis, R. (Ed.). (2005b). *Planning and task performance in a second language.* Amsterdam, Netherlands: John Benjamins.

Ellis, R., Tanaka, Y., & Yamazaki, A. (1994). Classroom interaction, comprehension, and the acquisition of L2 word meanings. *Language Learning, 44,* 449–491. doi:10.1111/j.1467-1770.1994.tb01114.x

Ferris, D. (1998). Students' views of academic aural/oral skills: A comparative needs analysis. *TESOL Quarterly, 32,* 289–318.

Ferris, D., & Tagg, T. (1996). Academic oral communication needs of EAP learners: What subject-matter instructors actually require. *TESOL Quarterly, 30,* 31–58.

Flavell, J. H. (1979). Metacognition and cognitive monitoring: A new area of cognitive-developmental inquiry. *American Psychologist, 34,* 906–911.

Gateway Harmonica Club. (1993). *First step harmonica course.* St. Louis, MO: Author.

German Shepherd Rescue of New England. (2003–2008). *Holling.* Retrieved from http://www.gsrne.org/Holling.htm

Gitsaki, C., & Taylor, R. P. (2001, January). Web-assisted language learning for EFL. *La Scuola Che Cambia,* 22–27. Retrieved from http://fds.oup.com/www.oup.com/ pdf/elt/it/InternetEnglish.pdf?cc=it

Google. (1999–2009). *Blogger.* Retrieved from http://www.blogger.com/

Grabe, M., & Grabe, C. (2000). *Integrating the Internet for meaningful learning.* Boston, MA: Houghton Mifflin.

Graves, D. H. (1992). Portfolios: Keep a good idea growing. In D. H. Graves & B. S. Sunstein (Eds.), *Portfolio portraits* (pp. 1–12). Portsmouth, NH: Heinemann.

Graves, K. (2000). *Designing language courses: A guide for teachers.* Boston, MA: Heinle & Heinle.

Hadley, A. O. (1993). *Teaching language in context.* Boston, MA: Heinle & Heinle.

Hall, J. K., & Walsh, M. (2002). Teacher-student interaction and language learning. *Annual Review of Applied Linguistics, 22,* 186–203. doi:10.1017/ S0267190502000107

Hedge, T. (2000). *Teaching and learning in the language classroom.* Oxford, England: Oxford University Press.

Herrington, J., Oliver, R., & Reeves, T. (2003). Patterns of engagement in authentic online learning environments. *Australasian Journal of Educational Technology, 19*, 59–71. Retrieved from http://www.ascilite.org.au/ajet/ajet.html

Hobbs, J. (2005). Interactive lexical phrases in pair interview tasks. In C. Edwards & J. Willis (Eds.), *Teachers exploring tasks in English language teaching* (pp. 143–156). New York, NY: Palgrave Macmillan.

Holmes, H., & Guild, S. (Eds.). (1973). *A manual of teaching techniques for intercultural education.* Amherst: University of Massachusetts, Center for International Education.

Hong Kong Polytechnic University, English Language Centre. (2000–2009). *Seminar on the transition from school to university.* Retrieved from http://elc.polyu .edu.hk/EAP/Activities/seminartransition.htm

Iwashita, N. (1999). Tasks and learners' output in nonnative–nonnative interaction. In K. Kanno (Ed.), *Studies on the acquisition of Japanese as a second language* (pp. 31–53). Amsterdam, Netherlands: John Benjamins.

Izumi, S. (2000). *Promoting noticing and SLA: An empirical study of the effects of output and input enhancement on ESL relativization* (Unpublished doctoral dissertation). Georgetown University, Washington, DC.

Izumi, S. (2002). Output, input enhancement, and the noticing hypothesis: An experimental study on ESL relativization. *Studies in Second Language Acquisition, 24,* 541–577. doi:10.1017/S0272263102004023

Jacobs, G., Power, M., & Inn, L. (2002). *The teacher's sourcebook for cooperative learning.* Thousand Oaks, CA: Corwin.

Johnson, R. T., & Johnson, D. W. (1994). An overview of cooperative learning. In J. S. Thousand, R. A. Villa, & A. I. Nevin (Eds.), *Creativity and collaborative learning: A practical guide to empowering students and teachers* (pp. 31–44). Baltimore, MD: Brookes.

Jonassen, D. (1999). Designing constructivist learning environments. In C. M. Reigeluth (Ed.), *Instructional-design theories and models: A new paradigm of instructional theory* (pp. 215–239). Mahwah, NJ: Lawrence Erlbaum.

Joyce, B., Weil, M., & Calhoun, E. (2003). *Models of teaching* (7th ed.). Boston, MA: Allyn & Bacon.

Juvenile 3 Podcast. (n.d.). Retrieved from http://erikacruvinel.podomatic.com/

Kramsch, C. (1993). *Context and culture in language teaching.* Hong Kong: Oxford University Press.

Krashen, S. (1982). *Principles and practice in second language acquisition.* New York, NY: Pergamon.

Krashen, S. (1998). Comprehensible output? *System, 26,* 175–182. doi:10.1016/ S0346-251X(98)00002-5

Kumaravadivelu, B. (2003). *Beyond methods: Macrostrategies for language teaching.* New Haven, CT: Yale University.

Lantolf, J. (1996). SLA theory building: "Letting all the flowers bloom!" *Language Learning, 46,* 713–749. doi:10.1111/j.1467-1770.1996.tb01357.x

LaPierre, D. (1994). *Language output in a cooperative learning setting: Determining its effects on second language learning* (Unpublished master's dissertation). University of Toronto, Toronto, Ontario, Canada.

Lave, J., & Wenger, E. (1991). *Situated learning: Legitimate peripheral participation.* Cambridge, England: University of Cambridge Press.

Leaver, B., & Willis, J. (Eds.). (2004). *Task-based instruction in foreign language education.* Washington, DC: Georgetown University Press.

Levine, A. (2007). *The fifty tools.* Retrieved from http://cogdogroo.wikispaces.com/ page/diff/StoryTools/8139339

Literacyworks. (2006). *Learning resources.* Retrieved from http://literacyworks.org/ learningresources/

Little, D. (1991). *Learner autonomy. 1: Definitions, issues and problems.* Dublin, Ireland: Authentik.

Littlewood, W. (1997). Self-access: Why do we want it and what can it do? In P. Benson & P. Voller (Eds.), *Autonomy and independence in language learning* (pp. 79–92). London, England: Longman.

Long, M. (1985). A role for instruction in second language acquisition: Task-based language teaching. In K. Hyltenstam & M. Pienemann (Eds.), *Modeling and assessing second language acquisition* (pp. 77–99). Clevedon, England: Multilingual Matters.

Long, M. (1996). The role of the linguistic environment in second language acquisition. In W. C. Ritchie, & T. K. Bhatia (Eds.), *The Handbook of second language acquisition* (pp. 413–468). Orlando, FL: Academic Press.

Long, M. (1998). Focus on form in task-based language teaching. *Working Papers in ESL, 16*(2), 35–49.

Long, M. H. (2007). *Problems in SLA.* Mahwah, NJ: Lawrence Erlbaum.

Looking into the future: Can your perspective influence your motivation? (2007, November 1). *ScienceDaily.* Retrieved from http://www.sciencedaily.com/

Lopes, J. (2004). Introducing TBI for teaching English in Brazil: Learning how to leap the hurdles. In B. L. Leaver & J. R. Willis (Eds.), *Task-based instruction in foreign language education: Practices and programs* (pp. 83–95). Washington, DC: Georgetown University Press.

Lucas, S. E. (2007). *The art of public speaking* (9th ed.). New York, NY: McGraw-Hill.

Lynch, B. K., & McNamara, T. F. (1998). Using G-theory and many-facet Rasch measurement in the development of performance assessments of the ESL speaking skills of immigrants. *Language Testing, 15,* 158–180. doi:10.1177/026553229801500202

Lynch, T., & Maclean, J. (2000). Exploring the benefits of task repetition and recycling for classroom language learning. *Language Teaching Research, 4,* 221–250. doi:10.1177/136216880000400303

Lynch, T., & Maclean, J. (2001). A case of exercising: Effects of immediate task repetition on learners' performance. In M. Bygate, P. Skehan, & M. Swain (Eds.), *Researching pedagogic tasks: Second language learning, teaching, and testing* (pp. 141–162). Harlow, England: Longman.

MacEvoy, P. (1998). *Educating the future GP: The course organizer's handbook* (2nd ed.). Abingdon, England: Radcliffe Medical Press.

Maley, A., & Duff, A. (1989). *The inward ear: Poetry in the language classroom.* Cambridge, England: Cambridge University Press.

Malone, M. E. (2003). Research on the Oral Proficiency Interview: Analysis, synthesis, and future directions. *Foreign Language Annals, 36,* 491–497. doi:10.1111/j.1944-9720.2003.tb02138.x

Marshall, S. P. (2006). *The power to transform: Leadership that brings learning and schooling to life.* San Francisco, CA: Jossey-Bass.

Mayo, M. (Ed.). (2007). *Investigating tasks in formal language learning.* Clevedon, England: Multilingual Matters.

Messick, S. (1996). Validity and washback in language testing. *Language Testing, 13,* 241–256. doi:10.1177/026553229601300302

Michigan State University Board of Trustees. (n.d.). *Rich Internet applications for language learning.* Retrieved from http://clear.msu.edu/teaching/online/ria/

Mixbook.com. (2006–2009). *Mixbook.* Retrieved from http://www.mixbook.com/

Moran, P. (2001). *Teaching culture: Perspectives in practice.* Boston, MA: Heinle & Heinle.

Murphey, T. (1996). Increasing performance events in language learning: Examples and theory to play with. *Nanzan University LT Briefs, 5,* 22.

Murphey, T. (2001). Video recording conversations for self evaluation in Japan. In J. Murphy & P. Byrd (Eds.), *Understanding the courses we teach: Local perspectives on English language teaching* (pp. 179–196). Ann Arbor: University of Michigan Press.

Murphey, T. (2006). *Language hungry!* Rum (Innsbruck), Austria: Heilbling Languages.

Murphey, T. (2009). Some crucial elements of learning ecologies. In G. Goncalves, S. Almeida, V. Menezes, & A. Rodrigues-Junior (Eds.), *New challenges in language and literature: Selected works from the first international conference of ABRAPUI* (pp. 129–148). Belo Horizonte, Brazil: Faculdade de Letras da UFMG.

Murphey, T., & Arao, H. (2001). Changing reported beliefs through near peer role modeling. *TESL-EJ, 5*(3). Retrieved from http://tesl-ej.org/

Murphey, T., & Kenny, T. (1996). Learner self-evaluated video recording (LSEV). In G. van Troyer, S. Cornwell, H. Morikawa, & N. Aoki (Eds.), *On JALT 95: Curriculum and evaluation* (pp. 198–202). Tokyo, Japan: Japan Association for Language Teaching.

Murphey, T., & Kenny, T. (1998). Video recording conversations for self-evaluation. *JALT Journal, 20*(1), 126–140.

Murphey, T., & Woo, L. (1998a). Using student feedback for emerging lesson plans. *English Teachers Association of Switzerland Newsletter, 15*(2), 27–29.

Murphey, T., & Woo, L. (1998b). Video recording student conversations: Educational video's diamond in the rough. *Language Teacher, 22*(8), 21–24, 30.

Nation, I. S. P. (2001). *Learning vocabulary in another language.* Cambridge, England: Cambridge University Press.

Norton, B. (2000). *Identity and language learning.* New York, NY: Longman.

Nunan, D. (1989). *Designing tasks for the communicative classroom.* Cambridge, England: Cambridge University Press.

Nunan, D. (1997). Language teaching and research. In D. T. Griffee & D. Nunan (Eds.), *Classroom teachers and classroom research* (pp. 13–21). Tokyo, Japan: Japan Association for Language Teaching.

Nunan, D. (2004). *Task-based language teaching.* Cambridge, England: Cambridge University Press.

O'Malley, J. M., & Chamot, A. U. (1990). *Learning strategies in second language acquisition.* Cambridge, England: Cambridge University Press.

O'Malley, J. M., & Valdez Pierce, L. (1996). *Authentic assessment for English language learners: Practical approaches for teachers.* New York, NY: Addison-Wesley.

Ornstein, A. (1990). *Strategies for effective teaching.* New York, NY: HarperCollins.

Ortega, L. (2005). What do learners plan? Learner-driven attention to form during pre-task planning. In R. Ellis (Ed.), *Planning and task performance in a second language* (pp. 77–109). Amsterdam, Netherlands: John Benjamins.

Ortega, L. (2007). Meaningful L2 practice in foreign language classrooms: A cognitive-interactionist SLA perspective. In R. DeKeyser (Ed.), *Practice in a second language: Perspectives from applied linguistics and cognitive psychology* (pp. 180–207). Cambridge, England: Cambridge University Press.

Oxford, R. (1990). *Language learning strategies: What every teacher should know.* New York, NY: Newbury House.

Pageflakes. (n.d.). Retrieved from http://www.pageflakes.com/

Passos de Oliveira, C. (2004). Implementing task-based assessment in a TEFL environment. In B. L. Leaver & J. R. Willis (Eds.), *Task-based instruction in foreign language education: Practices and programs* (pp. 253–279). Washington, DC: Georgetown University Press.

Pica, T. (2005). Classroom learning, teaching, and research: A task-based perspective. *Modern Language Journal, 89,* 339–352. doi:10.1111/j.1540-4781.2005.00309.x

Pica, T. (2008). Task-based instruction. In N. Van Deusen-Scholl & N. H. Hornberger (Eds.), *Encyclopedia of language and education* (Vol. 4, pp. 71–82). New York, NY: Springer.

Pica, T., Kanagy, R., & Falodun, J. (1993). Choosing and using communication tasks for second language research and instruction. In G. Crookes & S. Gass (Eds.), *Tasks and language learning: Integrating theory and practice* (pp. 9–34). Clevedon, England: Multilingual Matters.

PodOmatic. (2009). *PodOmatic.* Retrieved from http://www.podomatic.com/

Poehner, M. E., & Lantolf, J. P. (2005). Dynamic assessment in the language classroom. *Language Teaching Research, 9,* 233–265. doi:10.1191/1362168805lr166oa

Prabhu, N. S. (1987). *Second language pedagogy.* Oxford, England: Oxford University Press.

Protopage. (n.d.). Retrieved from http://protopage.com/

Quia. (1998–2009). *Quia.* Retrieved from http://www.quia.com/

Reimann, A. (2005). Developing meta-cultural skills, strategies and awareness: Support for a meta-cultural approach. *Journal of International Studies, 20*(2), 73–79.

Richard-Amato, P. A. (2003). *Making it happen: From interactive to participatory language teaching.* White Plains, NY: Pearson Education.

Richards, J. C. (2003). Current trends in teaching listening and speaking. *Language Teacher, 27*(7), 3–6.

Richards, J. C., & Rodgers, T. S. (2001). *Approaches and methods in language teaching* (2nd ed.). Cambridge, England: Cambridge University Press.

Richards, R., Schmidt, J., Platt, J., & Schmidt, M. (2003). *Longman dictionary of applied linguistics.* London, England: Longman.

Rieber, R. W., & Carton, A. S. (Eds.). (1987). *The collected works of L. S. Vygotsky: Volume 1 Thinking and speech.* New York, NY: Plenum Press.

Roberts, C., Byram, M., Barro, A., Jordan, S., & Street, B. (2000). *Language learners as ethnographers.* Clevedon, England: Multilingual Matters.

Robinson, P., Strong, G., Whittle, J., & Nobe, S. (2001). Development of EAP discussion ability. In J. Flowerdew & M. Peacock (Eds.), *Research perspectives on EAP* (pp. 347–359). Cambridge, England: Cambridge University Press.

Roever, C. (2006). Validation of a Web-based test of ESL pragmalinguistics. *Language Testing, 23,* 229–256. doi:10.1191/0265532206lt329oa

Rogoff, G., Paradise, R., Arauz, R., Correa-Chavez, M., & Angelillo, C. (2003). Firsthand learning through intent participation. *Annual Review of Psychology, 54,* 175–203. doi:10.1146/annurev.psych.54.101601.145118

Rosenkjar, P. (2006). Teaching and learning how a poem means: Literary stylistics for EFL undergraduates and language teachers in Japan. In A. Paran (Ed.), *Literature in language teaching and learning* (pp. 117–131). Alexandria, VA: TESOL.

Rucynski, T., & Strong, G. (2007). *The small group discussion* [DVD]. Tokyo, Japan: Aoyama Gakuin University, English Department.

Samuda, V., & Bygate, M. (2008). *Tasks in second language learning.* Clevedon, England: Palgrave Macmillan.

Sato, K., & Takahashi, K. (2008). Curriculum revitalization in a Japanese high school: Teacher-teacher and teacher-university collaboration. In D. Hayes & J. Sharkey (Eds.), *Revitalizing a program for school-age learners through curricular innovation* (pp. 205–237). Alexandria, VA: TESOL.

Saville-Troike, M. (2003). *The ethnography of communication: An introduction* (3rd ed.). Oxford, England: Blackwell.

Schmidt, R. (1998). The centrality of attention in SLA. *Working Papers in ESL, 16*(2), 1–34.

Schmidt, R. W., & Frota, S. N. (1986). Developing basic conversation ability in a second language: A case study of an adult learner of Portuguese. In R. Day (Ed.), *Talking to learn: Conversation in second language acquisition* (pp. 237–326). Rowley, MA: Newbury House.

Sheehan, R. (2005). Language as topic: Learner-teacher investigation of concordances. In C. Edwards & J. Willis (Eds.), *Teachers exploring tasks in English language teaching* (pp. 50–57). Houndsmills, England: Palgrave MacMillan.

Shehadeh, A. (2001). Self- and other-initiated modified output during task-based interaction. *TESOL Quarterly, 35,* 433–457.

Shehadeh, A. (2003). Learner output, hypothesis testing, and internalizing linguistic knowledge. *System, 31,* 155–171. doi:10.1016/S0346-251X(03)00018-6

Shehadeh, A. (2004). Modified output during task-based pair interaction and group interaction. *Journal of Applied Linguistics, 1,* 351–382.

Shehadeh, A. (2005). Task-based language learning and teaching: Theories and applications. In C. Edwards & J. Willis (Eds.), *Teachers exploring tasks in English language teaching* (pp. 13–30). Houndsmills, England: Palgrave Macmillan.

Short, M. (1996). *Exploring the language of poems, plays and prose.* Harlow, England: Addison-Wesley Longman.

Siemens, G. (2005). Connectivism: Learning as network-creation. *Learning Circuits.* Retrieved from http://www.astd.org/LC/

Skehan, P. (1998). *A cognitive approach to language learning.* Oxford, England: Oxford University Press.

Skehan, P. (2003). Task-based instruction. *Language Teaching, 36,* 1–14. doi:10.1017/ S026144480200188X

Society for the Preservation and Advancement of the Harmonica. (1995). *How to practice the harmonica.* Troy, MI: Author.

Splitter, L. J. (n.d.). *On the theme of "teaching for higher order thinking skills."* Retrieved from http://www.chss.montclair.edu/inquiry/summ95/splitter.html

Spradley, J. (1979). *The ethnographic interview.* New York, NY: Holt, Reinhart & Winston.

Spradley, J. (1980). *Participant observation.* New York, NY: Holt, Reinhart & Winston.

Stefani, L., Mason, R., & Pegler, C. (2007). *The educational potential of e-portfolios: Supporting personal development and reflective learning.* New York, NY: Routledge.

Sternberg, R. J., & Grigorenko, E. L. (2002). *Dynamic testing: The nature and measurement of learning potential.* Cambridge, England: Cambridge University Press.

Sullivan, P. (2000). Playfulness as mediation in communicative language teaching in a Vietnamese classroom. In J. Lantolf (Ed.), *Socio-cultural theory and second language learning* (pp. 115–131). Oxford, England: Oxford University Press.

SurveyMonkey.com. (1999–2009). *SurveyMonkey.* Retrieved from http://www .surveymonkey.com/

Swain, M. (1995). Three functions of output in second language learning. In G. Cook & B. Seidlhofer (Eds.), *Principle and practice in applied linguistics: Studies in honor of H. G. Widdowson* (pp. 125–144). Oxford, England: Oxford University Press.

Swain, M. (1998). Focus on form through conscious reflection. In C. Doughty & J. Williams (Eds.), *Focus on form in classroom second language acquisition* (pp. 64–81). Cambridge, England: Cambridge University Press.

Swain, M. (2000). The output hypothesis and beyond: Mediating acquisition through collaborative dialogue. In J. P. Lantolf (Ed.), *Sociocultural theory and second language learning* (pp. 97–114). Oxford, England: Oxford University Press.

Swain, M., & Lapkin, S. (1995). Problems in output and the cognitive processes they generate: A step towards second language learning. *Applied Linguistics, 16,* 371–391. doi:10.1093/applin/16.3.371

Swain, M., & Lapkin, S. (1998). Interaction and second language learning: Two adolescent French immersion students working together. *Modern Language Journal, 82,* 320–337.

Swain, M., & Lapkin, S. (2001). Focus on form through collaborative dialogue: Exploring task effects. In M. Bygate, P. Skehan, & M. Swain (Eds.), *Researching pedagogic tasks: Second language learning, teaching and testing* (pp. 99–118). London, England: Longman.

TeacherTube. (2009). *TeacherTube.* Retrieved from http://www.teachertube.com/

Thornbury, S. (1999). *Teach grammar.* Essex, England: Pearson Education.

Tsutsui, M. (2004). Multimedia as a means to enhance feedback. *Computer Assisted Language Learning, 17,* 377–402. doi:10.1080/0958822042000319638

Twitter. (2009). *Twitter.* Retrieved from http://twitter.com/

Van den Branden, K. (2006a). Introduction: Task-based language teaching in a nutshell. In K. Van den Branden (Ed.), *Task-based language education: From theory to practice* (pp. 1–16). Cambridge, England: Cambridge University Press.

Van den Branden, K. (Ed.). (2006b). *Task-based language education: From theory to practice.* Cambridge, England: Cambridge University Press.

Vasquez, N. A., & Buehler, R. (2007). Seeing future success: Does imagery perspective influence achievement motivation? *Personality and Social Psychology Bulletin, 33,* 1392–1405. doi:10.1177/0146167207304541

VoiceThread. (2007–2009). *VoiceThread.* Retrieved from http://voicethread.com/

Voxopop/Chinswing. (2007–2009). *Voxopop.* Retrieved from http://www.voxopop.com/

Vygotsky, L. (1962). *Thought and language.* Cambridge, MA: MIT Press. (Original work published 1934)

Vygotsky, L. S. (1978). *Mind in society.* Cambridge, MA: Harvard University Press.

Wajnryb, R. (1990). *Grammar dictation.* Oxford, England: Oxford University Press.

Warschauer, M. (2004). Technological change and the future of CALL. In S. Fotos & C. M. Browne (Eds.), *New perspectives on CALL for second language classrooms* (pp. 15–26). Mahwah, NJ: Lawrence Erlbaum.

WavePad Sound Editor (Version 4.26) [Computer software]. (2009). Retrieved from http://www.nch.com.au/wavepad/index.html

Wenden, A., & Rubin, J. (1987). *Learner strategies in language learning*. London: Prentice Hall.

Wertsch, J. (1998). *Mind as action*. New York: Oxford University Press.

White, N. (n.d.). *Twitter collaboration stories*. Retrieved from http://onlinefacilitation.wikispaces.com/Twitter+Collaboration+Stories

Widdowson, H. (1987). Aspects of syllabus design. In M. Tickoo (Ed.), *Language syllabuses: State of the art*. Singapore: RELC.

Widdowson, H. (1992). *Practical stylistics*. Oxford, England: Oxford University Press.

Widdowson, H. G. (1998). Skills, abilities and contexts of reality. *Annual Review of Applied Linguistics, 18*, 323–333.

Williams, J. (1997). *The place of focus on form in collaborative learning settings*. Paper presented at the American Association of Applied Linguistics convention, Orlando, FL.

Williams, M., & Burden, R. L. (1997). *Psychology for language teachers*. Cambridge, England: Cambridge University Press.

Willis, D., & Willis, J. (2007). *Doing task-based teaching*. Oxford, England: Oxford University Press.

Willis, J. (1996). *A framework for task-based learning*. Harlow, England: Longman.

Willis, J. R. (2004). Perspectives on task-based instruction: Understanding our practices, acknowledging different practitioners. In B. L. Leaver & J. R. Willis (Eds.), *Task-based instruction in foreign language education: Practices and programs* (pp. 3–44). Washington, DC: Georgetown University Press.

Willis, J. (2005). Introduction: Aims and explorations into tasks and task-based teaching. In C. Edwards & J. Willis (Eds.), *Teachers exploring tasks in English language teaching* (pp. 1–12). Houndsmills, England: Palgrave Macmillan.

Wood, D., Bruner, J. S., & Ross, G. (1976). The role of tutoring in problem-solving. *Journal of Child Psychology and Child Psychiatry, 17*, 89–100. doi:10.1111/j.1469-7610.1976.tb00381.x

Woodward, T. (2001). *Planning lessons and courses*. Cambridge, England: Cambridge University Press.

Yahoo! (2008). *Yahoo! Groups*. Retrieved from http://groups.yahoo.com/

Yahoo! (2009). *Flickr*. Retrieved from http://www.flickr.com/

Yeh, A. (2006, November). *Using podcast for oral skills*. Paper presented at the 15th International Symposium on English Teaching, Taipei, Taiwan.

Yeh, A. (2007a). Learner autonomy in blended learning. In J. Egbert, E. Hanson-Smith, & K. Huh (Eds.), *CALL environments: Research, practice, and critical issues* (2nd ed., pp. 404–421). Alexandria, VA: TESOL.

Yeh, A. (2007b, March). *Vlogging students' oral speeches for assessment purposes.* Workshop presented at the 41st Annual TESOL Convention and Exhibit, Seattle, WA.

YouTube. (2009). *YouTube.* Retrieved from http://www.youtube.com/

Yule, G., & Macdonald, D. (1990). Resolving referential conflicts in L2 interaction: The effect of proficiency and interactive role. *Language Learning, 40,* 539–556. doi:10.1111/j.1467-1770.1990.tb00605.x

Zhao, Y., Zhang, M., Wang, S., & Chen, Y. (2005). Exploring constructivist learning theory and course visualization on computer graphics. In O. Gervasi, M. Gavrilova, V. Kumar, A. Lagana, H. P. Lee, Y. Mun, D. Taniar, & C. J. K. Tan (Eds.), *Computational science and its application: ICCSA 2005, part IV* (pp. 1–9). Berlin, Germany: Springer-Verlag.

Index

Page numbers followed by an *f*, *n*, or *t* indicate figures, notes, or tables.

A

Ability Checklist, 142–144, 142*f*, 143*f*, 144*f*, 146
Accuracy, 2–3, 145–146
Activities, instructional, 25*t*
Adaptability, 33
Adult Learning Activities (California Distance Learning Project, 2005), 19
Agreeing phrases, 20
American Council on the Teaching of Foreign Languages Oral Proficiency Interview (OPI), 182
Analysis and correction stage of the dictogloss task, 21, 29*t*. *See also* Dictogloss task
Appropriation concept, 106
Asking opinions phrases, 20
Assessment. *See also* Evaluation; Formative language assessment
   audience awareness task and, 154–156
   ethnography project and, 64–65
   introduction to, 6
   longitudinal self-evaluated video recording (LSEV) and, 104–105
   self-evaluated approach and, 141–144, 142*f*, 143*f*, 144*f*
   small-group discussion task and, 14–16, 17–18, 17*f*
Audience awareness
   context of, 150–151
   curriculum, tasks and materials for, 151–156
   exercises for writing survey questions, 158–160
   introduction to, 149–150
   practice speech forms, 157–158
   reflections regarding, 156–157
Autonomy, learner. *See* Learner autonomy

B

Balanced approach to teaching, 32
Beyond methods approach, 26
Binder use, 142–144, 143*f*, 144*f*, 146
Blackboard's Discussion Board feature, 154, 156–157
Blended learning, 162–163
Blogger, 162–163
Brazil, 113–118

C

CALLaborative (collaborative computer-assisted language learning) projects
   curriculum, tasks and materials for, 113–118
   example of, 120–121
   reflections regarding, 118–120
Center for Language Education and Research (CLEAR) at Michigan State University (MSU)
   context of, 175–176, 176*t*
   course management systems (CMS) and, 174–175, 175*t*
   curriculum, tasks and materials for, 176–181, 179*f*, 180*f*
   reflections regarding, 181–183
   worksheets used for, 184–185

Checklists, self-evaluated approach and, 142–144, 142*f*, 143*f*, 144*f*, 146

Clarifying phrases, 20, 81

Classroom task. *See* Tasks

CLEAR RIAs
    context of, 175–176, 176*t*
    course management systems (CMS), 174–175, 175*t*
    curriculum, tasks and materials for, 176–181, 179*f*, 180*f*
    reflections regarding, 181–183
    worksheets used for, 184–185

Cognitive perspective, 2–3

Collaboration in classroom practice
    CALLaborative (collaborative computer-assisted language learning) projects and, 113–120
    dictogloss task and, 30–32
    self-evaluated approach and, 147–148
    speech training classes and, 163–170, 168*f*

Communication, 145–146

Community unit in investigative tasks curriculum, 38, 40

Complexity, cognitive perspective and, 2–3

Confidence of students
    dictogloss task and, 24
    Harmonica Project and, 124
    longitudinal self-evaluated video recording (LSEV) and, 106

Constructivist principles, 163

Content-based investigative tasks, 5

Cooperative learning environment, 42–43

Correction stage of the dictogloss task, 21, 29*t*.
    See also Dictogloss task

Course management systems (CMS)
    curriculum, tasks and materials for, 176–181, 179*f*, 180*f*
    online tasks and, 174–175, 175*t*
    reflections regarding, 181–183
    worksheets used for, 184–185

CSI television show, 36–37

Cultural awareness, 5

Culture unit in investigative tasks curriculum, 38–40

Curriculum
    audience awareness and, 151–156
    CALLaborative (collaborative computer-assisted language learning) projects and, 113–118

dictogloss task and, 22–30, 23*f*, 25*f*, 29*f*

ethnography project and, 52–65, 52*t*, 53*t*, 55*f*, 56*f*, 57*f*, 60*t*, 62*f*, 63*f*, 64*f*

Harmonica Project and, 125–130

investigative tasks and, 36, 37–41, 44

longitudinal self-evaluated video recording (LSEV) and, 99–104, 99*t*–100*t*, 101*f*, 102*f*

multilevel classrooms and, 80–88

online tasks and, 176–181, 179*f*, 180*f*

poetry and, 69–74

self-evaluated approach and, 138–144, 140*f*, 142*f*, 143*f*, 144*f*

small-group discussion task and, 12–18, 17*t*

speech training classes and, 163–170, 168*f*

D

Dictation stage of the dictogloss task, 21, 29*t*.
    See also Dictogloss task

Dictogloss task
    challenges in implementing, 30
    classroom adaptation of, 22–30, 23*f*, 25*f*, 29*f*
    context of, 22
    curriculum, tasks and materials for, 22–30, 23*f*, 25*f*, 29*f*
    example of, 92
    introduction to, 21–22
    multilevel classrooms and, 83–85
    reflections regarding, 30–33
    stages of, 21, 28–29, 29*t*
    validating task-based learning and, 32–33

Disagreeing phrases, 20

Discussion Board, 154, 156–157

Dynamic assessment, 173–174. *See also* Assessment; Formative language assessment

Dynamic of inquiry, 112

E

Ecological systems theory, 37

E-learning, 162

Engagement, student, 23*f*, 31

English as a foreign language (EFL), 11–12

English as a second language (ESL), 11–12

Ethnography project
    context of, 51

curriculum, tasks and materials for, 52–65, 52*t*, 53*t*, 55*f*, 56*f*, 57*f*, 60*t*, 62*f*, 63*f*, 64*f*
introduction to, 49–51
reflections regarding, 65
Evaluation. *See also* Assessment; Formative language assessment; Self-evaluated approach
introduction to, 6
self-evaluated approach and, 141–144, 142*f*, 143*f*, 144*f*
speech training classes and, 167–169, 168*f*
Experiential learning, 32, 105–106
Explaining category in assessment, 17–18, 17*f*

F

The Fifty Tools (Levine, 2007), 121
Five Things I Did Yesterday (But One Is a Lie) activity, 25*t*
Flexible learning, 162
Flickr website, 121
Fluency, 2–3, 145–146
Focus of instruction, 17
Formative language assessment
context of, 175–176, 176*t*
curriculum, tasks and materials for, 176–181, 179*f*, 180*f*
introduction to, 173–175, 175*t*
reflections regarding, 181–183
worksheets used for, 184–185
Freedom of the students, 26

G

Giving reasons phrases, 20
Group awareness, 55–58, 56*f*, 57*f*

H

Harmonica Project
context of, 124–125
curriculum, tasks and materials for, 125–130
introduction to, 123–124
reflections regarding, 131–133
Hybrid learning, 162

I

Identification concept, 106
Identity unit in investigative tasks curriculum, 38, 39
Input perspective, 1–2
Integrated English Program (IEP), 12–14, 13*f*
Intercultural communicative competence, 5, 49
International Consortium on Task-Based Language Teaching (ICTBLT), 4
Interrupting phrases, 20
Investigative tasks
context of, 35–37
curriculum, tasks and materials for, 36, 37–41, 44
examples of lessons, 45–47
introduction to, 35
reflections regarding, 42–44
Investment concept, 106

J

Japan
dictogloss task and, 23–30, 25*f*, 29*f*
ethnography project and, 51
investigative tasks and, 37–41
Kanda University of International Studies (KUIS) in Chiba Japan, 35–37
small-group discussion task and, 11–20
Journal writing
example of, 90–91
Harmonica Project and, 128–129
multilevel classrooms and, 80–83

K

Kanda University of International Studies (KUIS) in Chiba Japan, 35–37. *See also* Japan

L

Learner autonomy
dictogloss task and, 23*f*, 32
longitudinal self-evaluated video recording (LSEV) and, 98
self-evaluated approach and, 147
Learner ethnographies. *See* Ethnography project

Learning Resources (Literacyworks, 2006), 19

Literature-based lessons, 5, 67–68. *See also* Poetry

Longitudinal self-evaluated video recording (LSEV)
context of, 98
curriculum, tasks and materials for, 99–104, 99*t*–100*t*, 101*f*, 102*f*
example of, 107–110
introduction to, 97–98
reflections regarding, 104–106, 104*f*

M

Materials
audience awareness and, 151–156
CALLaborative (collaborative computer-assisted language learning) projects and, 113–118
dictogloss task and, 22–30, 23*f*, 25*f*, 29*f*
ethnography project and, 52–65, 52*t*, 53*t*, 55*f*, 56*f*, 57*f*, 60*t*, 62*f*, 63*f*, 64*f*
Harmonica Project and, 125–130
investigative tasks and, 37–41
longitudinal self-evaluated video recording (LSEV) and, 99–104, 99*t*–100*t*, 101*f*, 102*f*
multilevel classrooms and, 80–88
online tasks and, 176–181, 179*f*, 180*f*
poetry and, 69–74
self-evaluated approach and, 138–144, 140*f*, 142*f*, 143*f*, 144*f*
small-group discussion task and, 12–18, 17*t*
speech training classes and, 163–170, 168*f*
Matrix graphic organizer, 80–83, 90
Mixbook website, 121
Motivation of students
dictogloss task and, 24
longitudinal self-evaluated video recording (LSEV) and, 106
self-evaluated approach and, 144–145
Multilevel classroom
context of, 80
curriculum, tasks and materials for, 80–88
dictogloss task and, 83–85
introduction to, 79–80
investigative tasks and, 37
matrix graphic organizer and, 80–83
reflections regarding, 89
survey activity and, 86–88

N

Nature vs. Nurture Reading and Discussion Task, 45–46
Nonverbal communication in assessment, 17–18, 17*f*

O

Online tasks
context of, 175–176, 176*t*
curriculum, tasks and materials for, 176–181, 179*f*, 180*f*
introduction to, 173–175, 175*t*
reflections regarding, 181–183
worksheets used for, 184–185
Oral presentations. *See* Presentation skills
Oral Proficiency Interview (OPI), 182
Oral training course. *See* Speech training classes
Organizational ability of the student, 146
Output perspective, 2

P

Perception, 54
Perspective analysis, 54
Podcast project
context of, 112–113
curriculum, tasks and materials for, 113–118
example of, 120–121
reflections regarding, 118–120
PodOmatic, 116, 163
Poetry. *See also* Literature-based lessons
context of, 69
curriculum, tasks and materials for, 69–74
introduction to, 67–68
reflections regarding, 75–78
Portfolios in assessment
audience awareness task and, 154–156
self-evaluated approach and, 142–144, 143*f*, 144*f*, 146
Postcard Clue Sample activity, 46–47
Preconceptions, 54
Preparation, teacher, 148
Preparation stage of the dictogloss task, 21, 29*t*. *See also* Dictogloss task
Presentation skills, 41, 64. *See also* Speech training classes; Speeches
Process approach, 23*f*

Public speaking. *See also* Speech training classes
audience awareness and, 151–156
practice speech forms, 157–158
presentation skills, 41, 64
reflections regarding, 156–157

Q

Questioning, 26
Questioning category in assessment, 17–18,
17*f*
Questioning phrases, 20
Questions, ethnography project and, 53
Question-writing activities, 153–154, 158–160

R

Reconstruction stage of the dictogloss task, 21,
29*t*. *See also* Dictogloss task
Repetition, 16, 79
Representational nature of literary language,
67–68
Research-practice interface perspective, 3
Rich Internet Applications (RIAs)
context of, 175–176, 176*t*
introduction to, 173–175, 175*t*
Routines, 79

S

SambaEFL podcast project
context of, 112–113
curriculum, tasks and materials for, 113–118
example of, 120–121
reflections regarding, 118–120
Scaffolding
dictogloss task and, 26, 31
sociocultural perspective and, 3
speech training classes and, 165
Scrambled Sentences activity, 25*t*
Second language acquisition (SLA) theory
dictogloss task and, 21–22
learning tasks and, 67
longitudinal self-evaluated video recording
(LSEV) and, 105
Self-awareness
ethnography project and, 55–58, 56*f*, 57*f*
longitudinal self-evaluated video recording
(LSEV) and, 98

Self-correction, 105–106
Self-evaluated approach
context of, 138
curriculum, tasks and materials for, 138–
144, 140*f*, 142*f*, 143*f*, 144*f*
introduction to, 137
reflections regarding, 144–148
Self-evaluation. *See* Longitudinal self-evaluated
video recording (LSEV)
Sleeping Sentences activity, 25*t*
Small-group discussion task
assessing, 14–16, 17–18, 17*f*
context of, 11–12
curriculum, tasks and materials for, 12–18,
13*f*, 15*f*, 17*t*
questioning and turn-taking phrases, 20
reflections regarding, 18–19
Social interactions in the classroom, 26
Sociocultural perspective, 3, 105
Speech training classes. *See also* Presentation
skills; Speeches
context of, 161–163
curriculum, tasks and materials for,
163–170, 168*f*
introduction to, 161
reflections regarding, 170–171
Speeches. *See also* Speech training classes
audience awareness and, 151–156
practice speech forms, 157–158
presentation skills, 41, 64
reflections regarding, 156–157
Static assessment, 174. *See also* Assessment
Stereotypes lesson, 115–116
Student autonomy perspective, 4
Student engagement, 23*f*, 31
Student-centered assessment, 141. *See also*
Self-evaluated approach
Student-centered instruction perspective, 4
Stylistic tasks
context of, 69
curriculum, tasks and materials for, 69–74
introduction to, 67–68
reflections regarding, 75–78
Survey activity
audience awareness task and, 151, 153–154,
156–157, 158–160
CALLaborative (collaborative computer-
assisted language learning) projects
and, 115

Survey activity *(continued)*
  example of, 93
  multilevel classrooms and, 86–88
  speech training classes and, 169

T

Task-based learning (TBL) approach overview,
  1, 2–3
Tasks
  audience awareness and, 151–156
  CALLaborative (collaborative computer-
    assisted language learning) projects,
    113–118
  dictogloss task, 22–30, 23*f*, 25*f*, 29*f*
  ethnography project, 52–65, 52*t*, 53*t*, 55*f*,
    56*f*, 57*f*, 60*t*, 62*f*, 63*f*, 64*f*
  Harmonica Project, 125–130
  investigative tasks, 37–41
  learning tasks overview, 67
  longitudinal self-evaluated video recording
    (LSEV), 99–104, 99*t*–100*t*, 101*f*, 102*f*
  multilevel classrooms and, 80–88
  online tasks, 176–181, 179*f*, 180*f*
  poetry and, 69–74
  self-evaluated approach and, 138–144, 140*f*,
    142*f*, 143*f*, 144*f*
  small-group discussion task, 11–20, 12–18,
    13*f*, 17*f*, 17*t*
  speech training classes and, 163–170, 168*f*
Teacher evaluation, 146–147
Technology use. *See also* Online tasks
  Harmonica Project and, 124–125
  introduction to, 5–6
  SambaEFL podcast project and, 113–120
  speech training classes and, 162–163
Testing, 6
Translation Teams activity, 25*t*
Turn-taking phrases, 20
Twitter website, 121

V

Validating task-based learning, 32–33
Video recording tasks. *See* Longitudinal self-
  evaluated video recording (LSEV)

Videotaping in assessment. *See also*
  Longitudinal self-evaluated video
  recording (LSEV)
  small-group discussion task and, 14–15
  speech training classes and, 162–163,
    166–167
Vocabulary, 84
VoiceThread, 163
Voxopop, 163
Vygotsky, Lev, 3

W

Web 2.0 tools
  context of, 111–113
  curriculum, tasks and materials for, 113–118
  example of, 120–121
  ideas utilizing, 121
  introduction to, 111
  reflections regarding, 118–120
Websites
  Adult Learning Activities (California
    Distance Learning Project, 2005), 19
  course management systems (CMS),
    174–175, 175*t*
  Learning Resources (Literacyworks, 2006),
    19
  online collaboration and, 121
  PodOmatic, 116
  speech training classes and, 162–163
  for surveys, 115, 169
Where in the World Is Carmen Sandiego? video
  game, 36–37
Writing activities, 154–156. *See also* Journal
  writing; Portfolios in assessment;
  Question-writing activities; Survey
  activity

Y

Yahoo! Groups, 162–163
Yakudoku method, 69

Z

Zone of proximal development (ZPD), 26

Also Available From TESOL

TESOL Classroom Practice Series
Maria Dantas-Whitney, Sarah Rilling, and Lilia Savova, Series Editors

Authenticity in the Classroom and Beyond: Children and Adolescent Learners
Maria Dantas-Whitney and Sarah Rilling, Editors

Language Games: Innovative Activities for Teaching English
Maureen Snow Adrade, Editor

Authenticity in the Classroom and Beyond: Adult Learners
Sarah Rilling and Maria Dantas-Whitney, Editors

Adult Language Learners: Context and Innovation
Ann F. V. Smith and Gregory Strong, Editors

Explorations in Second Language Reading
Roger Cohen, Editor

Insights on Teaching Speaking in TESOL
Tim Stewart, Editor

Multilevel and Diverse Classrooms
Bradley Baurain and Phan Le Ha, Editors

Effective Second Language Writing
Susan Kasten, Editor

Using Textbooks Effectively
Lilia Savova, Editor

Classroom Management
Thomas S. C. Farrell, Editor

❋ ❋ ❋ ❋ ❋

Language Teacher Research Series
Thomas S. C. Farrell, Series Editor

Language Teacher Research in Africa
Leketi Makalela, Editor

Language Teacher Research in Asia
Thomas S. C. Farrell, Editor

Language Teacher Research in Europe
Simon Borg, Editor

Language Teacher Research in the Americas
Hedy McGarrell, Editor

Language Teacher Research in the Middle East
Christine Coombe and Lisa Barlow, Editors

Language Teacher Research in Australia and New Zealand
Jill Burton and Anne Burns, Editors

❋ ❋ ❋ ❋ ❋

Collaborative Partnerships Between ESL and Classroom Teachers Series
Debra Suarez, Series Editor

Helping English Language Learners Succeed in Pre-K–Elementary Schools
Jan Lacina, Linda New Levine, and Patience Sowa

Helping English Language Learners Succeed in Middle and High Schools
Faridah Pawan and Ginger Sietman, Editors

❋ ❋ ❋ ❋ ❋

CALL Environments: Research, Practice, and Critical Issues, 2nd ed.
Joy Egbert and Elizabeth Hanson-Smith, Editors

Learning Languages through Technology
Elizabeth Hanson-Smith and Sarah Rilling, Editors

Global English Teaching and Teacher Education: Praxis and Possibility
Seran Dogancay-Aktuna and Joel Hardman, Editors

Local phone: (240)646-7037
Fax: (301)206-9789
E-Mail: tesolpubs@brightkey.net
Toll-free: 1-888-891-0041
Mail Orders to TESOL, P.O. Box 79283, Baltimore, MD 21279-0283
ORDER ONLINE at www.tesol.org and click on "Bookstore"